THE TRAVERSE THEATRE STORY
1963–1988

'The Traverse Theatre opened in James Court just off the Edinburgh Lawnmarket, on the night of 2 January 1963. The place was Kelly's Paradise, a crumbling former doss-house and brothel barely a stone's throw from the Castle; the play was Sartre's *Huis Clos*, presented in a double bill with Fernando Arrabal's *Orisons*; the weather was icy . . .' so begins Joyce McMillan's compelling history of the Traverse; how the tiny theatre, founded in the heady atmosphere of the Sixties, shot from nowhere to a pinnacle of international recognition when it could be described as 'the most successful theatre in Britain for new work' – Michael Ratcliffe, *Observer*.

JOYCE MCMILLAN was born in the west of Scotland in 1952, went to school in Paisley and to university in St Andrews and Edinburgh. Since then, she has worked as a freelance theatre critic for the *Scotsman*, *Scottish Sunday Standard* and *Guardian* newspapers. for BBC Radio Scotland and Radio 4. Today she is Scottish theatre critic for the *Guardian*, and has a regular radio review column in the *Glasgow Herald*. She has also, in her time, been a barmaid, an auxiliary nurse, a chambermaid, a BBC typist and a schoolteacher.

D0993998

The photograph on the front cover shows the entrance to James Court, Lawnmarket, Edinburgh, the site of the first Traverse Theatre. It is reproduced by courtesy of Scotsman Publications Ltd.

A METHUEN THEATREFILE

in series with

THE IMPROVISED PLAY; THE WORK OF MIKE LEIGH
by Paul Clements

THE PLAYS OF EDWARD BOND
by Tony Coult

ALL TOGETHER NOW: AN ALTERNATIVE VIEW OF
THEATRE AND THE COMMUNITY
by Steve Gooch

DARIO FO: PEOPLE'S COURT JESTER
by Tony Mitchell

THE JOINT STOCK BOOK
compiled by Rob Ritchie

THE TRAVERSE THEATRE STORY 1963–1988

by
JOYCE McMILLAN

with
A CHRONOLOGY

of productions mounted by
THE TRAVERSE THEATRE
during its first 25 years

Compiled by
JOHN CARNEGIE

Methuen Drama

A METHUEN THEATREFILE
First published as a paperback original in 1988
by Methuen Drama, 81 Michelin House,
Fulham Road, London SW3 6RW
and distributed in the United States by
HEB Inc, 70 Cork Street,
Portsmouth, New Hampshire 03801, USA.

British Library Cataloguing in Publication Data

McMillan, Joyce
   The Traverse Theatre story 1963–1988.
   1. Edinburgh. Theatres, Traverse Theatre,
   history
   I. Carnegie, John
   792'.09413'4

   ISBN 0-413 19250-4

Printed in Great Britain by Richard Clay, Bungay, Suffolk

CONTENTS

PART ONE

PART TWO

ACKNOWLEDGEMENTS

Special thanks are due to the nine Artistic Directors of the Traverse, all of whom gave most generously of their time in assisting with the preparation of this book; also to Richard Demarco, Joe Gerber and Tom Mitchell, for access to their private archives, and to Una Flett, for making available her MA thesis of 1967; to the staff and Board of the Traverse Theatre, for patient assistance over many months, and for open access to their archives and to their collection of production photographs by Diane Tammes, Joe McKeever, David Liddle and Sean Hudson; to the staff of the manuscripts and rare books department, National Library of Scotland; to the Photo Sales Department of Scotsman Publications, Edinburgh, for invaluable help in tracing photographs of the Traverse's early years; and to Alan Taylor of Edinburgh Central Library. The writing of this book was made possible by a Writers' Bursary from the Scottish Arts Council.

PART ONE
THE STORY

The Old Traverse wall-sign, James Court, 1966.
(Photo Scotsman Publications)

CHAPTER 1
Terry Lane and the Meeting of Friends

The Traverse Theatre opened in James Court, just off the Edinburgh Lawnmarket, on the night of 2 January 1963. The place was Kelly's Paradise, a crumbling former doss-house and brothel barely a stone's throw from the Castle; the play was Sartre's *Huis Clos*, presented in a double bill with Fernando Arrabal's *Orisons*; the weather was icy, so much so that the capacity audience of 60 invited guests shivered their way through supper in evening dress and heavy overcoats. At the second performance, the actress Colette O'Neil was accidentally stabbed on stage with a paperknife, and almost bled to death; the publicity was tremendous, advance bookings soared, and the theatre, in the words of its first director Terry Lane, 'never looked back.' Within three-and-a-half years of that opening night, this tiny theatre club – with no visible means of support except its membership, its bar, and a few generous patrons – produced a staggering total of 110 productions, including 28 British premieres, and 33 world premieres. During the Edinburgh Festivals of those years, all the great and the good of world theatre trooped through its cramped little auditorium, drinking in its louche and fervent atmosphere and its strange, exciting repertoire; critics in London and worldwide began to write effusive reports of what Allen Wright (*The Scotsman's* leading theatre critic from the mid-60s to the present day) dryly called the 'up-a-winding-staircase-in-a-17th-century-Edinburgh-tenement-you-will-find-the-most-exciting-threatre-in-Britain' type. By the summer of 1966, when the Traverse Committee fell out with and effectively dismissed Jim Haynes – the laid-back American who had been the theatre's presiding genius and second Artistic Director – Harold Hobson was prepared to suggest, in the columns of the *Sunday Times*, that the survival of the Traverse along the lines laid down by Haynes was a matter of vital importance to world theatre.

In a sense, the whole Traverse story still revolves around the passionate experience of those early years. The memory of the period when the theatre shot from nowhere to a pinnacle of international recognition, when it won the worldwide reputation and support that still sustains it today, haunts the Traverse like an irritating beat-generation ghost; and its history since 1966, like the story of many enterprises that began in the heady atmosphere of that time, is tinged with a faint sadness, as though at some level it were all about an attempt to recapture that first fine rapture of creativity. Of course the Traverse has changed direction many times since 1966. It has moved house; it has moulded itself, over two and a half decades, to the images and aspirations of seven more artistic directors, some of whom have felt nothing but antipathy to the Traverse legend, and to the mythology of the early days. But even the most sceptical of them have been living, to some extent, on the artistic credit built up at that time; and it's impossible to understand the later history of this strange, arrogant little theatre without knowing something about its extraordinary beginnings.

What most Traverse veterans will say, when you ask about the secret of its explosive impact in the 60's, is that the theatre was very small. You could rub knees with the actors, smell their sweat, see the gooseflesh on their bodies; and to a generation brought up on rigid proscenium arches and serried ranks of plush seats this in itself was sexy, exciting, electrifying. It seems almost impossible to overstate the importance of the original James Court space in creating the Traverse legend, both in its size, and in its unique atmosphere. It was a long, low-ceilinged first-floor room barely 15 ft. wide by 8 ft. high, and at a time when the theory of performing in 'real space' – as opposed to artificial settings – hardly existed in Britain, it was inescapably a real room, with blocked-up window embrasures along one wall, and a certain unobtrusive insistence about its two-sided layout. Jim Haynes describes it as being 'like a pressure-cooker – it really was practically impossible to make a bad production in that space.'

But it has to be said, mythology notwithstanding, that the Traverse was not the first intimate theatre in Britain. Post-war London had had its share of smoky little clubs, so much so that by 1966, when the Traverse was trying to set up a London outpost, Irving Wardle wondered in *New Society* whether the whole fashion for basement-and-garret theatre wasn't becoming a little passé; and there was something more to the Traverse's special success – recognised far and wide, even by commentators who were quite blasé about intimate theatre – than mere smallness. Clearly, the Traverse was fortunate in coming onto the scene at a time of extraordinary material expansion, when the resources existed – both in terms of private patronage and of public subsidy – to support a style and scale of theatre that could never be commercially viable. But it seems the factor that combined with the excitement of the space itself to attract those resources, and to create the special electricity of the early Traverse, was something relatively difficult to measure, namely its unusually intense relationship with its Edinburgh audience. If it wasn't the first intimate theatre in Britain, it certainly was the only one in Edinburgh, a focus for the avant-garde interests and bohemian impulses of a small but considerable swathe of the Edinburgh bourgeoisie; so that in its first few vital years, the Traverse was that most privileged, and historically most significant, kind of theatre – a theatre with a committed audience, questioning, combative, and absolutely engaged with its work.

It was an audience created by the special social atmosphere of the early 1960's. By the end of 1962 the whole of British society had reached a strange, tense condition, with the mood of timid conservatism and suburban apathy that had characterised the 50's about to be blown sky-high by the attitudes of a post-war generation that was young, healthy, well-educated, well-heeled and, historically speaking, exceptionally fearless – unafraid of poverty, disease, unemployment, and, as the pill era dawned, increasingly unafraid of sex. The city of Edinburgh seems to have experienced that tension in a particularly acute form. Paralysed in dour provincial respectability from September to August, it was nonetheless galvanised, for three weeks of the year, by what was then quite unrivalled as the world's greatest and most exciting arts festival; so that just beneath the unyielding surface of the city's life there flourished a lively and growing minority who went to avant-garde Fringe shows in intimate spaces like Riddle's Court, who patronised Jim Haynes'

Paperback Bookshop in Charles Street, and who knew that cultural forums existed where the things they experienced in private life – but somehow were not supposed to mention in public – could be discussed, enacted, and shared with strangers and friends.

So the special quality of the Traverse – pinpointed by Irving Wardle in that same article when he wrote about its 'community atmosphere' and the 'concentration of life in the building' – is that it emerged not only out of the desire of theatre professionals to create a certain kind of work (although that became part of it), but also out of a definite, tangible change in the lives of a large section of Edinburgh people, and out of their desire to see that change reflected in a public forum – a theatre, a gallery, a bookshop, a meeting-place – not for three weeks of the year, but always. The story of the Traverse's foundation and its first three years is the story of how that audience emerged, found its leaders and its home, and, for a brief moment, was held in a powerful mutual dependence with the institution it had created. The story has no single hero; but it has a dramatis personae, and a remarkable one at that.

The leading and most controversial character, then, is this Jim Haynes, a tall, soft-spoken American of exceptionally relaxed and genial manner, born in Louisiana in 1933. At the beginning of the story, he is a young U.S. serviceman, serving out his time at the Kirknewton USAF base just outside Edinburgh; but there is more to Jim Haynes than immediately meets the eye. He has asked most particularly – on beginning his national service in 1956 – to be sent to a small base near a beautiful European city with a university; he is a romantic about Europe, he has fallen in love with Edinburgh, he is attending classes at the university by day, whizzing back to the base in his little black Volkswagen to sit out long Air Force watches by night. He loves the Edinburgh Festival, but is depressed by the slide back into drab 50's provincialism that overtakes the city in the other 49 weeks of the year; he has, somewhere in the back of his mind, the idea of getting his well-off father back in Texas to help buy him out of the forces, and of setting up a little Paperback Bookshop, Edinburgh's first.

The next character – in order of appearance – is Richard Demarco, a flairful Edinburgh art-teacher not much older than Haynes. Demarco hates teaching, loves the idea of organising exhibitions, and shares – with a vehemence foreign to Jim's character but absolutely typical of his own – Haynes' feelings about the state of Edinburgh's cultural life in the period outside the Festival. It should be noted, in fairness, that art is not the only thing on Demarco's mind, and certainly not the only thing on Haynes'; both are great socialisers, and keen and unapologetic woman-fanciers of the kind that flourished briefly in the window of opportunity between the decline of Victorian morality and the rise of feminism. The lace-curtained limitations on Edinburgh's cultural life – the men-only pubs that close at 9.30 or 10.00, the good restaurants that are few, stuffy and expensive, the near-total absence of late night eating and drinking-places, the slightly creaky entertainment offered by the Lyceum and Gateway theatres – also cramp their social style. No-one has heard of the swinging 60's, but they are just around the corner. Edinburgh is full of students and au pairs and bright young academics and professionals with a little money between their fingers; so after their first meeting – on the corner of Blackfriars Street and the Royal Mile one Festival night in 1957, when Haynes pulls his Beetle to a halt and says (in American) 'Hey, can I give you people a ride?' – Demarco and Haynes begin, quite deliberately, to hold parties, where an amazing throughput of people – the men gifted, well-connected or rich, the women young and beautiful – talk the night away to the sound of Sinatra's *Songs for Swinging Lovers*. 'You would be wrong,' says Demarco, 'to think the Traverse idea was born to the sound of the Beatles. We were a pre-Beatles phenomenon . . .'

Demarco also says, more seriously, and quoting the English painter Cecil Collins, that art originates in the meeting of friends. 'The Traverse began,' he says, 'when the friends of Jim Haynes – students, au-pairs, young Americans on their junior year abroad – met the friends of Ricky Demarco, who were the kind of interested Edinburgh people who could finance things . . .' With Demarco's encouragement, Haynes leaves the Air Force, sells his Volkswagen, and buys with the proceeds a little ramshackle junk-shop in a part of Edinburgh's South Side now demolished by the University. He commandeers an old rhinoceros head from the junk-shop stock as his sign over the door, opens his Paperback Bookshop, sells every kind of paperback under the sun (including material still frowned on in those far-off days, like *Lady Chatterley's Lover*) and finds himself with a roaring success on his hands. Those around at the time – like Judy Steel, wife of the former Liberal leader, who held her graduation party at the shop in 1961 – says that the impact on the Edinburgh of the day of this liberal, easy-going meeting-place, where you could drink coffee for hours and never be 'hassled' to buy a book, is almost impossible to overstate.

The third character of significance is the splendid and enigmatic Tom Mitchell, a tall person from the North of England with a lovely, rolling Cumbrian accent. Mitchell is a 'designer' – to quote from various legal documents and leases – and a property developer; he is also Chairman of Workington Rugby League Club, and has inscrutable foreign commitments which keep him out of the country for long periods. He is in Edinburgh, so it seems, because one day, on a zebra crossing in Kendal, he has fallen in love wth an actress called Tamara Alferoff, who looks 'like Julie Christie, but prettier . . .' Tamara happens to live in Edinburgh, and knows Richard Demarco; for her sake, Tom spends considerable amounts of time in the city, and triumphantly acquires a large flat overlooking the Meadows, totally run-down, and inhabited by a large colony of pigeons. To celebrate the purchase, he totters into the Laigh Coffee House in Hanover Street (owned by the well-known Scottish actor Moultrie Kelsall, and about as much of a headquarters as Edinburgh's Bohemia has back in 1960) and sits down, quite by chance, at a table occupied by an artist called Pete McGinn, who agrees to move into the flat and renovate it during one of Tom's absences.

It is worth pausing, here, to note that the drabness of Edinburgh at this time extends beyond the natural conservatism of a British provincial town in the 50's. Despite its history, despite its international Festival, despite its remarkable beauty, the city of Edinburgh has somehow become suburban and bungalow-crazed to the point where much of its glorious New Town is regarded as slum property, the University is cheerfully bulldozing large areas of the historic South Side and George Square for its 60's expansion programme, and what is now the chic and fashionable Old Town along the Royal Mile is so grossly run down and undervalued that a centuries-old five-storey building in the shadow of the Castle can be acquired for a few hundred pounds. The people who are coming together in Edinburgh to support the Traverse are a motley crowd, and some of them have only the most tenuous interest in theatre. But one thing they emphatically share is their love for the fabric of the old city, and their willingness to place a much higher value on it than is common at the time; so that when Pete McGinn one day leads Tom Mitchell up to the Lawnmarket, shows him a picturesque tumbledown pile in James Court with a strange long room on the first floor, and says 'It's coming down, you know . . .', Mitchell rises instantly to the challenge of buying it from its five scattered owners, and saving it from demolition. Mitchell, who, according to Demarco, 'fancied himself as an art patron', wants initially to convert it into studios and a flat for struggling artists; but that plan falls through, and the building lies temporarily empty.

At this stage, then, what we might call the inspired amateur section of the cast is assembled. Between them – what with the parties and the Bookshop and the little exhibitions Demarco was beginning to mount in its basement – Haynes and Demarco know hundreds of interested people in and around Edinburgh (even today, when people are asked why they became involved in the Traverse in the 60's, they tend to answer, 'Well, I knew Jim . . .'). Behind them stand not only Mitchell, the man of property, but also the publisher John Calder, who has a lively professional relationship with Haynes via the Bookshop, and runs his own special dinner-theatre in his Scottish house at Ledlanet, outside the city; beyond that there are dozens of valuable acquaintances like John Martin, a successful commercial artist, secretary Sheila Colvin (now Associate Director of the Edinburgh Festival), Andy Muir, Calder's Scottish agent and a gifted amateur actor, and a young lawyer called Andrew Elliott, who, together with Martin and an accountant with biscuit interests called Jim Walker, will help bankroll the Traverse through its early years.

But despite the generalised goodwill towards the idea of a permanent Fringe arts centre or club that floats around at Haynes-Demarco parties, it takes a few more strokes of fate, and a decisive intervention from the professional side of the theatre business, to bring the Traverse to life. In the early summer of 1962, someone telephones Richard Demarco from Cambridge to say that Cambridge University Theatre Company is looking for a venue for the Edinburgh Festival Fringe. Demarco suggests James Court, Mitchell agrees, Pete McGinn and his sidekicks in Mitchell's band of impecunious but artistic labourers start to clear out the first-floor space for them. In that year's Festival, 15 James Court becomes the Sphinx Club, and the Cambridge group acquire an influential fan in the shape of Lord Kilbrandon who lives – unusually for a member of the establishment at that time – just round the corner in Lady Stair's Close, and later becomes a dedicated patron of the idea of theatre in James Court, and of the Traverse.

It's at this point – during the Festival of 1962 – that the fourth character enters, a real actor, the least known and in some ways the most important character of all. His name is John Malcolm, he has a strong record of good work in Scottish theatres, he also has a reputation as a moody, manic, hot-tempered and, when he chooses, hugely energetic personality. He has left Pitlochry Festival Theatre in high dudgeon in the middle of the 1962 summer season, and he is appearing – at his agent's suggestion – in a Festival Fringe production of Fionn MacColla's *Ane Tryall of Heretiks*, which is being staged in the basement of Jim Haynes' bookshop. The atmosphere of this Festival is peculiarly exciting; Jim Haynes and the publisher John Calder have mounted an International Writers' Conference which has attracted dozens of distinguished literati to Edinburgh. The show in Jim's basement naturally attracts more than its share of attention from this glittering crowd; it – and John Malcolm – receive a glowing review from Harold Hobson in the *Sunday Times*.

And this is the crucial moment when the idea of some kind of arts club to keep the Fringe atmosphere alive in Edinburgh all the year round – kicked around in the Haynes-Demarco circle for years, known to John Calder with his extensive interest in avant-garde drama, discussed over months with Tom Mitchell, energetically prefigured by the student Sphinx Club in James Court – suddenly takes root in the mind of an ambitious and radically-minded young theatre professional with the sheer physical energy and hard practical knowledge to push it through to fruition. As both Demarco and Haynes emphasise, their idea of a meeting-place or arts centre was not particularly focused on the notion of a theatre; books and paintings and music and good food and company were at least as important to them, and Haynes had already been involved in an abortive folk-club venture called The Howff, a little way down the Royal Mile.

So it is John Malcolm, in that Festival of 1962, who sees the Sphinx Club in full swing, who hears the talk of a permanent 'fringe' centre, who makes up his mind that it will take the form of a professional theatre, and who determines that it will happen then and there, that autumn. After the Festival, he goes to see Tom Mitchell, laid low in a city hospital with a bout of typhoid contracted in Algeria. From the regulation six-pace distance he expounds the idea of professional theatre in James Court, vows that what with ticket sales and cafe proceeds it won't cost Mitchell a penny, and gets Mitchell's consent to the project. And he summons onto the scene the fifth and final leading character, his young actor/director friend Terry Lane, Stage Manager at Pitlochry during that summer. Lane shares Malcolm's frustration with what they feel is the tired, outdated, dispirited and blasé quality of most of the rep theatre in which they had worked; and when the telegram summons reaches him in London in mid-October, Lane packs a few necessaries (some clothes and a typewriter), and sets off for Edinburgh with nothing in his pocket but a last £5 of unemployment benefit.

With Lane's arrival, the cast was complete, and in the last weeks of 1962, fuelled by Malcolm's driving energy, Lane's cool organising professionalism, Tom Mitchell's capricious but substantial commitment to the use of the building, and the all-embracing enthusiasm of Haynes, Demarco and friends, the Traverse project suddenly reached critical mass. At Malcolm's behest, Terry Lane had already had a look at the James Court Building (keys obtainable from the Paperback Bookshop) before he went south at the end of the Pitlochry season. In London, Lane, who had worked for several seasons at the Stephen Joseph Theatre-In-The-Round in Scarborough, and had often discussed with Joseph the different kinds of staging used in America and on the Continent, had roughed out a suggested layout for the long, narrow theatre space, with two raked banks of seating at either end, and a small playing-area running across the auditorium between the two banks of spectators. He thought this layout was called a 'traverse' stage, and after some haggling between Lane, Malcolm and their newly-formed Committee – headed by Tom Mitchell as Chairman and Jim Haynes as Vice-Chairman – it was decided that 'the Traverse' would be as good a name as any for the new theatre; although Mitchell, who had wanted to revive the name 'Sphinx Club' in memory of happy Festival nights there in 1962, was slightly disappointed by the decision. It was only some months later that Lane realised he had got it wrong, and that the technical term for his staging was 'transverse'; by that time, fortunately, the name was too famous to change.

Lane and Malcolm moved quickly on the basis of almost no funds, printing up headed notepaper to give themselves credibility, and ordering timber and lighting for the theatre space; they acquired five dozen old red plush tip-up seats from the disused Palace Cinema further down the Royal Mile, and an interested architect was invited in to redesign the cafe-restaurant space on the floor above the theatre. There never seems to have been any doubt that the new theatre would have to be a private members' club. Club status made the whole project much easier to license, in terms of fire safety, drink sales and, above all, the censoring activities of the Lord Chamberlain's office, still in full operation in 1963; and in any case, the Committee desperately needed the operating capital that advance membership subscriptions would provide.

The Committee began to co-opt new members; Mitchell, Haynes, Lane, Malcolm and Andy Muir were soon joined by Demarco, his friend Sheila Colvin, and gentle John Martin, who became the first cash patron of the Traverse when he gave £50 towards the initial expenses and persuaded Tom Mitchell to do the same. Demarco – who knew from earlier experience at the Gateway Theatre that he had a great talent for drumming up support ('Honest to God, you used to end up going to his damn theatre because you felt sorry for him . . .' reports one Edinburgh worthy much harrassed at the time) – appointed himself as a kind of recruiting agent, and bustled about trying to acquire the 500 members at a guinea apiece (ten shillings and sixpence for students) that were thought to be needed for the Club to succeed. By the time the theatre opened just after New Year, there were almost 300 members, and income was flowing in; but according to Terry Lane – possibly the most level-headed and business-minded of the whole group – no-one ever sat down and worked out a budget. 'Everyone just *wanted* us to succeed,' he remembers, and the whole project proceeded on a vague and, as it turned out, completely mistaken assumption that if 500 members materialised, and the cafe/restaurant was reasonably successful, then the theatre would break even, and would never need any subsidy at all.

In a sense, that failure even to consider the possibility of looming financial crisis tells us all we need to know about the extraordinary atmosphere in which the theatre was born; the assumption was that the members wanted the theatre enough to finance it, that the professionals wanted it enough to work for next-to-nothing, and that when the chips were down enough cash could be found in private pockets to bail it out. The sense of a head of steam, of a shared wish to 'come out' with an alternative view of the world, seems to have been almost irresistible at the point when the Traverse burst on the Edinburgh scene. It not only embraced the social, sexual and creative longings of Jim Haynes, Richard Demarco and friends; it also, crucially, touched on the real professional discontents of men like Malcolm and Lane, trapped in a conservative theatre culture where Stephen Joseph could be, in Lane's words, 'mocked and derided – really, mocked is not too strong a word . . .' for his interest in working in-the-round.

It's therefore hardly surprising that the question of who, exactly, founded the Traverse remains an emotive one for everyone who was involved. The truth is that they all founded it, that the idea of this new, alternative kind of place – a theatre or an arts centre, a restaurant or just a meeting-place – was alive, at different intensities, in all of these five principals and in dozens of their friends; and it was because it was in all of them that it had such unstoppable force. It is probably true that Jim Haynes – in his inimitably relaxed personality, his easy warmth, his openness, his obvious and confident rejection of the rigidities of rules, regulations, appointments, timetables, accounts and all the paraphernalia of conventional life – embodied and promoted this spirit more than any other single person. But as many of his detractors are eager to point out, and Haynes himself freely admits, he wasn't even in the country when the Traverse opened; he had succumbed to a £400 cheque from his father, sent to finance a Christmas trip home for Jim, his new wife Viveka and baby son. And yet the process of opening the theatre never paused, rolling straight on through his absence, drawing more than enough strength from the dedication of Lane and Malcolm and the rest of the committee. Richard Demarco, Haynes' loyal friend to the last, says that 'Jim wasn't resolute enough about the Traverse; he set up all the energy for it, and then let it slip away . . .' But the energy that was around in 1962 wasn't any one man's to set up; and the mild acrimony that remains today over the question of who founded the Traverse arises, purely and simply, from misguided attempts to claim as a private inspiration something that was more like a small force of history, and all the more remarkable for that.

Even before the Traverse opened, though, it became obvious that the alliance of interests that had come together in the Club had its weak points and, in particular, that Lane's tolerance for the radicalism and openness of the Traverse idea was limited. In the middle of December – one bleary-eyed night when everyone was hard at work in the theatre screwing down the new seats – Terry Lane and John Malcom became involved in a row (about Lane's prerogatives as director of *Huis Clos*) so ferocious that it became clear one or other of them had to go. Lane assumed that it should be him, since the project was 'Malcolm's baby', but the Traverse committee felt it had no choice but to sack the actor and back the director, who seemed, with only two weeks to go before opening night, the more indispensable of the two. Tom Mitchell was detailed to take Malcolm to lunch, and persuade him to leave Edinburgh without making any damaging public comments; an actor called Clyde Pollitt was summoned up at short notice, and formed, with Colette O'Neil and Lane's fiancée Rosamund Dickson, the first acting company ever to tread the Traverse boards.

Under the circumstances – and in the absence of Jim Haynes, who had left for America – the Committee, which had no practical experience of theatre at all, probably made the right decision. But in giving its firm backing in that first conflict to a director who was insisting on the traditional prerogatives of the job, the Committee made an involuntary lurch towards the conventional and the orthodox in theatre practice that had to be corrected with some difficulty before the Traverse could reach the full iconoclastic potential of its early years. It wasn't that Terry Lane was any kind of conventional theatre hack; his presence at the Traverse made it clear that he was not. He had unusual experience for a young English director of working in-the-round, he knew the Continental and American avant-garde repertoire well enough to have no difficullty in putting together a programme for the first year, he was seriously frustrated by the poor, off-hand, conventional quality of acting he saw in English rep.

But he was no cultural revolutionary in the Jim Haynes mould, and his patience with Traverse radicalism stopped short of any tinkering with the normal demarcation lines of theatre structure – the lines between professionals and amateurs, theatre workers and committee members, director and cast. In fact, he seems to have found the persistent blurring of those distinctions at the Traverse – made inevitable both by the strong organic relationship between the theatre and its membership, and by the Traverse's inability at that stage to afford professional catering and administrative staff – increasingly threatening and disturbing. In his bright pink 'participatory autobiography' *Thanks for Coming* – written partly by himself and partly by those who have known him – Jim Haynes says that Lane seemed to look down his nose at the enthusiastic volunteers and committee members who clustered round the Traverse, to dismiss them as 'a bunch of amateurs, whereas they (the company) were professionals . . .'. But Lane's apparent attitude had more to do with the insecurity of a young, sensitive actor-director, placed rather abruptly and unexpectedly in a high-profile position of considerable responsibility, and subjected – without the benefit of a university education, a lack of which he was acutely conscious – to the scrutiny of one of the most intellectually sophisticated audiences in Britain. In the end, Haynes is probably nearer the mark when he says, today, that he and his associates at the time were slightly 'crazy people . . . and the whole social thing around the Traverse just wasn't Terry's scene.'

But it's an index of the strength of the impulse for change at the time that for a crucial moment, the Traverse project succeeded in bringing together such opposites in personal politics and style as Jim Haynes and Terry Lane. In fact, at the time of the opening the nature of the new theatre's mission seems to have been so obvious to those involved that no-one saw much need to articulate it. The newspapers in the run-up to opening night carried simple policy statements about 'plays which, for economic and other reasons, are not being staged elsewhere in Scotland,' and 'plays which are interesting both for actor and audience'; but so clear was the need to put Edinburgh audiences back in touch with the latest thinking in world theatre that for the first year or two there hardly seems to have been any debate over policy and repertoire. John Calder's drama list was bristling with interesting small-scale drama previously unperformed in Britain; Terry Lane's programme for the first year included eight British premieres and one world premiere, and covered the work of Arrabal and Sartre, of Jarry, Ionesco, Grabbe, William Snyder, Yukio Mishima and Ugo Betti, as well as a brand new play – *The Balachites* – by the Edinburgh academic and writer Stanley Eveling, who became the first Traverse playwright.

One critic at the time described this programme as 'suicidally ambitious'; but Terry Lane himself now says that it was 'safe, within the theatre's remit . . .', a programme designed to found the new theatre's reputation on respected work of acknowledged quality, albeit relatively unfamiliar in Britain. In that first year, as the programme unfolded, there was no nudity, no scandal, none of the freewheeling naughtiness for which the Traverse became known in the mid-60's; just a steady sequence of productions of avant-garde classics, some adequate, some good, some – like the festival productions of Jarry's *Ubu Roi* and Grabbe's *Comedy, Satire, Irony and Deeper Meaning* – of outstanding quality. The theatre averaged 60% attendances in its 60 seats, and membership, following the stabbing scandal and the consequent publicity, moved rapidly up towards the 2,000 mark. During the 1963 Festival, Jim Haynes and John Calder organised a Drama Conference, made notorious by the split-second appearance of a naked girl on the balcony of the McEwan Hall, under the unimpressed eye of the then Festival Director Lord Harewood; many of the attendant famous faces – from Kenneth Tynan to J.B. Priestley – appeared in the audience at the Traverse, and the theatre began for the first time to attract national and international attention.

By the time he left the Traverse in January 1964, Terry Lane had carried through the essential job of establishing the Traverse as a professional small-scale theatre, showing how its little auditorium could be made to work excitingly for a wide range of plays, and establishing the beginnings of a reputation beyond Edinburgh. His final row with the Committee – now dominated by Jim Haynes, who had returned from his U.S. trip early in 1963, taken one look at the burgeoning success of the theatre, and thrown himself into a heavy involvement with its day-today running – was as acrimonious as one might expect in a situation involving such an intensity of commitment. Public accusations of 'petty personal dislike' were made, and countered by a long and rather bitter press statement in which the Committee suggested that Lane had taken too much credit for the Traverse's collective achievements, and (in a complaint that was to become almost a permanent refrain between Traverse directors and their committees) that he had become too interested in making the Traverse into a cheap try-out theatre for transfers to London.

Towards the end of Lane's directorship, when Lane himself was exhausted by the double task of directing and administering the company without a break for an entire year, there seems to have been a complete breakdown of relations between the amateur committee members and the professionals at the Traverse. Lane felt that the Committee took an absurd amount of credit for what he saw as voluntary work on the periphery of the theatre's real activity, and that they understood very little of what was involved in professional production; the Committee were outraged by Lane's stand-offishness, by his tendency to underrate the very real financial and practical burdens willingly accepted by the Committee at that time, and by his dismissive attitude to the social and recreational functions which they saw as integral to the nature of the place. John Martin, briefly Chairman of the Club during that year, remembers an appalling row when Lane appeared, quivering and white-faced with rage, to reprimand some hapless helper for dropping a plate on the cafe floor – which was also the theatre ceiling – during a performance. In the end – after a year during which the tensions among the Traverse's founding group had been subordinated to the priority of getting the theatre off the ground – the radical questioning of conventional forms and structures which had been a part of the Traverse impulse began to reassert itself, and to kick against the rigidities of Terry Lane's personality and attitude; and on the 19 January 1964 he left, taking with him his fiancée Rosamund, whose appearance in almost every Traverse production to date had been another bone of contention. He never returned to the Traverse again.

24 years on, Lane remains understandably bitter about his Traverse experience. He worked on in the theatre for a few years, returning to seaside rep and the wider audience he had come to feel he preferred; but in the late 60's, when he and Rosamund Dickson married and began to have children, he gave up the theatre, taught drama for a while in Strathclyde, and eventually settled in the Clyde coast town of Helensburgh where, by a strange circular twist of fate, he opened a small, bright, informal bookshop called Bookworms. He is still convinced – as he sits in his little back office among piles of spiked invoices, a tense, dapper, incongruously grand figure in a perfectly-tailored three-piece suit – that his removal from the Traverse was engineered over a period of months by Jim Haynes, who had been aiming to take over the leadership of the Traverse ever since his return from America. Certainly, Haynes was the most radical figure on the Traverse Committee at the time, quite explicitly hostile to what he later called 'creeping professionalism' in the theatre, and to the kind of conventional theatre

structures for which Lane had come to stand.

But it is unlikely that Haynes could have disposed of Lane if his attitude had not struck a chord with other members of the Committee. What had happened, in reality, was that the phenomenon Terry Lane had helped create at the Traverse had simply outgrown him and his personality; the impact of the theatre and its atmosphere had been such that by early 1964, a whole world of radical theatrical talent was homing in on James Court, and the Traverse began to need a director who could respond to those ideas openly, enthusiastically, and without any competing need to reserve the stage for himself and his company. The theatre was also beginning to feel pressure – from the Arts Council, from playwrights who were sending in scripts, and from its own programme, which was gradually running out of steam – to move on from the established repertoire of American and Continental chamber drama, and to begin to create new work. Lane himself recognises that the Traverse, at this stage, probably needed an Artistic Director of a less 'safe' turn of mind, with more vision and risk-taking flair. But his bitter departure is nonetheless one of the saddest episodes in the Traverse story, for he was its first Artistic Director, and it was his commitment, his professionalism, his experience, and his high sensitivity to the space he had designed, that brought the Traverse safely through the rapids of its first year, with its professional reputation high and rising, and its future relatively assured.

CHAPTER 2
Jim Haynes and the Blue Carrot Era

With Terry Lane's departure, the Traverse rapidly became what it had
not been until then; it became Jim Haynes' baby, and the atmosphere of
the organisation underwent an immediate, subtle change. By January
1964, Haynes was Chairman of the Traverse Committee; more
significantly, he had established himself – as much through his
Paperback Bookshop and the Festival Writers' Conferences as through
the Traverse – as an internationally recognised cultural phenomenon, a
man who in some way epitomised the laid-back, receptive, anything-goes
spirit of the arts in the 1960's. Whether Haynes had done anything
substantial to deserve this status is still a subject of intense debate
among his friends and enemies, but in a sense it hardly matters. By 1964
he was becoming a well-known figure from Moscow to Los Angeles, and
in allowing itself to be increasingly identified with a man who was seen
as embodying the very spirit of the age – and who had so many contacts
among its key artists – the Traverse put itself right in the epicentre of the
crazy, exuberant, mid-60's explosion of avant-garde art and performance
that swept across America and into Europe. Jim Haynes may not have
been the Traverse's founding father, but in that sense he was its destiny.

Not that there was any sharp change of policy on Lane's departure; in
fact, the transition from Lane's artistic directorship to Haynes's – which
did not formally begin until August – was of the smoothest, for reasons
which had as much to do with good luck as good guidance. Whatever
else Jim Haynes may have claimed for himself, he has never claimed to
be a professional man of the theatre, a writer, a director or, in any
conventional sense, an administrator; so when Terry Lane walked out of
rehearsals in the first week of January, the pressing need was to find
someone to take over his forthcoming production (a Strindberg double-
bill of *The Stronger* and *Playing with Fire*), and to defuse the rebellion
among Lane's company, who understandably felt that they ought to
walk out in solidarity. Legend has it that the problem was solved by the
Edinburgh journalist W. Gordon Smith, who had taken a warm interest
in the Traverse – and the good copy it provided for his column – from
the outset. Walking up the Lawnmarket one January day, he met a
fraught Committee member who poured out the story of the row with
Lane, and quick as a flash Smith suggested that the Traverse approach
the Scottish actor and director Callum Mill, who had recently finished a
successful period as Director at the Citizens' Theatre in Glasgow.

Now Callum Mill is one of the great unsung heroes of the Traverse
story and of Scottish theatre generally, a man whose productions of
classic texts (now only to be seen among drama students in Edinburgh)
are pure, brilliant dynamite. Mill was and remains absolutely passionate
about the need for Scottish theatre to stop contemplating its own grubby
navel and – without losing its distinctive Scottish accent – to become
sophisticated, forward-looking and cosmopolitan in style and repertoire;
his career has been limited by a chronic dislike of the administrative
burdens of artistic directorship ('Callum just wasn't a Committee man,'

says Tom Mitchell sadly of his eventual departure from the Traverse. 'Hated all that, just wanted a place to put on plays . . .'), and by a sneaking preference for acting rather than directing.

In 1964, though, Mill welcomed the invitation to step in at the Traverse with open arms, like a man famished for opportunities to work in a sophisticated theatre-de-poche atmosphere, and to direct the European chamber repertoire he knew and admired. He not only took over Terry Lane's company and his Strindberg double-bill with a flourish; he stayed on at the Traverse for almost eight months, directing half-a-dozen shows (including four double-bills) and playing in three more. His repertoire included Strindberg, Albee, Robert Pinget, Michael de Ghelderode's *Escorial*, and a double-bill by Slawomir Mrozek. His company was made up of top-class Scottish actors including David McKail, Isobel Black, Tom Conti and Alex McAvoy; and as well as producing successfully himself, he also collaborated warmly, at least for a time, with some of the new Traverse directors that Jim Haynes – advised by John Calder – was beginning to introduce from the south. In February, Michael Geliot – who had directed opera for John Calder's Ledlanet Nights – created a production of Harold Pinter's *The Caretaker*, with Callum Mill in the cast, that was one of the great Traverse successes in James Court, playing to capacity audiences, and taking the princely average of £106 a week at the box office – enough, at 1964 rates, to pay the cast twice over. Mill also appeared in a quintuple-bill of short Chekhov pieces directed by Anne Stutfield.

There seems to have been a sense, at the time, that the quality of the Traverse's work at this period was particularly high. Jim Haynes, in his Chairman's address to the Traverse's first AGM in March, talked warmly about the 'improvement in standards' since the beginning of the year; and although Haynes and the Committee may have had a vested interest in justifying their decision to get rid of Terry Lane, the fact that audiences moved up from 60% to 90% of capacity in the club's second year, and that membership rose steadily past the 3,000 mark, suggest that it was a particularly successful season. It's also noticeable that many Traverse veterans – including Jim Haynes himself, in *Thanks for Coming* – identify this year, and particularly the summer of 1964, as the high point of the whole experience; and with hindsight, there are several clear reasons why that should have been so.

For one thing, the Traverse was at a happy stage in its development; it was reaping the artistic benefits of the success of its first year, it had become a magnet for talent and for audiences, and it had not yet hit the limits of the financial tolerance of its bankers and guarantors. At the end of 1963, the organisation had a total deficit of £3,700, which showed little sign of being reduced; but it hadn't yet acquired the sense of doom and harassment about its financial plight which soon became a permanent drain on its energy. For another, it's an observable fact about the Traverse that it often works extremely well under a two-handed leadership, provided the two come together involuntarily and not because one is the sidekick and appointee of the other. What developed by chance, in the early months of 1964, was a kind of double artistic leadership, with Callum Mill providing a strong backbone of professional productions of avant-garde classics, and Jim Haynes and his associates feeding in stimulation in the shape of guest directors – like Geliot and, later, Charles Marowitz – and of ideas for new plays, which began to mature later in the year.

What's more, this was one of the few periods in the history of the Traverse when it fully acknowledged and exploited its roots in Edinburgh and in Scotland. One of the most powerful undercurrents in the whole Traverse story is the recurring tension between the theatre's Scottishness, its Britishness, and its internationalism. John Malcolm, the actor who pulled the Traverse idea together in the autumn of 1962, had wanted it to be an international theatre created 'for Scotland by Scotland', but that aspect of his policy disappeared with the Committee's decision, just before the opening, to sack him and back Terry Lane. Jim Haynes is fond of saying that 'the Traverse isn't in Scotland, it's in the world', and it's easy to see what he means. But the fact is that it is in both; and like all Scottish-based institutions, it's subject to the sod's law of cultural domination, which says that any organisation in Scotland which does not strive to stay Scottish ends up, not international, but Anglicised. Scots – particularly Edinburgh Scots – tend to react enthusiastically to anything that smacks of true internationalism. But creeping anglicisation – and the traditional British insularity that sometimes comes with it – is something they justly resent. In the summer of 1964, the Traverse was offering a real interface between Scotland and the wider world, between Scottish actors and directors and the international theatre scene, and the audience responded to that; the trouble is that none of the English and American directors who followed Mill into the Traverse was in a position to see what had made this formula so successful.

At any rate, by August 1964 Callum Mill was beginning to feel he had had enough of the Traverse. More than any other Traverse director, he seems to have been both seduced by and wary of the glamour of the little, intimate space; he had then, and still retains, a strong feeling that intimate theatre, while thrilling in its potential, can easily become indulgent and voyeuristic, and that both directors and actors need to temper their experience of theatre-de-poche with the bigger, more distinctly theatrical disciplines of large-scale performance. In any case, tensions were building up again. Jim Haynes, increasingly intrigued by the stars of the London Fringe, probably underestimated the value of the powerful, audience-building machine he had in Callum Mill's company; Mill was irritated by the high expenditure involved in flying in actors and directors from the South at a time when the organisation was increasingly short of cash. At the end of the Edinburgh Festival he left, on cordial enough terms to return in 1965 as a guest director; and Jim Haynes was confirmed by the Committee as both Chairman and Artistic Director.

His regime began in tremendous style, with a Festival production – at the old Pollock Hall in the South Side – of the British premiere of the Brecht/Weill musical *Happy End*; Michael Geliot directed, the designs were by Ralph Koltai and Nadine Bayliss, and the 20-strong cast was led by John Calder's wife, the singer Bettina Jonic. Excursions outside its own tiny auditorium have always been important to the Traverse as a way of generating extra box-office income, and this first attempt at a larger-scale production was a roaring success. It was also a prime example of one of the main strands of Jim Haynes' directorship, namely his determination to open the place up to new, innovative theatrical talent wherever it sprang from; over the next two years, Haynes' Traverse became a home from home for the artists like Charles Marowitz, Lindsay Kemp, Geoff Moore (a Traverse stage manager in 1965, later founder-director of Moving Being) and the American George Mully, all of whom directed successful productions there.

But Haynes' most substantial and lasting contribution to Traverse policy lay in his commitment to new writing. Neither Lane nor Mill had been particularly interested in the idea of doing brand new work; but Haynes was thrilled by it, and he had also worked out – possibly with the help of the former Scotsman critic Ronald Mavor, who had been a warm supporter of the Traverse from the start, and had recently become director of the Scottish Committee of the Arts Council – that while the Council might have reservations about giving outright revenue grants to a private members' club, it could certainly provide guarantees against loss for any new plays they might produce. In November 1964, Jim Haynes' new-play policy produced its first fruit, in the shape of John Antrobus' lusciously-named comedy *You'll Come to Love your Sperm Test* (or, 'You gave her a thorough examination, Doctor?'); and although this was only the second new play the Traverse had ever produced, in the next 19 months, up to Jim Haynes' departure, no fewer than 30 world premieres were staged in James Court, 25 of them Traverse productions, and one of them created by the Children's Theatre Workshop which Haynes had encouraged.

Some of the plays were instantly forgettable and forgotten, of course; with such a volume of new work passing through the theatre, the Traverse enjoyed a right to fail unheard of before or since. But they included the Robert Burns monologue *There Was a Man*, written by Tom Wright and performed by John Cairney; Paul Ableman's *Green Julia* with Jonathan Lynn and Philip Manikum, thought by many to be the best single play of the Jim Haynes era; a Saul Bellow double-bill called *The Wen* and *Orange Souffle*; Heathcote Williams's *The Local Stigmatic*; and a first Traverse play – *Happy Days Are Here Again* – from C. P. Taylor, who became, with Stanley Eveling, almost a resident Traverse playwright.

All of this begs the question of Jim Haynes' precise role in relation to these productions. After he left the Traverse in 1966, it was suggested by some – presumably anxious to lay his ghost, and legitimise the new regime – that Haynes never, in fact, did any work; and he certainly was not an Artistic Director in the conventional modern mould, directing productions with one hand and frantically trying to run a theatre with the other. Technically, his job involved selecting plays, choosing guest directors, identifying and encouraging new writers, preparing advance programmes and presenting budgets for them to the Committee, and 'fronting' the organisation to press and public; in reality he did the first three pretty well (with the help of his friends and advisors), the fourth hardly at all, and the fifth quite brilliantly.

What he did, in essence, was to create a unique ethos for the place, and although the precise value of it is hard to quantify, and even harder to evoke at more than twenty years' distance, only a fool would say that such an atmosphere is worthless, particularly in the arts. Allen Wright, of *The Scotsman*, treasures a little breathless note from Haynes, scrawled shortly before his departure in 1966: 'Allen – Both Harold Pinter and Heathcote Williams are coming up, but I am not sure when yet, but I will let you know as soon as I do hear – I just called London and Harold Pinter and Heathcote Williams are coming up on Monday afternoon and staying for dress rehearsal and first night and perhaps longer Cheers! – Jim'. Irving Wardle writes of how 'conceivably you might see three indifferent productions in a row, devour a limp omelette in the restaurant, and still have a good night out . . .' Tom Mitchell remembers how Jim would meet people at the door, enfold them in a hairy embrace, and make them feel marvellous to be there; and Ronald 'Bingo' Mavor, of *The Scotsman* and the Arts Council, wrote this most famous account of what it was all about.

'A great feature of those days was Jim, everybody's easy friend, and always on the verge of getting Orson Welles to play King Lear with music by either Lionel Bart or Stravinsky on a cart in James Court. Jim's greatest gift was to believe anything possible and, by gentle enthusiasm, to keep everybody's daft notions alive until, as often as not, they took shape. Everybody went to the Traverse, and Jim would introduce you to Timothy Leary, the Lord Provost, and a man who was growing blue carrots in the interval between acts . . .'

And for a year or two at least, the Haynes aura worked. In 1965, membership and box office income moved onward and upward; the Traverse was invited to mount an official production for the 1965 Edinburgh Festival, and although the end result – after some ridiculous haggling with the Festival management over various proposals for new plays – was an Assembly Hall production of *Macbeth* which Allen Wright of *The Scotsman* remembers as 'an all-time disaster', the theatre continued to flourish. Press reaction to the rest of the Traverse programme was enthusiastic, and productions began to transfer to London; *Happy End* and *You'll come to Love your Sperm Test* had already gone to the Royal Court and Hampstead Theatre respectively, and in the aftermath of the 1965 Festival six Traverse shows transferred to the Arts Theatre, where *Green Julia*, in particular, made a strong impression, although the Traverse lost money on the season.

But beneath the surface, the Traverse's growing success was beginning to create its own strains. For one thing, it was becoming impossible to administer the operation – the visits from guest directors and actors, the transfers of productions to other theatres, the scripts to be read and processed, the Festival commitments, the growing membership – on the voluntary and casual basis the members had come to expect. In the summer of 1966 the Scottish writer Una Flett, then a sociology student in Edinburgh, researched and compiled a fascinating MA thesis on the development of the Traverse, which makes it clear that the transition from an informal association of friends – banding together to deal with practicalities like catering and membership enquiries, fund-raising events and the supervision of the building – to a fully professional theatre organisation was a traumatic one, marked by a jolting series of rows and adjustments which were often personally painful.

Sheila Colvin, the Traverse's Honorary Secretary in its first two years, pointed out a poignant little example in the shape of the box office telephone, which everyone had been able to use at will when the Traverse was a small community of friends. Later, when the theatre became bigger and busier, she hardly knew how to tell people that the box office was out of bounds to everyone except staff. It seemed against the spirit of the place, but the alternative was chaos; and little nerve-grating instances like this were multiplying during 1965. In fact, some members of the original Traverse Committee – and Jim Haynes in particular – disliked this kind of formality so much that they fought a long and determined rearguard action against the forces of 'professionalism' in the organisation; and it's highly characteristic of that Committee's determination to preserve the special atmosphere of the Traverse that the first General Manager they appointed – in September 1964, just after Jim Haynes was made Artistic Director – was no outsider, but Sheila Colvin herself.

But if voluntary administration could no longer meet the Traverse's needs, then neither could voluntary finance in the form of members' subscriptions, ticket sales, and fund-raising events like the famous Black and White Ball of 1964; and by mid-1965, the organisation was running into serious financial trouble. The Club more or less broke even during 1964; but in the Haynes year of 1965 – with the financially abortive visit to the London Arts Theatre, and various other ambitious projects – another £2,200 was added to the accumulated deficit, bringing the total close to £6,000; in fact revised figures presented to the Committee after Haynes' resignation suggested the real deficit at the end of March 1966 was as high as £9,000.

The three guarantors of the Club's overdraft – John Martin, Jim Walker and the lawyer Andy Elliott, co-opted onto the Committee in 1963 – began to make anxious noises, and the search for new sources of finance was on. As early as August 1964 – only 19 months after the Club's foundation – the Committee had discussed the possibility of ceasing to be a private club, so as to attract more substantial support from the Arts Council; they turned the idea down flat on the grounds of one practical objection (licensing difficulties) and three intangible ones to do with atmosphere, members' loyalty to the Club, and the Committee's sense of obligation to them. Nevertheless, the Arts Council contribution to the Traverse – in guarantees for new work and small equipment grants – had grown from zero in 1963 to £2,500 in 1965; and in 1966 they felt able to offer the Traverse a full revenue grant of £7,000, including guarantees. But the growing involvement of the Arts Council in Traverse funding increased the pressure to 'normalise' the Club's administration and budgeting, and the conflict between the need for responsible management on the one hand, and the freewheeling Haynes style on the other, grew sharper. In September 1965 – in the shadow of an astonishing debacle in Cardiff, where Haynes and Jack Henry Moore had undertaken to present C.P. Taylor's new play *Of Hope and Glory* at the Commonwealth Arts Festival and apparently failed to deliver a presentable production – John Calder proposed that Haynes step down from the Chairmanship of the Club and remain as Artistic Director only, re-establishing the formal distinction between staff and lay members of the Club. He was replaced in the Chair by Andrew Elliott, a Committee member strongly identified with the attempt to clarify and regularise the Club's financial position.

If relations between Jim Haynes and the Committee had remained warm and communicative during this period – and in particular if he had kept them more fully in touch with his artistic plans, instead of leaving them to struggle with the dust and ashes of shoestring finance – it might have been possible for the Traverse to work out a strategy for resolving these inevitable tensions, and meeting the need for a minimum of formal structure and financial control without totally destroying the freewheeling, creative atmosphere Haynes had been so successful in generating. But instead, Haynes and his Committee had begun to drift apart on a personal level, and the pace of that drift accelerated after Elliott took over the Chair. Haynes had been experiencing his own pressures as Artistic Director, particularly from the writers, actors, and directors with whom he now worked. He came to feel strongly that in order to increase the impact of the Traverse's work, to maximise its earning power and to offer an attractive prospect to actors, directors and writers, the Traverse had to be able to guarantee a London transfer for successful Edinburgh productions; and he began to set up various schemes – culminating in the London Traverse idea of 1966, based at the Jeanetta Cochrane Theatre in Holborn and co-directed by Haynes, Michael Geliot and Ralph Koltai – which would provide the Traverse with a London sister-theatre.

This scheme – sensible enough, from Haynes' increasingly metropolitan point of view – was unfortunate in two ways. Firstly, it annoyed the Traverse Committee in principle, partly since Haynes, never particularly interested in formal lines of communication, neglected to keep them well informed about his plans. The idea that a show can only be considered 'successful' after it has conquered London is bound to irritate an Edinburgh committee, and the idea that the theatre could only survive by attracting the kind of actors, directors and writers who insist on London exposure must have been threatening to their sense of the Traverse's intrinsic value as an Edinburgh organisation. In more practical terms, Jim Haynes' increasing absorption in the London operation meant that he spent longer and longer periods away from the Traverse; in the summer of 1965, he disappeared for several weeks without leaving any information on where he could be contacted or what he proposed by way of an autumn season, and the Committee were so distraught that they actually started the process of finding a stop-gap director in case Haynes should fail to return. Sheila Colvin resigned from the post of General Manager at the end of the 1965 Festival, saying that she remained firm friends with Jim Haynes but would never work with him again; she couldn't stand the unpredictability. Her replacement was a

tidy and orthodox theatre administrator called Eric Jenks, and he and
Haynes seem to have loathed one another cordially on sight, increasing
the general tension within the organisation.

The most damaging conflict of all, though – the one which led to
Haynes' dramatic resignation – arose when he produced his own
solution to the problem of his long absences from Edinburgh in the
shape of Jack Henry Moore, whom he hoped to appoint as his Associate
Director. Moore was an enigmatic and highly abrasive character, a
young American whom Haynes had met on a trip to Dublin, where
Moore apparently ran either a detective agency (according to Jim
Haynes) or a domestic cleaning agency (according to the Scottish poet
and playwright Tom McGrath, who was hanging out in Dublin in 1964
and introduced Haynes to Moore). Like the mime artist Lindsay Kemp –
with whom he co-devised a version of Dylan Thomas's *A Child's
Christmas in Wales*, first presented at the Traverse at Christmas 1964 –
Moore was overtly and unashamedly homosexual, at a time when
homosexual acts were still technically illegal. Perhaps for this reason –
but also because he believed passionately in his theatrical talent as a
director and talent-spotter – Haynes took Moore unreservedly under his
wing during 1965, and encouraged him to become heavily involved in
the work of the Traverse, acting as stage manager, reading scripts
(which he apparently did voraciously and conscientiously – Haynes says
it was Moore who first spotted the talent of C.P. Taylor) and directing
several shows, including, in December 1965, a hugely successful
production of the musical *The Fantastics*. 'Can't say I liked Jack Henry,'
says Tom Mitchell. 'Nobody did, except Jim. But I nearly forgave 'im
everything when I saw that . . .'

Despite this notable hit, though, Jack Henry Moore remained
unpopular with the Traverse staff and Committee, who found him rude,
uncommunicative and extremely hard to work with. Jim Haynes
maintains that some of this dislike boiled down to prejudice against
Moore's sexuality, and to judge from the records and photographs of the
time – which show lots of doe-eyed, short-skirted 'girls' draped around
the place in traditional servicing roles, typing, catering, serving coffee,
being decorative in the bar – sexual politics in the modern sense certainly
wasn't the organisation's strong suit. Sex was all the rage at the
Traverse, and sexual frankness a strong motif of many of the early
productions; but the ethos at the time was very much to do with
uninhibited access to pretty young women, and it's easy to see how the
presence of an unabashed homosexual might have disturbed it a little.
Tom Mitchell says there were actual threats of police raids on Moore; at
any rate, what with Moore's unpopularity, and his persistent problems
in obtaining clearance to work in Britain from Equity, the Committee
were reluctant to allow Haynes to employ him as his permanent
associate.

Meanwhile, back at the balance-sheet, the tired and disgruntled
Committee were becoming increasingly inclined to blame Haynes for the
Club's financial problems. In fact, although his artistic programme was
sometimes extravagant, there was never any real suggestion that he
spent the Club's money improperly, or that he was solely responsible for

the funding crisis it faced. But he certainly was not the man to co-operate in a period of stricter financial control. He was vague about which till his salary and expenses should come from, he lived on the Traverse premises and wandered off leaving bills unpaid, his dedication to spontaneity made budgeting almost impossible, his penchant for casting and rehearsing in London was expensive in itself and persistently annoying to the Committee, and by the Spring of 1966 – with the guarantors threatening to withdraw from the organisation altogether unless Haynes was brought to heel – it was clear that a crisis couldn't be avoided.

Finally, and crucially, Haynes began to lose touch with the thinking of an influential section of the membership. Audiences dwindled in early 1966, bar profit slumped, and criticisms of the Club's ethos and artistic policy began to be heard. According to Una Flett there was an increasing division between 'beat' types and 'responsible' members of the Club, with 'responsibles' tending to stay away, and complaining about the 'beat' appearance of the premises, the clientele and Jim Haynes himself. There were also complaints, so Andrew Elliott told the press in the run-up to the 1966 Annual General Meeting on 27 April, about the 'crude type of plays being performed', and requests for more varied productions, more classics and British premieres on the Terry Lane/ Callum Mill pattern, and a programme with broader appeal. According to a list of complaints prepared for the Committee in February, one member said that 'pelvic regions are self-limiting as areas of explanation, and the Traverse seems to be stuck there . . .'

So far as Haynes was concerned, though, the Committee under Elliott's Chairmanship had simply taken a wrong turning in their anxiety to improve the Traverse's situation, had allowed 'the balance of control to move from the artistic to the financial sector', and had forgotten – in the words of a circular he sent out to members early in 1966 – that the Committee's job was to find ways of financing what the Artistic Director wanted to do, not to tell him that he couldn't do it. In the run-up to the 1966 AGM, he invited his new friend Nicholas Fairbairn – now a Scottish Tory MP and ex-Solicitor-General, then a flamboyant young advocate well known for his astonishing waistcoats – to stand for election as a replacement Chairman, on the understanding that Fairbairn would be strongly supportive of his artistic directorship and would make sure that Haynes 'never had to worry about money'. Together with the publisher John Calder – who was about to resign from the Traverse Committee, and was anxious to see a new line-up that would support the Haynes policy while offering some strong positive control – Haynes assembled a slate of supportive candidates for the Committee, and at the huge crisis AGM in the Pollock Hall – attended by almost four hundred Traverse members – Haynes effectively won a vote of confidence by appealing over the Committee's heads to his electorate, and by making a strong pitch on the issue of artistic freedom as opposed to nit-picking financial constraint. Nicky Fairbairn was elected Chairman, with Richard Demarco continuing as Vice-Chair. Only two members of the old Committee – John Martin and Demarco – remained, and Martin resigned within a day or two when he realised that Haynes' position was substantially unchanged.

After this miniature Traverse coup – which effectively flushed out of the organisation the entire group of friends that had come together to form it three years before – Jim Haynes believed that his position was secure, and that his new friends on the Committee would give him a free rein. But while the new Committee were broadly well-disposed to him, they were also a strong-minded and highly confident bunch of professionals (lecturers, doctors, a journalist), capable of making up their own minds about the best interests of the Traverse, and relatively indifferent to its romantic history. During May, an unpleasant difference of opinion developed within the Committee – or between the Committee and Richard Demarco – over the fate of the Traverse Art Gallery. Demarco's art exhibitions – mounted in the cafe-bar space directly above the theatre, and, on one memorable occasion during the Festival of 1964, in some handsome rooms in George Street belonging to the Bank of Scotland – had been an integral part of the Traverse's work from the outset, and over the years between 1963 and 1966 he had shown an impressive range of artists, including Elizabeth Blackadder, Mark Boyle, Douglas Craft, Jasper Johns, William Johnstone, Patrick Heron, and many more, Demarco claims that the gallery sold £10,000 worth of art in its first year of operation, a remarkable figure at 1964 prices. But he had become increasingly frustrated by the limitations of space at the Traverse, and when in May 1966 several of the old Traverse guarantors – John Martin, Andrew Elliott, Jim Walker – agreed to set him up in a spacious new gallery in Melville Crescent, he was anxious to accept their offer, but to continue to operate his gallery in conjunction with the Traverse and under the Traverse banner.

In a series of remarkably graceless discussions during May, the new Traverse Committee quibbled at the scheme, picked holes in it, and persistently implied that they were being asked to do the new gallery a favour in allowing the Traverse name to be used; and eventually they decided to refuse permission. The new gallery, as the Richard Demarco Gallery, took shape and prospered in its fashion; but this decision, and the manner in which it was made, shows how little sympathy the new Committee had with the old Haynes-Demarco sense of the 'Traverse spirit' as something that was everywhere and nowhere, that could flourish in James Court and in Melville Crescent without a hint of competition.

Haynes, significantly, had opposed the Committee's decision on the Gallery; and within six weeks of the AGM, the whole fragile settlement was finally broken over Haynes' insistence on reopening the question of Jack Henry Moore. At a long and agonising final meeting on 6 June, Haynes gave the Committee an ultimatum; if they refused to appoint Moore as his Associate, he would have no option but to resign. The Committee considered, recalled Haynes into the room, pleaded with him not to wreck his relationship with the Traverse on unreasoning loyalty to a man there were good reasons not to employ (Moore still had no Equity clearance), begged him to see that he was making his stand on a most unfortunate issue; but Haynes stood firm on his commitment to Moore, and in the end, in a mood of shocked disbelief on both sides, the Committee accepted his resignation.

The events of the night rapidly deteriorated from crisis into pure melodrama, with Haynes rushing distraught from the meeting (after telling his friend Demarco that he simply didn't believe the Committee could sack him from what he felt was his own theatre, his 'child'), travelling back with Nicky Fairbairn to the Fairbairn castle at Fordell in Fife, climbing out of a first-floor window at dead of night, and hitch-hiking back into Edinburgh, where he burst into Ricky Demarco's house – Demarco was sitting up with friends, mulling over the disaster – weeping and almost literally beating his breast. However obvious it may have been that the Traverse was heading for some kind of crisis, the final catastrophe came as an appalling shock to Haynes. He retreated to the London Traverse to lick his wounds, but over the next few weeks he repeatedly rang the new Traverse Secretary, Una Maclean, and eventually sent a telegram begging the Committee to allow him to withdraw his resignation; he seems to have felt that his work at the Traverse was far from over, and Demarco, too, feels that he should have stayed at least another year, and that he left with terrible sadness and regret. In fact, given the traumatic circumstances of his departure, it is to Haynes' credit that he appears to bear no grudges, and that he felt able to reappear in Edinburgh within a few years, as a regular Festival visitor to his old stamping ground.

In the end, so far as a large and influential section of the membership was concerned, Jim Haynes simply went too far both artistically and financially, and something had to give. But as the shock surrounding his resignation showed, by 1966 Jim Haynes and his style, his aura, his attitude, had become permanently and irrevocably associated with the Traverse and its public image. For one thing – and as much through what he was as through anything he articulated – Haynes stood without reservation for the idea of freedom, in the arts and everywhere else; for the notion that no footling considerations of censorship or law or regulations or administrative tidiness or, above all, of finance (for what was lack of money but the biggest censor of all?) should be allowed to get in the way of the business of self-expression. As far as he was concerned, if art came first, money should and would follow. He simply had no time for what Una Flett calls in her thesis 'the rational calculation of economic means'; he knew that if anyone had stopped to do a rational economic calculation, the Traverse would never have opened at all. It was an extreme position, but it's one that must find a small echo in every creative organisation; and it's because he embodied that reckless, essential, 'let's-do-it' instinct so completely and unhesitatingly that the Haynes era will be remembered as long as the subsidised arts survive.

More subtly, Haynes approached his theatre work from the radical perspective – almost unique, in post-war British theatre – of someone who was not a theatre professional, and had no vested interest in becoming one. This left him free to take a completely open view of the relationship between theatre and the world outside it, and of the need for theatre to be flexible in form and organisation – perhaps even to metamorphose into something else entirely – if that audience-relationship is to stay alive. To him, he says now, theatre was 'just a means to an end, whereas to most people who work in professional theatre, the thing is an end in itself. To us it was also about books, and folk songs . . . we were trying to transfer an attitude, create kindred spirits, spread joy, and theatre seemed like one way to create that change in people.' Haynes's instinct was to take the Traverse back to its social origins, as a meeting-place that was perhaps only incidentally a theatre, and it was that feeling that the show was part of some much larger life-experience that made the work itself seem so exciting. As the playwright Stanley Eveling puts it, 'the thing about the Traverse at the beginning was that it was more like an anti-theatre than a theatre . . . then it got famous for putting on plays, and everyone thought it must be a theatre, then. But the original idea was that people came to the place not to *see* but to *live*. The play was the centre, but just the centre, of a more generalised thing that was happening to them. They were being liberated, that's what. Then they would straighten their ties and fix their hair and go back to their nice Edinburgh flats. But it had an effect . . .'.

Of course, that sense of fluidity about the Traverse's role was bound to fade with time. As the world recognised its theatrical achievements, the Traverse increasingly accepted that definition of itself, and got on with the business of putting on plays; after Jim Haynes left, it would be run without exception by proper, professional theatre directors, in the manner of every other subsidised theatre of the day, and in that sense 'professionalism' triumphed early. But the old anarchic image of a place where literally anything could happen was too vital to die completely; and together with that old revolutionary defiance against the 'rational calculation of means', it lives on in modified form at the heart of the Traverse idea, and perhaps in the heart of every worthwhile artist who has ever battled with a Board and a budget.

Haynes was and remains a strange, elusive character, and many have detected a kind of vacuum at the centre of him. In 1988 (after a career that took him to London, where he founded the Arts Lab., and Amsterdam, where he edited an amazing early-70's magazine called *Suck*) he lives in a run-down but vaguely alluring atelier in Paris – full of unmade beds and transient friends – which many have described as 'a 60's time-warp'; Jack Henry Moore is in the basement, running a video company. There, he runs a small publishing imprint, holds soirées, entertains, animates, but in a style that finds less response than it did in Edinburgh 25 years ago. Stanley Eveling says Haynes is like a guest at some huge worldwide party, who never goes home to get on with life; Charles Marowitz, in a brilliant, half-exasperated contribution to Haynes's book ('What is a participatory autobiography,' he writes, 'but a renunciation of self-definition . . .?') goes so far as to say that the Haynes psyche is so remarkable, in its uncritical enthusiasm for everything and everyone, that it ought, after his death, to be 'preserved in ectoplasm and kept on permanent exhibition at the Smithsonian Institute.'

Marowitz also says that Haynes' extraordinary receptivity is fundamentally 'irreconcilable with art', which requires discipline, aggression, discrimination. But if ever there was proof that art requires both – in different measures at different times – it lies in the Traverse in space for the world's creative efforts built in his own image; and the energy that rushed in to greet him – modified through other, sterner minds, including Marowitz's own – was enough to create art Haynes himself could not have imagined.

CHAPTER 3
Gordon McDougall

The news that Jim Haynes had left the Traverse was greeted with dismay in the British theatre world. It was in the immediate aftermath of the row that Harold Hobson wrote his emotional *Sunday Times* piece declaring that the Committee could do no better for world theatre than to welcome their prodigal director back with open arms, and Allen Wright recalls that many Edinburgh observers believed the Traverse would never survive the loss of the man who had become its social and psychological lynchpin.

But from inside the Traverse organisation, things looked less gloomy. For one thing, people within the Traverse had more reason than outside observers to understand the tremendous strains that had been weakening the organisation towards the end of Jim Haynes' directorship. For another, the notion that Jim Haynes was the sole proprietor and protector of the Traverse idea had always been a convenient simplification of the truth; and just as the theatre had managed – with the imaginative support of some influential Edinburgh citizens, and the dedicated effort of a few radical theatre professionals – to launch itself in Haynes' absence, so it now set out, with the same resources plus Arts Council backing, to survive his departure.

Of course, something was broken when the Traverse parted company with its founding group; the early Traverse had embodied the idea that the medium – this strange, free-flowing place, where performance and the lifestyle of the members tended to merge – was the message, whereas the new Committee accepted a more conventional framework of operations. But they wanted a successful experimental theatre in Edinburgh all right, and in Nicky Fairbairn the Traverse had acquired a skilful and, in his way, charismatic Chairman, who had no intention of allowing his new protégé to come to grief. In the weeks following the Haynes resignation, the Traverse Committee met, as Fairbairn joked at the time, 'more often than the Cabinet,' and according to Una Flett's notes of committee meetings she attended, it soon became apparent that they were an impressive and decisive group, including – in Kenneth Ireland of Pitlochry Festival Theatre – one experienced theatre professional. Within a couple of weeks, they had determined that there was no point in reopening the painful matter of Haynes' resignation, that they wanted to look to the future, and that they would advertise for a new Artistic Director; in the meantime, they set themselves to work to pull together some kind of programme for the 1966 Festival, now less than two months away.

They had every reason for optimism, for on the staff side of the organisation, the prospects looked very bright indeed. The Jim Haynes era may have left the Traverse in financial difficulties, but it had been stacking up priceless artistic reserves, in that by 1966 the place had become a kind of lodestone, a symbol of the radical potential of modern theatre, a place where a whole generation of bright young professionals wanted to work; and it's significant of the way in which the Haynes dragnet scooped up talent that by the time he left, three future Artistic

Directors of the place had already become involved in its work. Mike Ockrent, a physics student at Edinburgh University, had directed a huge pro-am production of Peter Weiss's *The Investigation* in early 1966, and Haynes' successor Gordon McDougall, a trainee director at Granada Television on attachment to the Royal Court, had been Assistant Director on the London transfer of *Happy End*.

But the most significant presence of all – and the one without which the Committee's best efforts to assemble a 1966 Festival programme might have come to nothing – was that of Max Stafford-Clark, who had been drawn into the magic atmosphere of the Traverse as a young theatre-struck student, visiting Edinburgh in the winter of 1964–65 with his Trinity College Dublin rugby team. In the summer of 1965, he came back to the Traverse with a classy student revue called *Dublin Fare* (later *Stewed Irish*), which was revived during the Edinburgh Festival of that year; and in the Festival he was also encouraged to direct the world premiere of *Oh Gloria!*, a new play by the American writer Robert Shure. So by the Spring of 1966, when the row between Haynes and the Committee came to a head, the personable young Stafford-Clark (then just 25, and well liked by almost everyone except the General Manager, Eric Jenks) was already ensconced in the Traverse as an Assistant Stage Manager, occasionally sallying forth to present shows like *The Paterson's Shortbread Show* of March 1966, put together, no doubt, in homage to the biscuit interests of Traverse patron and guarantor Jim Walker.

Shortly after the Haynes sacking, the Committee hurriedly called in Stafford-Clark (who had been given his marching orders by Eric Jenks a few weeks before, on grounds of general sloppiness), and asked him to supervise the production of some stop-gap shows, and to help compile a Festival programme, a task which he seems to have fulfilled with great enterprise and dexterity. In early July, Eric Jenks was taken ill, and went on extended sick leave (Derek Salberg's Arts Council report on the Traverse organisation, compiled in that summer as a condition of the Council's increased grant to the theatre, paints a most vivid picture of the impossible number of routine administrative tasks with which Jenks had to wrestle in the tiny Traverse box-office, and unlike many Traverse people he wasn't the man to shrug his shoulders at a modicum of chaos). In his absence, the young Max was promptly appointed acting General Manager, a post in which he was confirmed just after the Festival; and by late July he and the Committee had finalised a Festival programme which included world premieres of James Saunders' *Double Double* (directed by Stafford-Clark himself), John Hall's *The Little Woman* (directed by Alan Vaughan Williams), and a new show about Lorca by Bettina Jonic, with music by Harrison Birtwistle. There was also a British premiere of Roland Dubillard's *The Swallows*, a visit from Liverpool Everyman Theatre with an enterprising quadruple bill of pieces by Rene de Obaldia and Eugene Ionesco, and a healthy sprinkling of late-night shows and revues, including many appearances by The Scaffold.

It was into this rather strange situation – a powerful Committee pleased with its achievement in keeping the show on the road, a popular young General Manager already established in the place and effectively acting as Director – that Gordon McDougall walked during the Festival of 1966. He was only 25 (exactly the same age as Stafford-Clark), had been involved in successful student theatre at Cambridge in the early 60's, had won a traineeship in television direction at Granada in Manchester, and had had theatre experience – on attachment from Granada – at Barrow-in-Furness (where he worked with Giles Havergal) and at the Royal Court in London; he also carried with him an academic record of a distinction unusual in theatrical circles. In coming to the Traverse, he faced not only the usual difficulties of taking over after a successful interregnum, but also a crushing weight of conflicting expectations about the direction the Traverse should take. On one hand, there were powerful external pressures – from the critics, from fans of the old Traverse, from Ronald Mavor and the Arts Council – to emulate and sustain the Jim Haynes achievement; on the other, there was a strong Committee, quite convinced that whatever it wanted, it was nothing like Jim Haynes.

In fact, right from McDougall's first contact with the Traverse, he had been identified by the Committee as a kind of sober alternative to Haynes. In the summer of 1965, as a keen young trainee, he had written around to several interesting theatres in search of an assistant director's job, and the Traverse, at its wit's end for a stop-gap director during one of Jim Haynes' absences, had invited him north to talk. In the course of a hideously embarrassing summer day, McDougall managed to miss the Committee members Andrew Elliott and Alan Daiches, who had gone to meet him at the airport, and wandered into town and into the Traverse, where he met, in the box-office, some lanky American whom he did not know, and to whom he explained that he had been invited up to talk about being Artistic Director. After chatting to McDougall at some length about his ideas for the place, this character revealed that he was in fact Jim Haynes, that he had just returned from his holiday, that he was Artistic Director of the Traverse, and intended so to remain.

At this point Elliott and Daiches turned up in confusion and bore McDougall off to lunch, but he remains to this day understandably irritated by the Haynes legend, and he cannot have relished the fact that throughout his period at the Traverse he had to wrestle with a combination of problems created by the Haynes regime, and problems created by the ending of it. On one hand, there was the spectacular financial confusion, and a massive £2,000 loss on the restaurant somehow incurred during the interregnum of 1966. On the other, there were persistent public-image problems caused by the loss of Haynes' charismatic personality, and it must have been galling to McDougall to hear the same Committee that had dispensed with Haynes' services complaining – in the spring of 1967 – that the Traverse's image was becoming 'too dull and conservative', and that membership figures were drastically down (which they were – membership income dropped by almost a third between 1965 and 1967) because of 'the loss of Jim Haynes' catalytic presence'. Basically, whoever succeeded Jim Haynes was bound to be cast as the 'straight man', the boring theatre professional called in to give the repertoire a more solid, reliable look, to keep his financial nose clean, and to professionalise the whole operation; and at first Gordon McDougall seemed to fit that bill so neatly that some of the admirers of the Traverse in its earlier, maverick incarnation were concerned that the place would dwindle into nothing more than a small-scale rep.

For a start, McDougall looked the part; he was short-haired, softly-spoken and reserved, in a typically English manner that contrasted sharply with Haynes's transatlantic exuberance. Then, he was absolutely dedicated to the idea that the Traverse should be a fully professional outfit, offering the members a standard of production on which they could rely; he had heard some of the (no doubt exaggerated) horror-stories about Haynes' irresponsibility that were circulating in the Committee after his resignation, rumours of half-rehearsed, unscripted shows being allowed to wander on stage on the strength of a friendly telephone call, and he felt compelled to present a strongly contrasting attitude. 'I think one thing Max and I did in that period,' he says, 'was to establish that whatever you saw at the Traverse – and you would almost certainly go not knowing what it was, what it was about, or who the writer was, or anything about the actors' track-records – you would know that you were going to get a solidly interesting professional evening, and that it wasn't going to be something just put together at the last minute.'

He was also less ecstatic than Haynes about the idea that the Traverse should do nothing but new plays. At his first press conference in Edinburgh, shortly after his appointment in July, he said that the theatre would do new plays, 'but because they are worthwhile, not just for the sake of doing them'. Like Callum Mill, he was fascinated by the unique properties of the Traverse space, and excited by the idea of using it as a forum for re-examining classic texts, as well as a nursery for new talent. Again, this must have been music to the ears of the element in the Traverse membership that had been pleading for more classics, and worrying to those who treasured the Traverse's unique commitment to the risk of the new; and McDougall played into the hands of his critics by choosing, as his opening productions in September/October 1966, a pair of John Osborne plays – *Look Back in Anger* and the more recent *Inadmissible Evidence* – neither of which was new, and one of which was rapidly becoming standard repertory material.

In fact, the productions – starring Scottish film actor John Fraser, then something of a young matinée idol – worked outstandingly well in the Traverse space, and were so successful in audience terms that they were transferred to a larger hall at the YMCA in South St. Andrew Street; but the doubts about McDougall's intentions towards the Traverse remained, and were not allayed either by his first new play at the Traverse – David Storey's first stage play *The Restoration of Arnold Middleton*, done in November 1966 on a carefully-contrived living-room set – or by his next production, a memorable version of D.H. Lawrence's *The Daughter-in-Law*, featuring the great and much-loved Scottish actress, Lennox Milne.

Apart from the mood of the Committee, there were also powerful external reasons why the atmosphere of Gordon McDougall's Traverse was bound to be different. In 1964, Jim Haynes became Artistic Director of an organisation that drew more than 80% of its income from subscriptions, box office, and private fundraising, and less than 10%

from public subsidy. By 1966, the Arts Council was providing over 40% of income, and as the Traverse members ceased to pay the piper, the theatre's relationship with them, and its Club character, inevitably weakened. The theatre's response to the world outside it became more premeditated, more conscious, more intellectual; there was less of the organic, instinctual sense of giving the members what they needed.

Beyond that, the whole theatre life of Edinburgh had changed in the three years of the Traverse's existence. The Lyceum had developed from a tired, underused Victorian relic (under threat of demolition to make way for a car-park in 1962) to a thriving new civic theatre under Clive Perry and Richard Eyre, who were appointed around the same time as McDougall. The theatre therefore had to think much harder and more clearly about its role. It no longer had the automatic kudos of being the only serious, internationally-aware theatre in the Festival city, and a vague sense of mission was no longer enough to guarantee public support or funding; and what is remarkable about the McDougall era – and he is, perhaps inevitably, the most undervalued of all Traverse directors – is that this young graduate, in his first attempt at running a theatre or anything else, somehow mustered the personal and intellectual resources to meet most of these demands for greater clarity and rigour in the organisation, while managing to sustain the old spark of Traverse radicalism and controversy.

The biggest single factor in that success lay in the relationship he was able to strike up, right from his first day in Edinburgh, with his General Manager and future Associate, Max Stafford-Clark. On the day of McDougall's interview – a glorious July day, as he recalls it – the two young men went for a stroll round the Castle Esplanade, while Stafford-Clark explained his attachment to the Traverse and his ambitions as a director. McDougall had his interview, argued vigorously and at length with Nicky Fairbairn (who liked him on sight) and was offered the job; and he seems to have recognised almost immediately that Stafford-Clark's was a talent he should accommodate and collaborate with, rather than try to assert his superior status as Artistic Director. Of course Stafford-Clark's notorious charm may have had something to do with McDougall's willingness to accept this arrangement; it's intriguing to read Una Flett's contemporary impressions of him as a young man who already combined an impeccable background with an exceptionally disarming and democratic manner, great social skills and many useful contacts. At any rate, once again, by chance, the Traverse acquired that complementary two-handed leadership that seems to suit it best, with McDougall co-ordinating policy and directing a solid diet of new plays and classics, and the flairful Stafford-Clark providing a link back to the wilder avant-garde mood of the Haynes/Demarco era, and on to a new and exciting relationship – with the experimental La Mama company of New York – which was to set the tone for the Traverse's development up to the end of the decade.

And as it turned out, it was this McDougall/Stafford-Clark team that led the Traverse into the single most controversial period in its history. It's worth recalling, here, that when Jim Haynes left Edinburgh, the 60's as we remember them had barely begun. It was during Gordon McDougall's time – 1966–68 – that student protest began to be a serious feature of British and American life, that demonstrations against the Vietnam War began to gain momentum, that hippies and yippies and the first hints of Flower Power began to waft across the Atlantic, bringing with them the beginnings of the drug culture that would eventually discredit the whole 60's movement; and although McDougall wasn't a gut cultural revolutionary in the Haynes mould – his attitude to politics was more structured and intellectual – he was a serious young radical, strongly receptive to the changes in the air.

So during his time at the Traverse, he responded enthusiastically to Stafford-Clark's growing interest (prompted by the publisher John Calder) in the American avant-garde writer Paul Foster, and in the La Mama group with whom Foster worked. In the spring of 1967, following McDougall's relatively conventional opening season, he and Stafford-Clark directed a series of Paul Foster plays, including a notorious piece called *Balls* – in which the cast consists of two tennis balls swinging above an empty stage – which won what McDougall calls a 'bricks-in-the-Tate-style' editorial in the *Daily Express*; and at the 1967 Edinburgh Festival, the Traverse spent more than it could reasonably afford on a terrific programme of La Mama shows at the Barrie Halls, backed by their official Festival production of Foster's *Tom Paine*. It was one of the La Mama shows – *Futz*, about the tender relationship between a man and his pig – that produced the famous Scottish *Daily Express* headline "Filth on the Fringe", and a searing Traverse Talk-In (the Traverse was running a series of vigorous midnight debates during this Festival, chaired by the likes of Nicky Fairbairn, Gillian Reynolds, David Frost) featuring the entire La Mama company versus Brian Meek, the journalist who had written the story without, alas, seeing the show.

In that same wild Festival – in which the Traverse presented no fewer than 22 shows – McDougall also directed what he calls a 'disastrous' production of Jarry's *Ubu in Chains*, a British premiere and a homage to Terry Lane's great Festival success four years earlier with *Ubu Roi*. This quintessentially 1960's event had outrageous designs by Gerald Scarfe ('Ma and Pa Ubu got up as a huge hairy cunt and huge hairy prick, and everyone wearing Sergeant Pepper uniforms and Mars Bar insignia because Marianne Faithfull had just been busted at that party with a Mars Bar . . . all wonderful contemporary stuff . . .'); it also had music by the Soft Machine, who finally turned up on the morning of the first night and, according to McDougall, sat in their van until lunchtime arguing with their road manager (who was against it) about whether they should do this ludicrously ill-paid 'gig' or not. After the first performance, McDougall had to contend with further wrath and disappointment from the press, to whom he had rashly suggested that *Ubu* would be even filthier than *Futz*, but after a kindly *Guardian* review the production became something of a cult success, and McDougall retired for a two-week holiday.

Thus it was that the Traverse, under the supposedly mild-mannered McDougall, actually reached the height of its notoriety in Edinburgh, with wildly exaggerated stories circulating about the drinking, dope-smoking, drug-dealing and lurid sexual practices that were supposed to take place there. At the time, the Traverse was a powerful focus for respectable Edinburgh's fantasies and fears about the new 'permissive' age. McDougall tells a story of an actor climbing on a bus at the bottom of the High Street, telling the conductress he wanted to get off at the Traverse, and being rewarded with a big nudge and an 'Ooh, you naughty boy!'; and in February 1968 the most threatening scandal of the Traverse's whole history erupted when a student company called Edinburgh Experimental Theatre, who had already appeared at the theatre with some success, staged a production (which neither Stafford-Clark nor McDougall had managed to vet) called *Mass in F*, in which a young girl sat on stage stripped to the waist and recounted her sexual history, to the accompaniment of superfluously horrible goings-on on the floor around her.

The scandal was enormous and the press coverage excessive, with threats of closure for the Traverse, of sendings-down from the university for the students, and of peremptory withdrawal of the Edinburgh Corporation's minuscule £350 grant ('as if we cared!' says McDougall); Councillor J. Kidd, then Edinburgh's leading scourge of permissiveness in drama, moved into overdrive, and for a few days it seemed as though the theatre might have fatally overplayed its hand. The production was withdrawn in order to protect the students from academic discipline, and Nicky Fairbairn – in an unequivocally supportive gesture typical of the Committee's attitude at the time – joined McDougall in penning and performing a hasty riposte called *F in Mass*, which amused audiences mightily. The row simmered down and the Traverse survived, but by the time McDougall left in April 1968 – having been tempted by a dazzling offer to become Head of Drama at Granada – no-one would have dared complain that the Traverse's image was 'too dull and conservative'. As a parting gift, the Committee gave him a glass goblet engraved with one of Councillor Kidd's more memorable quotes: 'I do not approve,' it read, 'of drama as such.'

But alongside all this, there was also a more serious strain of radicalism in McDougall's own work. Like Haynes, in this if in nothing else, McDougall is not interested in theatre for its own sake; he believes it should be a means for 'communicating that there are things that need doing about the way people live.' At his first press conference in July 1966, he had expressed a wish to prise the theatre free of its traditionally middle-class audience, and to use Joan Littlewood-style documentary techniques to produce shows which related to contemporary issues; and this remained a strong subtext of his Traverse work. In the conventional sense, he encouraged new writing by making sure that the Traverse in his time provided a forum for writers like David Storey, Stewart Conn, Ranald Graham, Ellen Dryden, Stanley Eveling, Don Taylor and David Gregan. But in the documentary area he seems to have had an unusually active approach to commissioning and working with writers, often hatching ideas himself and bringing in writers to work on them. At the beginning of his time at the Traverse, he compiled late-night documentary pieces on subjects like *The Vietnam Hearings* (December 1966) and *The Denning Report on the Profumo Affair* (January 1967), and later he produced shows like *A Life in Bedrooms* (based on the Rector of Stiffkey scandal of the 1930's), Ranald Graham's *Aberfan*, a memorable quasi-documentary performed by children from the thriving Theatre Workshop group, linking the stories of the Tay Bridge and Aberfan disasters, and *Would You Look at Them Smashing All the Lovely Windows*, a frighteningly prescient play (in March 1968) about the Irish Rebellion of 1916, written by David Wright.

At Christmas 1967, he directed an intense production of *Waiting for Godot*, which the cast (John Shedden and Richard Wilson) researched by spending a whole day in the Grassmarket with the down-and-outs, whose presence in the heart of this self-consciously respectable city disturbed McDougall. 'We did it,' he says, 'to remind people of what the Traverse building had been, and that the tramps were still there.' And as well as expressing these concerns in his work, McDougall brought them into the Traverse in more explicit ways, running Talk-Ins on local issues, and developing links with an Edinburgh student body that was just moving into the forefront of protest with the Malcolm Muggeridge affair. McDougall still remembers a particularly depressing Talk-In on the then ring-road scheme, which would have run through the Meadows and sliced a great swathe through the classical beauty of the New Town; even now, he speaks with passion about the struggle to conserve classical Edinburgh at that time, and he seems to have inherited in full the love for the fabric of Old Town and New Town that was common to all the Traverse founders.

It would be wrong to suggest that McDougall passed through his two years at the Traverse without friction. Like all ambitious young directors, he tended to be slightly obsessive about London recognition and the possibility of London transfers. In the summer of 1967, he invested a frightening amount of Traverse money in a huge London-rehearsed production of O'Neill's *Mourning Becomes Electra*, destined for the Arts Theatre and then the Baalbek Festival in Lebanon; when the Six Days' War broke out and prevented the Lebanon trip, £3,000 of Traverse money hung in the balance for days while the Lebanese government decided whether to pay up, and McDougall's attempts to cover the cost of the next summer's re-production, which did go to Baalbek and also to the Edinburgh Festival, caused some financial haggling with the Board after he left. He was also jealous of his reputation for financial reliability – although in fact the Traverse finances were so fraught at this period that it's impossible to tell with confidence how much of the £13,000-plus deficit the Traverse was carrying by the end of 1967 had been accumulated before McDougall's time, and how much during it.

McDougall was also less than diplomatic about the Scottish dimension of the Traverse and about Edinburgh as a city. He reacted with some irritation to questions about his casting and commissioning policy (raised both at the 1967 AGM and in the press), asserting (rather foolishly) that the Traverse had 'always been run by Englishmen and Americans' and that 'no Scottish director had ever worked there'. McDougall was in fact part-Scottish by birth, and he employed more Scottish actors than many of his successors at the Traverse. But he seems also to have felt a kind of native antipathy to the hypocrisy of lace-curtained Edinburgh, compounded by his disgust at the philistinism of the ring-road scheme and by his encounters with the Councillor Kidd lobby; and at his final Edinburgh press conference he declared – with great justice but little tact – that Edinburgh was basically a cultural desert, and that to most of its people the Festival was a bore and the Traverse a strip club.

But despite occasional outbreaks of abrasiveness, ambition, and financial nit-picking McDougall brought some essential and attractive qualities to the Traverse, including the intelligent political awareness of his own work, the receptivity to others' talents which he quickly learned in his relationship with Stafford-Clark, and something deeper, a kind of youthful romance with the whole idea of the Traverse that marks him out as belonging, far more than his style suggested, to the early pioneering days of the place. The best single indication of the survival of that spirit is the terrific volume of work that passed through the Traverse in McDougall's time. In the 21 months of Haynes' directorship the Traverse presented 50 separate shows, including 32 world premieres. In the 19 months of McDougall's it presented 54 shows, including 35 world premieres, and that kind of output – in an organisation that was constantly in serious debt – is not the mark of a conservative approach. According to McDougall, it literally never crossed his or Stafford-Clark's mind (nor, for that matter, was it put to them by the Arts Council) that cutting the number of productions might help to balance the books. The bond between the theatre and its membership was beginning to weaken, but at that stage the whole ethos still had to do with keeping the doors open, keeping the show on the road, providing enough changes of programme to keep the members loyal and interested. 'I think we all felt,' says McDougall, 'that if we went for three or four weeks without the members having something to see, then we'd lose them; they'd just never come back. That if we once let the place close, it would never open again.'

In order to achieve that relentless output of productions, the Traverse staff, including McDougall and Stafford-Clark, went to the most romantic lengths of commitment, working seven days a week, and often running round wealthy supporters with a begging-bowl on Friday nights to raise cash for the wages; in June 1967, the Committee actually heard that Stafford-Clark had been paying wages out of his own pocket. Both he and McDougall occasionally acted in productions in order to save money, and there were moments when they were driven to mount student productions (McDougall's *The Hessian Corporal*, co-directed with young Mike Ockrent and Ian Mandleberg, was one conspicuous example) because they couldn't afford professional ones; the whole idea of using children to play *Aberfan* was born out of a cash crisis. In his last four months at the Traverse, as well as forming a company and directing a heavyweight series of plays including *Waiting for Godot, Women Beware Women, Would You Look at Them Smashing All the Lovely Windows* and *Uncle Vanya*, McDougall organised – and to a large extent carried out – the redecoration of the upstairs bar to create a little weekend nightclub, in order to maximise the amount of income the building could produce; and that kind of total physical commitment to the place was not the mark of the slick young professional moving through on his way to better things. In fact, those who knew McDougall in Edinburgh are more likely to use phrases like 'the nicest of the lot of them', and 'not egotistical enough, too serious for his own good . . .'.

McDougall left the Traverse to take up a unique challenge at Granada Television, setting up and running the Stables Theatre Company, and also taking responsibility – with the same company of actors – for the company's broadcast play output. After the Stables experiment was wound up in 1971, McDougall put in a long, successful stint at Oxford Playhouse, which he directed (with Nicholas Kent) from 1974 to 1984. Today, he lives in deepest Worcestershire, a startlingly youthful 47-year-old with a young wife and family, commuting across the Atlantic on lucrative teaching-directing contracts at North American universities, and still deeply nostalgic for the radical atmosphere, the politics and the idealism, of the 1960's; he unhesitatingly described his time at the Traverse as the happiest of his life. Perhaps he never was diplomatic and flexible enough to climb the highest greasy poles in British theatre; perhaps his strong academic intellect – which has kept him in demand as a university teacher throughout his career – is a mixed blessing in a profession where craft and instinct still tend to matter most.

But what is clear is that he was the right man for the Traverse in 1966, and that it was the right place for him. He loved the theatre and its atmosphere, he understood its tensions better than most of his successors, he respected and admired a Committee that was likewise loyal to him, he enjoyed his relationship with Max Stafford-Clark, he steadied the theatre and its reputation after the thrills and spills of the Haynes era without crushing its radical identity. The Traverse will always be in his debt; it seems unlikely, given the arbitrary swings and roundabouts of theatrical success, that the debt will ever be paid in full.

CHAPTER 4
Max Stafford-Clark

There's something deeply romantic about the story of Max Stafford-Clark
and the Traverse, from the day in the winter of 1964–5 when he escaped
from the 'hearty male atmosphere' of his college rugby team, wandered
up to James Court, met Ricky Demarco, and found himself upstairs
stuffing envelopes and talking about his plans for that summer's *Dublin
Fare* revue, to the moment in 1972, well into the reign of his successor
Mike Rudman, when he began to wind up the Traverse Workshop
Company he had formed in association with the theatre, and left
Edinburgh to become a founder-member of Joint Stock, and later Artistic
Director of the Royal Court. As he says himself, he arrived at the
Traverse 'an unwritten-on blackboard,' the most junior of assistant stage
managers with no experience beyond student revue, and left seven years
later with 'quite a stance, quite a creed about theatre.' Like the fast-
moving little rugby half he was, he simply picked up the concept of the
magic, open-to-anything theatre space and ran with it, moving and
learning all the time, through the end of the Jim Haynes era, through the
threats and tackles of Gordon McDougall's time, into his own
experimental regime as Artistic Director, past the arrival of Michael
Rudman, through his Traverse Workshop Company and on into the
1970's; in a sense, he's running with it still.

For there's no doubt where Max Stafford-Clark stands on the spectrum
of Traverse directors. He was the one most clearly and unabashedly
dedicated to the idea of the Traverse as an experimental theatre, a
workshop for the exploration of what Jim Haynes called 'whatever's
coming next in theatre', no matter how bizarre that next thing might be.
Where his commitment to the idea of experiment came from is obscure; it
certainly seems, at least at first, to have been almost wholly a matter of
instinct, and not at all of deliberate policy. In *Thanks for Coming*, Jim
Haynes rather shrewdly remarks that whereas traditionally, British
society had been all about 'working-class kids with their noses against
the window-pane, looking in on the upper-class kids having a good
time', in the 60's the picture was suddenly reversed, with upper-class
kids longing to do a bit of slumming, and annoy their parents; perhaps
Max Stafford-Clark, as the well-bred and comfortably-off son of an
eminent psychiatrist, owed his early interest in the odd and the new
simply to that kind of rebellious urge. Tom Mitchell – who enjoyed a
warm relationship with Stafford-Clark because of their shared
enthusiasm for rugby, and because Max lived for a while in a flat at
Harvieston, Mitchell's gloomy chateau near Edinburgh – describes him
as a 'provocative' lad, and tells a story of how he once popped his head
into a Stafford-Clark rehearsal, saw that the play opened with a
prolonged scene of a woman extravagantly picking her nose, and said he
wasn't having that kind of infantile snook-cocking going on in his
premises. Returning a fortnight later, he went in to inspect the show,
and found that Stafford-Clark had obediently replaced it with an equally
long scene of a woman digging wax out of her ear. The playwright
Stanley Eveling, with whom Stafford-Clark enjoyed a long and

productive professional relationship, likewise remembers him as 'a wilful bugger', cheerfully 'deconstructing' perfectly normal plays that could have done with perfectly conventional productions; but hardly anyone ever seems to have been seriously annoyed.

At any rate, Stafford-Clark's feeling for the weird and the innovative in theatre began to assert itself fairly soon after his arrival at the Traverse. He was a young, enthusiastic theatre buff, and he had fallen in love with a theatre-space that was not only revolutionary in itself (in challenging traditional images of what a theatre should look and feel like), but which had also become a forum – in its first few seasons – for all the most radical, absurd and surrealist drama in the international canon, from Jarry to Pirandello and back again. So by the autumn of 1966 – when he had just been confirmed as General Manager and Assistant Director under Gordon McDougall – Stafford-Clark was busily introducing plays like Wolfgang Borchert's *The Man Outside*, remembered by McDougall as 'a very weird evening indeed'; and by early 1967 – when the *Edinburgh Evening News & Dispatch* profiled him under the headline 'Rugby And Greasepaint Do Mix!' (he played for Edinburgh Wanderers throughout his time in the city) – he had developed a strong interest, under John Calder's influence, in the work of the American Paul Foster, a writer in whom he sees the same Ionesco-like influences that attracted him to the work of Samuel Beckett, Edward Bond, Stanley Eveling and Caryl Churchill. In February of that year, he directed the Traverse triple-bill of Foster plays, including the notorious *Balls*. Later that year, Paul Foster came to Edinburgh, and by the summer plans had been made for the La Mama Troupe of New York – with whom Foster habitually worked – to visit Edinburgh during the Festival, to mount four productions at the Barrie Halls (including plays by Lanford Wilson and Sam Shepard, both still almost unknown), and to create one new show – Foster's *Tom Paine* – as the Traverse/La Mama contribution to the official Festival.

The *Futz* scandal, and the roaring controversy it generated, ensured that La Mama made a terrific impact on that year's Festival scene, and for Stafford-Clark the experience seems to have been crucial. La Mama's style of theatre – based as much on music, movement, mime, atmosphere and image as on the spoken word, conceived as 'happenings' rather than plays, developed within a company rather than written by some solitary playwright – seemed to him to open up a new world of possibilities in theatrical expression. 'That work,' he says, 'just hit a nerve with us, then. I think we felt we were in a period of revolution – not so much in content, as in *form*'; and after an autumn trip to the Mickery Theatre in Amsterdam (with a revised version of a programme of 'mini-plays' by new writers, which the Traverse had successfully presented cartoon-theatre-style during the Festival) he asked for leave of absence in the New Year of 1968, and went to America for six weeks to operate a follow-spot at La Mama performances, to watch their work, and to 'be part of their world.' Just before Christmas, the Traverse Committee went into a huddle and decided, in view of Stafford-Clark's 'obvious excellent qualifications', to appoint him Artistic Director in succession to Gordon McDougall, who had said he would be leaving at the end of the Spring season.

Whether the Committee – at this stage a noticeably distinguished and well–heeled body, led by Nicky Fairbairn, and including the banker Ian Noble, accountants James Ferguson, Joe Gerber and Ivison Wheatley, and Deirdre, Lady Primrose – knew exactly what they were getting when they appointed the youthful Max is hard to say. In his first two years at the Traverse, as well as expressing an interest in avant-garde American theatre, he had also shouldered a great deal of responsibility in working with apprentice writers around the Traverse, and had directed new plays or mini-plays by James Saunders, Ranald Graham, Stewart Conn, Stanley Eveling, Michael Jones, Ellen Dryden, Olwen Wymark, Carey Harrison, and Brian McMaster (whose short play *The Inert* was one of the few pieces ever given a full production at the Traverse after popping unsolicited through the letter-box). It may be that the Committee fancied they had found a junior, improved version of Jim Haynes, who would encourage new work and generate an exciting atmosphere while at the same time directing plays, saying the right things in polite society, and not indulging in financial anarchy – although Stafford-Clark himself says he had been 'the most dreadful and irresponsible General Manager', employing the time-honoured method of paying any bills that said the bailiff was on his way round, and ignoring the rest.

At any rate, they soon found out that things were not to be so simple. Stafford-Clark returned from America in the spring of '68 bursting with new theatrical ideas formulated under the influence of La Mama, and hit the Committee, at its March meeting, with the idea that the Traverse should form a permanent workshop company, and start working with writers in a completely new way. The Committee asked for more information, and the result – typical of Stafford-Clark's regime as Director – was a couple of lucid, well-written and altogether disarming documents, designed to explain his artistic thinking to the Committee and to win them over to it.

The first document – a list of possible objections to the scheme, under headings like *All Paul Foster and Balls!* and *Paying Actors for Doing Nothing* – demonstrated one of Stafford-Clark's most engaging characteristics as Artistic Director, namely his unfailing ability to see and acknowledge the difficulties his policy entailed. Under the final objection – 'We may get no return at all, artistically or financially, from this venture' – Stafford-Clark simply wrote 'Absolutely true'. In the second document – a longer and more complete statement of intent – he wrote firmly and with feeling about the theatre's commitment to new writing, and made it clear that encouraging and developing new playwrights must remain the most important single aspect of the Traverse's work; then went on to argue that the Traverse must, nevertheless, open its mind to the possibility of different kinds of formal innovation, which writers could not generate on their own. 'For some time,' he wrote, 'different groups in Europe and America have been trying to find a new theatre language . . . Simply, there's a growing dissatisfaction with actors standing on stage speaking speeches, and people sitting in the audience listening; this 'movement' is groping towards additional methods of expressing emotion and feeling; through noises, through dance movement, and through a much greater physical involvement.' Stafford-Clark urged that the development of this 'new language' could only be done through a permanent company working on a longer time-scale, 'developing' plays instead of simply rehearsing them and putting them on stage.

What Stafford-Clark was asking for – and he mentioned Peter Brook's work in the course of the document – was really a much more leisurely, Brook-style method of working, with long-term research and collaboration between writers, actors, designers, directors, musicians; and the Committee correctly perceived that it must be an expensive one, particularly since Stafford-Clark readily conceded that his workshop group would not be able to generate enough shows to keep the Traverse ticking over. It would mean more guest directors, more visiting companies, and the employment of other actors apart from the workshop group. However, Stafford-Clark won them over by promising that his workshop actors would be paid only £5 a week during rehearsal periods (he expected them to take evening jobs as 'waiters or something', he said), and by arguing that the Traverse, now on a solid artistic basis, had to 'strike out in a new direction' if it didn't want to be left in the artistic rearguard within a year or two. Ben Lassers and Ben Steen, reporting for the artistic Sub-Committee, said they felt that artistic policy should be, fundamentally, the province of the Artistic Director, and that provided Stafford-Clark promised to keep his whole operation within budget (£240 a week was the sum mentioned), the Committee should not stand in his way; and within a month or two of their decision Stafford-Clark had started to build up a fine company of actors, some of whom stayed with him for the next four years. At the 1968 AGM, in June, he told the members of the Club that his aim was 'to maintain an avant-garde theatre in Edinburgh, not just a small theatre with a new-play policy'.

During his 20 months as Artistic Director, Stafford-Clark and his company created eight shows, seven of them involving new plays and one – Megan Terry's *Comings and Goings*, which they chose as their first production in May 1968 – taking the form of an elaborate series of games for actors and audience, designed to elicit different relationships between them. In 1968 they produced Stanley Eveling's *The Lunatic, The Secret Sportsman and the Woman Next Door*, David Mowat's *Anna-Luse*, and – at the end of the year – Rosalyn Drexler's *The Line of Least Existence*; in 1969 they worked on the multi-author piece *Dracula*, Leo Lehmann's *Another Town* (paired with Samuel Beckett's *Play*), Eveling's *Dear Janet Rosenberg, Dear Mr. Kooning*, and Robert Nye and Bill Watson's *Sawney Bean*.

The rest of the Traverse programme – about three-quarters of it, in a period when the theatre still tended to operate for at least 11 months of the year – was made up of new work directed by visitors (David Benedictus directing his own play *Angels and Geese*, Carey Harrison's *In a Cottage Hospital*, C.P. Taylor's *Lies About Vietnam/Truth About Sarajevo*), student shows, little incidental pieces mounted by Workshop Company members, and visiting productions from companies like Open Space, the Freehold, American Theatre Project, and – overwhelmingly – the People Show, whose work seems to have dominated the Traverse programme during 1968; Allen Wright of *The Scotsman* describes these early People Shows as 'truly subversive and probably very good – it just so happened I couldn't stand them.' As Stafford-Clark points out, the theatrical movement that had come to Britain with La Mama and the Open Theatre in the mid-60's was beginning to gather momentum, and that momentum was expressing itself mainly through the avant-garde touring groups, to which the Traverse became a northern base and second home in the late 60's and early 70's.

Allen Wright wasn't alone, though, in his reservations about the People Show, or in his doubts about the whole trend of Stafford-Clark's work. He had taken considerable trouble to understand Stafford-Clark's thinking, even going so far – in June 1968 – as to attend one of his early workshop sessions, which he described as 'a curious mixture of a keep-fit class and a nursery-school music and movement session', and he was intrigued by the possibilities inherent in Megan Terry's *Comings and Goings*, which allowed the audience to stop and start the action by raising a baton at will. But he remained anxious about the relegation of language and text from its pre-eminent position in the hierarchy of theatrical expression, and to judge from Stafford-Clark's response to a thoughtful Scotsman piece on the subject – in which Wright expressed a hope that the Traverse would not lose the ability to handle 'words and ideas, which are the stuff of drama' – Stafford-Clark was indeed working through a phase when he felt that writers were failing to keep up with the latest developments in theatre, which were being generated by directors like Grotowski and Jerome Savary. In fact, Stafford-Clark never stopped working with writers, and only sought to suggest that writers, actors and directors would have to collaborate in different ways in future. But the merest suggestion that there are no good plays lying around waiting to be produced always sticks cruelly to a Traverse director in a nation of frustrated scribblers and closet Shakespeares; and by the beginning of 1969, doubts about aspects of the Stafford-Clark policy were also being expressed inside the Traverse.

The source of most of the criticism was Rosalind Clark, the leading figure in the successful – and increasingly autonomous – Children's Theatre Workshop, who had been elected to the Traverse Committee in 1968. At the first Committee meeting of the New Year, she produced a series of complaints about Stafford-Clark's attitude to visiting companies (including the Children's Workshop, which had appeared at the theatre in December), saying that the Traverse staff were uncooperative and gave preference to the Director's own actors, that the dressing-rooms were dirty, that the place was inefficiently run, and that the whole unpleasant atmosphere could be traced back to the 'policy and attitudes of the present Director and company', which were also reflected in their work and choice of plays; that the continuity of the company led to 'monotony or selfishness' in the work, and that audiences had stopped enjoying their visits to the Traverse because the productions were either offensive or meaningless.

According to Stafford-Clark, tension between him and the Theatre Workshop went back as far as 1965, when one of the members of his Dublin revue company, in a fit of middle-class hooliganism, added obscene graffiti to what turned out to be a children's art exhibition in the Workshop rehearsal-room, and by the end of 1968 – only a few months after the happy collaboration between Traverse and Workshop that had produced the *Aberfan* show, with Ros Clark herself appearing as the children's teacher – Clark and Stafford-Clark between them seem to have laid the foundations of an antagonism between the two organisations that survived to haunt the Traverse into the 1980's. But it also seems clear that Ros Clark's criticisms had some real force, and the Committee went so far as to agree with her that 'plays which were more comprehensible or attractive to a general audience were wanted, in the framework of the Director's artistic policy'.

In fact, the Committee later tried to back-peddle on this implied criticism of Stafford-Clark, saying that the minutes of the discussion were too detailed and definite; but there was some concrete evidence that all was not well at the Traverse in early 1969. During the first seven or eight months of Stafford-Clark's experiment, the Traverse audience had held up well; Stanley Eveling's *The Lunatic, The Secret Sportsman and the Woman Next Door* played to 91% of capacity, David Benedictus' *Angels and Geese* – in the graveyard month of June – to over 70%; the Eveling play had won a Scottish Television drama award, and had been acclaimed on a short visit to the Brandeis Interact festival in the USA. Membership had recovered from a low of around 1,300 in January 1968 to a total of 2,700 (including joint members) by the end of the year; the Arts Council had come through with another increase in basic revenue grant (to £10,000), and the Traverse had taken on a strong administrator in Andrew Leigh, who stayed with the organisation from September 1968 until the beginning of 1970. But in the Spring of 1969, both audiences and membership began to slide. In February there was a debacle over the general obscenity of the People Show's *Walter*, several performances of which were cancelled; audiences through the first half of the year struggled around the 50% mark, and despite Andrew Leigh's efficiency in chasing up renewals, membership drifted back and stuck at around 2,300.

Before criticism of the policy could gather any momentum, though, the Traverse was hit by a crisis that would transform its style and atmosphere almost beyond recognition. Over the six years of the theatre's existence, the Traverse building in James Court had itself been through some highly dramatic episodes, from the early discovery that the beautifully-designed new coffee-bar over the theatre couldn't be used during performances because of noise problems, through various traumas regarding the use or abuse of the flat at the front of the building overlooking the Lawnmarket, to the conversion of the second-floor flat into a bar, lounge and nightclub in an attempt to maximise revenue. In Gordon McDougall's time there had been several attempts – from the nefarious to the farcical – to get the building closed, on the grounds not only of the obscenity of its activities, but also of fire risk (the theatre eventually passed its inspection, with the help of many lurid exit signs and huge fire bells) and structural insecurity. Edinburgh University, which owned the neighbouring Milne's Court and was anxious to develop the whole area for student flats and residences, tried repeatedly to persuade Tom Mitchell to sell the building for redevelopment, and then sought to have it declared structurally unsafe; according to

McDougall, the subsequent inspection revealed that the main cause of structural stress was a huge hole in Milne's Court dug by the University builders themselves.

Obviously, the building was much loved by most of those who used it, but no-one denied that it had some glaring inadequacies. Harold Pinter paid it one visit in the spring of 1966, and said it was a disgusting place in which no actor should be expected to work or audience to sit. The Scottish actor Duncan Macrae mellifluously dismissed it as 'a dirty little rat-hole'; Allen Wright, who loved it, felt it was nonetheless a 'death trap' in terms of fire safety; and Stanley Eveling – who likewise doted on the theatre space – says it was 'an 'orrible little room. And the bar was horrible, and there was a terrible smell on the stairs – I think it was the cats that used to come in. It was just great.' So one of the most cheering events of 1968 had been the theatre's success – prompted by the Arts Council, which wanted to make capital improvement grants available – in persuading Tom Mitchell, who apparently loved his now-you-see-the-landlord-now-you-don't relationship with the Traverse, to sign a secure ten-year lease on the property. By the end of 1968 the Arts Council's capital grant had come through, a full programme of improvements was in hand, and a structural survey had been commissioned; but when the surveyor's report appeared before the Committee, in March 1969, what it said, in essence, was that the internal floors of the building were unsafe, and that it was quite unfit for use as a theatre club or restaurant.

The Committee reacted to this bombshell with extraordinary speed. By the time the March Committee meeting took place, the Chairman Nicky Fairbairn, together with Andrew Leigh and other Committee members, had pinpointed an old stone-built property around a courtyard at 112 West Bow, at the east end of the Grassmarket, into which the Traverse could move if necessary; and had ascertained that the owner, a Dr. Butterworth, was willing to bear some of the costs of conversion of what had been an old warehouse, in return for a reasonable rent guaranteed over 11 years. At the April Committee meeting, Tom Mitchell – now life President of the Club – fought a stout rearguard action to keep the Traverse in James Court, or to persuade them that they could return there after rebuilding work had been carried out. But a few days later Fairbairn, who seems to have felt that indecision in this situation could be fatal, convened a special meeting of the Committee to confirm the decision to move to West Bow, and the race was on to open the new theatre in time for the Festival of 1969.

The story of how the Traverse met this deadline – and in particular of the last few days before the opening on the 24 August, when Committee members, actors, staff, Max Stafford-Clark and his predecessor Gordon McDougall, Tom Mitchell, Andrew Leigh and above all Nicky Fairbairn himself worked for days and nights without sleep to complete the new theatre, slashing through red tape at every turn and passing a final building inspection half an hour before the Arts Minister Jennie Lee arrived to open the building – is legendary. Max Stafford-Clark says he still has the T-shirt he wore, 'covered in paint and blood'; Gordon McDougall – back in Edinburgh for the Festival with his Stables Theatre company – remembers laying flooring for a solid day with Nicky

Fairbairn, and Susan Carpenter, then a member of Max Stafford-Clark's company, now married to Mike Ockrent, says the company had to take a whole week out of rehearsal to help with the building. Tom Mitchell – who acquired bricks from the north of England to get round a Scottish brick shortage – remembers Fairbairn 'up in the rafters like a monkey, hammering away'; a concrete staircase exit from the theatre was laid in the last 24 hours before the opening. People who sauntered up to inspect the new theatre (including Mavor of the Arts Council) went away again, convinced that Miss Lee would have nothing to open; yet somehow, by some miracle of collective effort, by the time she arrived in her flowing lemon-yellow evening dress, to pick her way over the duck-boards in the muddy courtyard and up into the new loft-shaped theatre space on the second floor, the new Traverse was fit to open, and that week's performances of the company's multi-author extravaganza *Dracula*, and of Stanley Eveling's *Dear Janet Rosenberg, Dear Mr Kooning*, went ahead as planned.

Max Stafford-Clark saw the Traverse into its new home, and through its first autumn season there, which included interesting guest productions, such as a double-bill of Olwen Wymark plays directed by Michael Meacham, and the first appearance at the Traverse – like a tall, thin harbinger of things to come in the new building – of Chris Parr, directing Michael Almaz's *Monsieur Artaud*. In fact, the 1969 Festival was a considerable success for the Traverse, with the new 100-seat theatre bringing a 50% increase in paid attendances and box office income over the Festival of 1968; Eveling's *Dear Janet Rosenberg, Dear Mr. Kooning*, played by Tony Haygarth and Susan Carpenter of the Stafford-Clark company, became one of the most popular Traverse productions ever, transferring almost immediately to the Royal Court Theatre Upstairs. But the problems inherent in the Stafford-Clark working method were beginning to become obvious; in the autumn, while the resident company toured their current repertoire and then took a break, the theatre seemed abandoned and poorly attended, particularly since it had not yet been possible to arrange a restaurant space and art gallery in the new building. In October Andrew Leigh warned the Committee of low membership and looming financial problems; there was talk of trying to appoint an Assistant Director to help fill the gaps in the organisation, and sometime in November Stafford-Clark decided – but in typically original fashion – that the time had come to step down as Artistic Director. He explained himself to the Committee in one of his free-flowing, thought-in-action documents, thus.

'The Artistic Director of the Traverse divides his time between directing plays himself and acting as a theatrical entrepreneur arranging and choosing the plays, directors, companies and actors which fill the rest of the programme. The first director of the Traverse, Terry Lane, spent his whole time directing plays. After Lane's dismissal by the Committee, Jim Haynes spent his whole time acting as entrepreneur and never directed anything. After Haynes' dismissal by the Committee, first Gordon McDougall and then myself have both directed plays as well as arranging others. Recently, as you know, I felt that single-handed, I could no longer both direct the Company and undertake the job of

Artistic Director, and for this reason, it was decided to appoint an assistant. I have come to feel that this would not be a feasible solution, as no amount of assistance can take away from the responsibility and the drain on emotional energy involved in the job of Artistic Director. It is for these reasons that I sent a letter of resignation to Nicky, and that I have decided to form a company of my own in Edinburgh to continue the kind of work which the Traverse Company has been doing. Although I intend to pursue this scheme with or without the blessing of this Committee, I firmly believe that if it could be linked in some way to the Traverse's Empire, it would be to great mutual benefit. . . .'

And Stafford-Clark went on to explain how he would use the old James Court building as a base for his workshop group, that the Arts Council was interested in providing independent funding for it (in those days the Arts Council, whose Scottish resources increased more than six-fold *in real terms* between 1962 and 1972 could fund expansion and new initiatives with a minimum of heart-searching), and that his hope was that this Traverse Workshop Company would provide a part of the Traverse programme each year, broadening the scope of what the theatre could offer at relatively small cost to the Traverse itself – 'i.e.,' he wrote 'the relatively "mainstream" bias of the rest of the year's productions would be offset by the comparatively "avant-garde" work of the company.'

The document is written with all Stafford-Clark's usual panache, and his customary list of anticipated objections, all very shrewd. '1. The allocation of part of the season to the Company may not fit in with the new Artistic Director's plans. 2. The Company may be bad, rude, talentless and awful, and the association of the Traverse's name may therefore be detrimental. 3. The Company may be good, charming, talented and brilliant and rivalry may spring up between their work on one hand and the Traverse's ordinary programme on the other.' But despite its light tone, it represents, bearing in mind the unseemly rows that had accompanied the departures of the first two Traverse directors, a quite exceptional feat of self-awareness and creative thinking. Stafford-Clark had always been adept at understanding and disarming criticism; now he had come to accept the full force of the argument that a director at his stage of development – absorbed in the work of an avant-garde ensemble, dedicated to working with a small group of writers and actors in the most detailed and concentrated way – was not ideally placed to run and to 'front' a theatre with so many public responsibilities, particularly at the point when it had just accepted the commercial and organisational challenge of moving into an auditorium twice the size of its previous home; and he was determined to create a framework of operations such that he could still belong to and contribute to the Traverse idea, while passing on that central outward-looking responsibility.

The reasons why Stafford-Clark's approach ultimately became incompatible with his role as Artistic Director are complex and interesting. It certainly was not a matter of being 'too experimental'; indeed Stafford-Clark's openness to new thinking about ways of making theatre gave the Traverse one of the most exciting creative periods, and some of the best productions, in its history. Nor was it the case that his ensemble approach prevented him from carrying on the Traverse's commitment to new writing. In proposing the Traverse Workshop Company idea to the Committee, Stafford-Clark gave it as his first intention 'to act as a laboratory company for writers working in Scotland . . .'; he went on to list seven writers – including Benedictus, Eveling, Conn, and C.P. Taylor – who wanted to work with the company, and explained, in a particularly fine phrase, that 'the playwright is the only artist who uses people – actors – as his materials. Our intention is to bring the materials into his garret.' ,

The problem was, to some extent, financial, in that the British arts funding system was then, and remains now, unwilling to support the kind of long-term, slow-burning, totally involving new work in which Stafford-Clark was interested. The Traverse simply could not afford to stay dark while workshop productions materialised, or to fill the gaps between them with rich enough material; and though the throughput of shows remained high, the programme sometimes acquired a thin look during Stafford-Clark's directorate. There was also the undeniable fact that Stafford-Clark had, by his own admission, 'left his heart' in the old Traverse space, which – in its pressurised room-like intimacy – had helped form his ideas about the detailed truthfulness in performance he tried to achieve through the workshop process. With his wholehearted acceptance of the 'experimental' idea, Stafford-Clark also accepted and enjoyed the Traverse's club atmosphere, and the sense that it would always attract an unusually committed and strictly limited audience. He was what he laughingly calls a 'confirmed exclusivist, not a populist at all', and could see no advantage in increasing the theatre's capacity; on the contrary, he was acutely aware that to change the 'geography' of the theatre would be to change the nature of its work, and he suspected (wrongly, he now thinks) that a larger space would mean a move towards the mainstream which he could not, at that stage, have supervised with any enthusiasm.

But in the end, the crucial problem was that Stafford-Clark, by temperament, occupied too extreme a position not on the spectrum between "mainstream" and "experimental" work, but on the spectrum between creative and receptive attitudes, between the Marowitz notion of art fuelled by discontent with what already exists, and the Jim Haynes notion of art made possible by an endless nurturing receptivity to ideas. Stafford-Clark strongly resembled Haynes in his challenging attitude to the whole conventional structure of theatre and its relationship to reality; Stanley Eveling, writing in *The Scotsman* in January 1988, remembered him as a 'Jim-type person', given to smashing traditional barriers and indulging in a bit of anarchy. But he differed crucially from Haynes in that he was, himself, a strongly creative personality. His increasing absorption in his own work, and in the dynamics of his own company, meant that the Traverse building came to lack a heart, a host, a central welcoming personality to make audiences and brand new writers and visiting companies feel that the door was open to them, as the door of Haynes' Traverse had been open to Stafford-Clark back in 1965; and when the theatre moved to its raw new building, that lack of home-making flair became so obvious that something had to give.

In 1988, Max Stafford-Clark is still Artistic Director of the Royal Court Theatre, still working with new plays, still weaving and bobbing in the endless search for the right theatrical tack at any given moment in history. More than any other ex-director, he seems to find it difficult to consider his own Traverse experience in isolation; he is still deeply interested in the work of the Traverse 18 years on, and his conversation is peppered with comments on its recent productions and latest writers. But when he does talk about his own time at the Traverse, his language is all to do with learning, with movement from one state to the other. If his predecessor Gordon McDougall was a young man interested in radical ideas whose understanding of form was jolted by contact with the American avant-garde, Stafford-Clark was a boy fascinated on sight by the formal excitement of La Mama's work, who worked his way only slowly towards a critique of it as lacking in the substance of good innovative writing to match its formal boldness. In his later work, particularly with Joint Stock, he went on to tackle much more substantial political argument on stage, and – in parallel – to confront more fundamental questions about theatrical structures and director power than had ever crossed his mind at the Traverse. 'A political idea would have died of loneliness in there, wouldn't it?' he says drily, when I read him one of his early policy statements.

Today, he can say with confidence that just as new ideas without new theatrical forms make dull plays, so formal experiment without tough new ideas is pure indulgence; and he acknowledges that 'Edinburgh put up with a lot' from him while he was working towards that conclusion. But it was in that very fluidity of thought, in his instinctive, sometimes alarming exploration towards the way of working that seemed right to him at the time, that he so perfectly expressed the ideal of the Traverse itself. There are those who wonder why Stafford-Clark – for all his fits and starts and indulgences and financial vagueness – was so well tolerated and even loved by most of his Committee; it was because they recognised, in the bright integrity of his movement towards new kinds of theatrical truth, the very thing for which their theatre had been made.

nn Malcolm (*left*) and Terry Lane in the Traverse auditorium in James Court, November 1962. The eatre opened six weeks later. (Photo: Scotsman Publications)

t to right: Terry Lane directing Clyde Pollitt, Rosamund Dickson, and Colette O'Neill in a rehearsal the Traverse's opening production of *Huis Clos*, December 1962. (Photo: Scotsman Publications)

Below: Jim Haynes as Chairman and Artistic Director of the Traverse, 1965. (Photo: Scotsman Publications)

Right: Edinburgh 1960: a lady missionary burns a copy of *Lady Chatterley's Lover* outside the Paperback Bookshop in Charles Street, Jim Haynes (centre with beard) looks on. Note the rhinoceros head! (Photo: Alan Daiches)

Above: The entrance to the old Traverse from James Court, 1966. (Photo: Scotsman Publications)

Above right: The Traverse production of the Brecht/Weill musical *Happy End*, August 1964. (Photo: Alan Daiches)

op left and right: The actor/director: ıllum Mill (with John Shedden) in ıchael Geliot's production of *The retaker*, 1964. (Photo: Alan Daiches)

low: The Haynes era: Wendy Brierley d Gordon Whiting in Jack Henry ore's production of *The Fantastics*, ecember 1965. (Photo: Alan Daiches)

ght: Oliver Cotton (*left*) with Toby laman in Peter Gill's production of eathcote Williams' *The Local Stigmatic*, 66. (Photo: Alan Daiches)

low right: Max Stafford-Clark (*left*), as young actor/stage-manager, with nstantin de Goguel and Mike Newling *The Paterson's Shortbread Show*, March 66. (Photo: Alan Daiches)

Centre left: Sue Lefton and Toby Salaman in Max Stafford-Clark's production of *Dracula*, which moved from the old Traverse to become the first production in the new building. (Photo: Traverse Theatre)

Top right: Max Stafford-Clark (*centre*) rehearsing Philip Manikum (*left*) and Ronald Falk in Olwen Wymark's mini-play *The Gymnasium*, 1967. (Photo: Diane Tammes)

Tony Haygarth (*centre*) with Colin McCormack and Sue Lefton of the Stafford-Clark company in Ann Jellicoe's *The Sport of My Mad Mother*, 1969. The director was Paul Tomlinson. (Photo: Diane Tammes)

Lower right: Antonia Pemberton in Michael Meacham's production of Olwen Wymark's *Stay Where You Are*, New Year 1969–70. Michael Rudman saw this production on the evening of his interview, and fell in love with the new Traverse on the spot. (Photo: Traverse Theatre)

Top left: Richard Wilson as Vladimir in Gordon McDougall's Christmas 1967 production of *Waiting for Godot*. (Photo: Diane Tammes)

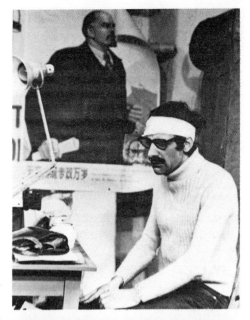

Top left: Rowan Wylie, Neil Johnstone and Arwen Holm of the Freehold Company in Michael Rudman's production of Michael de Ghelderode's *Pantagleise*, 1971. (Photo: Diane Tammes)

Centre left: *Left to right*: Hugh Fraser, Lindsay Kemp and Richard Harboard in Kemp's version of *Woyzeck*, 1971. (Photo: Diane Tammes)

Lower left: Mike Ockrent's company, *left to right*: Lesley Joseph, Simon Callow and Jim McManus in Hanoch Levin's *Hefetz*, 1974. (Photo: Joe McKeever)

Top right: Peter Kelly in Mike Ockrent's production of C. P. Taylor's *Allergy*, 1973. (Photo: Joe McKeever)

Lower right: Carole Hayman and Kevin Costello in the Traverse Workshop Company production of Howard Brenton's *Hitler Dances*, 1972. (Photo: Diane Tammes)

Top left: Patrick Malahide and Tammy
Ustinov in Tom McGrath's *Android Ciruit*,
1978. (Photo: David Liddle)

Top right: Peter Kelly and Frances Low in
Tom McGrath's *The Hardman*, 1977. (Photo:
David Liddle)

Below left: *Left to right*: Pat Doyle, Jim Byars
and Billy McColl in David Hayman's
première, production of *The Slab Boys* by
John Byrne, 1978. (Photo: David Liddle)

Below right: Chris Parr's acclaimed
production of Tom McGrath's *Animal*,
Edinburgh Festival 1979. (Photo: David
Liddle)

Top: Patience Tomlinson and Russell Hunter in Tom Buchan's *Over the Top*, 1980. (Photo: David Liddle)

Centre left: Jimmy Chisholm as Boswell and Jonathan Adams as Dr Johnson in Dusty Hughes' *Heaven and Hell*, 1981. Design and painting (*behind*) by John Byrne. (Photo: David Liddle)

Centre right: Simon Callow at the Traverse in the Almeida Theatre production of *Melancholy Jacques*, Edinburgh Festival 1984. (Photo: David Liddle)

Left: Sarah Collier (*left*) and Valerie Fyfer in Marcella Evaristi's *Wedding Belles and Green Grasses*, 1981. (Photo: David Liddle)

Above left: *Left to right*: Andrew Wilde, Simon Donald and Bernard Doherty in Jenny Killick's touring production of John Clifford's *Losing Venice*, 1986 (Photo: *Traverse Theatre*)

Above right: *Left to right*: Tilda Swinton, Kate Duchêne and Ken Stott in Steve Unwin's production of *White Rose* by Peter Arnott, 1985. (Photo: David Liddle)

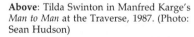

Above: Tilda Swinton in Manfred Karge's *Man to Man* at the Traverse, 1987. (Photo: Sean Hudson)

Above right: Sam Graham (*left*) and Ralph Riach in John McKay's *Dead Dad Dog*, directed by Steve Unwin, May 1988, in a Traverse auditorium again stripped back to bare stone walls and original windows. (Photo: Sean Hudson)

CHAPTER 5
Michael Rudman

'The Traverse,' said Max Stafford-Clark, resigning as Artistic Director in December 1969, 'now stands uneasily somewhere between an Arts Lab and a conventional repertory theatre.' So it did, or at any rate somewhere between an Arts Lab and the 'small theatre with a new play policy' which Stafford-Clark had said he did not want in 1968; and in its uncertainty about its future, it perhaps reflected a general unease among organisations that had grown up in the 60's as the decade drew to an end. On one hand there were those – like Stafford-Clark himself – who had taken the revolutionary attitudes of the 60's to heart, and were not going to abandon them lightly. On the other, there were those who had thoroughly enjoyed the 60's – particularly as a long overdue rebellion against sexual guilt and inhibition – but were now ready to return to business as usual. In withdrawing from the Traverse, and recognising that the theatre needed a more 'mainstream' programme for part of the year, Stafford-Clark was, perhaps unconsciously, acknowledging that fragmentation of purpose and shift of mood, which was clearly reflected within the Traverse Committee. Avant-garde theatre was moving, physically and politically, away from building bases and on to the road, and Stafford-Clark followed that trend.

Ironically, though, his continued association with the Traverse – which had been agreed at the end of December 1969, just as the search began for a new Director – freed the Committee from the need to try to resolve this tension between the radical and experimental on one hand, and a more conventional new-play policy on the other. The Artistic Director's job description drawn up in January 1970 was the only one in the theatre's history to refer not at all to the artistic content of the work; what the Committee clearly had in mind was a Director who would do all the things that Stafford-Clark was no longer going to do – i.e. planning the programme, directing 'straight' productions of new plays, taking care of the budgets, supervising the staff, locking up at night, generally husbanding and caring for the theatre in its new building. In other words, the selection process was programmed to institutionalise the split in the theatre's psyche, and to produce a new Artistic Director who would contrast with and complement Stafford-Clark at every point; small wonder that it resulted in one of the cleanest breaks, and sharpest changes of mood, in the whole Traverse story.

For Michael Rudman, who was appointed at the beginning of February 1970 and finally took up the job on 1 May, was quite a different proposition from any previous Traverse director. At 31 he was half-a-decade older than most of them, an experienced theatre director of some six years' standing who had worked with the Royal Shakespeare Company in Stratford and London, at Glasgow Citizens' Theatre, at major rep theatres all over England, and – most extensively – as Associate Director to John Neville at Nottingham playhouse from 1964–68. Uniquely among Traverse directors, he had had no previous professional connection with the place, although he had enthusiastically admired its work and its atmosphere on visits to the Edinburgh Fringe with his Oxford student company in the early 60's; like many literature students drawn to theatre, he had always been more interested in directing classics than new work, seeing theatre as 'literature made accessible.'

When the Traverse job came up in January 1970, he was too busy directing a production of *Henry IV* at Sheffield Playhouse to take much notice. But he had been on the lookout for the chance to run a theatre of his own for some time, and when his agent – prompted by the enterprising Ros Clark, who was anxious to ensure that there were strong candidates of a non-Stafford-Clark kind – suggested the Traverse, he leapt at the opportunity, flew to Edinburgh in a daze (his wife had thrown a party in London the night before), overdosed on coffee in the Caledonian Hotel, buzzed into his interview 'stoned' on caffeine, talked volubly and without interruption for half an hour about his detailed plans for the Traverse as jotted on the back of an envelope, and was immediately offered the job against strong opposition. 'I didn't think I had a hope of getting it, and that made me very relaxed,' he remembers, with a characteristic mixture of self-mocking Jewish fatalism and expansive Texan charm. 'The strange thing is, I found the envelope a couple of years later, and I had actually done almost everything I'd said I would . . .'.

Part of Rudman's immediate appeal for the Committee lay in his obvious resemblance to Jim Haynes. Like Haynes he was anglophile American with a warm Texan drawl, like Haynes he offered an extrovert, welcoming presence of the kind the new Traverse desperately needed; Richard Demarco once described him as a 'Jim Haynes lookalike,' and Nicky Fairbairn introduced him, at his first Press Conference, as 'another American at the Traverse'. Of course the likeness was strictly limited. Where Haynes' welcoming manner was based on an endless, anarchic openness to people and ideas, Rudman's concealed a most acute and discriminating eye for marketable talent in writers and actors, for audience preferences, for visiting productions that would strike a chord with the Traverse public. In Michael Rudman, the sensible, businesslike, no-nonsense element in the Traverse's make-up had in fact found its ideal candidate; he was no revolutionary, no great innovator, no disturbing, irresponsible creative presence, and in many ways he justified Alistair Moffat's description of him, in his book on the Edinburgh Festival Fringe, as the first 'orthodox' director of the Traverse. Unlike previous directors, he spent no energy questioning or attacking the system, but simply played it for all it was worth, and in that sense those older Traverse members who saw him as somehow alien to the tradition of the place were right. But within those terms of reference, Rudman proved himself right from the start as that most rare and valuable character in post-war British theatre, an Artistic Director who applies himself to every aspect of the theatre business – from the direction of major productions to staffing problems in the bar and small fund-raising stunts – with equal intelligence, flair and good humour, and is more amused and stimulated than ground down by the insane complexity of the job.

What Rudman did share with Haynes, though, was his powerful sense of the Traverse as a centre, a focus for creativity from other sources; and he also had the personality to enable him to play the role of lynchpin in that kind of operation. What's more, he had fallen in love with the new Traverse auditorium, in which he had seen Michael Meacham's production of an Olwen Wymark double-bill on the night of his interview. The Traverse in the Grassmarket is a large, oblong garret (with an oddly-shaped foyer and bar on the floor below) about three times the size of the old Traverse, and capable of seating twice as many people on flexible black seating 'modules' – three-tier banks of cushioned seating – which can be rearranged at will to change the shape of the playing-area. It is more of a relaxed, blank space, much more passive than the old auditorium; where the James Court theatre was a hot, insistent little pressure-cooker, squeezing intensity out of the most unlikely situations, the new Traverse is a black hole of a space, requiring to be filled, and from his first sight of it Rudman was not only thrilled by its technical possibilities – as a tiny, intimate theatre nonetheless fitted out (thanks to the Northern Lights Company of Committee member Neil, Lord Primrose, who had taken over from his wife Deirdre in 1969) with the possibility of sophisticated lighting and sound effects – but seduced by its oddly receptive quality. In his Festival programme for 1971, Rudman wrote with great eloquence about this aspect of the Traverse's personality, describing how 'the building and all the people in it seem to take on a new form from the mind of each writer who enters . . . every month the seating units shift, the poster reflects the new arrival, the audiences become unrecognisable and the performers completely different . . . This flexibility is our policy. We . . . keep ourselves open enough to receive and respond. No make-up, painted black in fact, cushioned by our audience, we'll play the whore to any man's truth.'

In fact, this is a pretty simplistic model of what happens when a writer comes into contact with a theatre and its staff; it reduces the creative process to a kind of wham-bam one-way transaction (writer deposits seminal work in theatre space) rather than a process of cohabitation, gestation and birth. But ever since the days of Jim Haynes, it has had a fine, straightforward potency in making creative people feel that the Traverse is an open space on which they can converge; and it also freed Rudman from the task of articulating a specific artistic policy. For he makes no bones about the fact that new plays were not particularly important to him before he came to Edinburgh; he arrived thinking that he might perhaps take the Traverse on for six months or so, and began to work on new plays simply out of a sense that that was what a Traverse director should do, only later developing a passion for the unique process of bringing a play to life for the first time.

Unlike Stafford-Clark – who had been painstakingly deconstructing and re-constructing the idea of what a 'good play' and 'good acting' might be in modern terms, and under what working conditions they were likely to emerge – he therefore cherished no complex or radical ideas about how the Traverse should operate; he simply set out, without hesitation, to get hold of the best new plays around, and to persuade the best available actors to play in them. Unlike previous Traverse directors, he had a rich range of contacts in the upper echelons of English acting, and he demonstrated impressive skill in persuading them to come up to Edinburgh for a month, and act themselves into the ground for £17 a week. At his first Committee meeting, in March, Rudman said that he hoped there would be something familiar about each production – either the title or the author or an actor's name – to attract audiences; and he minimised the risks of a new-play policy not only by casting as well as he could, but by trying to pick up existing unperformed plays, rather than commissioning brand new ones. 'If you're going to commission a play,' he says, 'better commission one that's already written. In my experience, you don't often get a very good play from a commission. . .'.

And in his first year at the Traverse, he clocked up an impressive list of successes and transfers, including (from his own productions) a successful triple-bill of plays by David Halliwell, a variation on Shakespeare's *Henry IV* plays called *Stand for my Father* (written under pseudonyms by the actors Mike Gwilym and Nigel Hawthorne), Tom Mallin's *Curtains* with Nigel Hawthorne and Antonia Pemberton, Syd Cheatle's *Straight Up* with Polly James and William Franklyn, and David Snodin's *A Game Called Arthur* with Timothy Dalton and Judy Loe. In 1971 he directed Mallin's *The Novelist* with Barbara Jefford, and John Antrobus' *The Looneys* with Barbara Atkinson and John Shrapnel; in 1972, C.P. Taylor's *The Black and White Minstrels* with Tom Conti, Alan Howard and Patti Love, Vanbrugh's *Relapse* with Fenella Fielding and Philip Guard, and Stanley Eveling's *Caravaggio Buddy* with Ian Holm. The Traverse has never had a casting policy like it, and Allen Wright remembers actors like Hawthorne and Holm as unforgettably impressive in the close quarters of the Traverse auditorium. Nor was Allen Wright alone in his strong appreciation of Rudman's productions, which were conspicuously popular and well-reviewed throughout his three years at the Traverse. From a standing start as an interpreter of new work in a confined space, Rudman had rapidly evolved a powerful Traverse style which he describes as 'rather spare in terms of set, with a terrific concentration on the detail of the words and the acting'; and like his successor Mike Ockrent, he found that the meticulous, concentrated approach he developed at the Traverse remained as a strong artistic backbone to his work, even when he moved on to much larger and more conventional auditoriums.

Taken by itself, this Rudman programme might have looked rather conventional, if imposing; but by this stage in its history, the Traverse itself was mounting less than half the productions staged there (only 20 of a total 53 shows in 1970), and Rudman used both Traverse Workshop productions and touring shows by fringe companies like Nancy Meckler's Freehold, the Lindsay Kemp Theatre Troupe, the Open Space Theatre and Low Moan Spectacular, to give an edge of innovation and outrage to the work. At his first press conference in February 1970 – true to his sense of the Traverse as a passive vehicle for playwrights' efforts – he had allowed himself the obligatory sideswipe at the outgoing artistic policy, talking about his intention to 'choose actors to suit plays' rather than have a permanent company that might restrict material, rejecting the word 'experimental', talking about concentrating on 'texts rather than improvisation', and generally portraying himself as the playwright's friend. In May, he told Allen Wright that the Traverse had become a showcase for groups who imposed their ideas and style on texts; he said the Traverse should rather be highly sensitive to the writer, that the writer was the most creative person in theatre, and that all the great developments in theatre had come from writers – all of this in direct contradiction to the explicitly collaborative policy of the Traverse Workshop.

But despite some public sniping, Rudman (unlike some of his Committee, who continued to attack the quality and style of Stafford-Clark's shows long after his resignation) was quick to grasp that the Workshop productions were both strong in themselves and attractive to audiences. With some effort ('I was the past incumbent, and instead of retiring gracefully, I was still around,' as Stafford-Clark puts it) the two directors developed a reasonable working relationship, and over the next two years – relieved of the burdens of Artistic Directorship – Stafford-Clark went on to produce some of his best work at the Traverse, including Stanley Eveling's *Our Sunday Times* – a real-life story of a lone English yachtsman who suffered a breakdown in the South Atlantic, and floated around broadcasting desperate lying messages back to base about his progress round the world – John Spurling's *In the Heart of the British Museum*, and Howard Brenton's *Hitler Dances*.

And in fact, some of the most exciting productions in which Rudman himself was involved came out of collaborations or co-productions with similar experimental companies. In March 1971, Rudman directed a much-admired production of Michael de Ghelderode's *Pantagleise* with the Freehold Company, and a few weeks earlier the Pip Simmons Theatre Group premiered their outrageous show *Do It* at the Traverse. *Do It* was based on the writings of Yippie revolutionary Jerry Rubin and on an idea dreamed up by Rudman, who had known Rubin at college; and the show apparently caused no concern at all to the Episcopalian Bishop of Edinburgh, who calmly lit up a cigarette in the front row as writhing bodies simulated sex a few inches from his nose, and later told Rudman he had enjoyed the show very much. (Bobby Younger, the Traverse Secretary of the day and a minute-writer of great drollery and style, recorded a strangely inconsequential committee discussion on the subject. 'Paul Broda plus a bishop enjoyed *Do It*. Jim Ferguson said it merely blasted the emptiness of Rubin's position. Someone else said that Lord Eccles (the new Tory arts minister) would be replacing socialists with conservatives on the Arts Council. . .'). Later that year, the Traverse sensation of the 1971 Festival was the Portable Theatre co-production *Lay By*, a piece written collaboratively by Howard Brenton, Brian Clark, Trevor Griffiths, David Hare, Stephen Poliakoff, Hugh Stoddart and Snoo Wilson which no other theatre wanted to premiere because it involved distributing hard-core Swedish porn to the audience – and of course, as the front-of-house staff vividly remembers, trying to get it back again before they left the theatre.

In his campaign to maximise the Traverse audience (which he admired for its open-mindedness and studied with great energy; he could never work out whether the theatre had different audiences for different kinds of show, or the same audiences differently dressed), Rudman deliberately mixed and matched these elements in his programme with great cheek and panache. In January 1971, after a successful year of what he said were mainly 'small intelligent plays', he announced that the forthcoming programme would be 'considerably fleshier, more offensive, more experimental and slightly more expensive . . .' In May, after *Do It, Pantagleise*, the Low Moan Spectacular and three shows from the Traverse Workshop (including the Eveling double bill *Oh Starlings* and *Sweet Alice*), he told the Committee he would now be setting out to recapture the steadier members of the audience. 'Do you know what?' he says, with a dolorous street-trader's wisdom, after a long conversation about the problems entailed in a particular and very definite artistic policy pursued by one of his successors. 'I just tried to give them variety. You know, a three-piece suite here, a play with nothing but one of the modules for a set there, a bit of sailing around on the ocean in *Our Sunday Times*. It sounds simple, but it works. . .'

And by and large it did work, often spectacularly well. At the 1971 AGM, after Rudman had been at the Traverse for a full year, the theatre announced an unheard-of surplus on the year of £3,722, including bar profits which soared, under the close supervision of Rudman's dedicated General Manager Penny Richardson, from £800 to £4,000; the theatre's accumulated deficit, which had stood at £12,000 when Rudman took over the job, plummeted to just over £8,000 and went on downwards. The theatre had mounted 55 shows in the financial year, of which 29 were British or world premieres, and membership was surging upwards. A year later, in 1972, the figures showed a·doubling of paid attendances at the theatre in the three years since 1969, another reduction in the overall deficit, and membership standing at a high of 3,500. 'It's the two-hit theory,' says Rudman. 'In any theatre, anywhere, if you can get two hits in a season, then suddenly you've got all sorts of income you never had before. . . '.

If anything, Rudman was even better at managing the theatre's external relations than he was at programming. According to Allen Wright, he handled the press with tremendous geniality and skill, issuing dire threats to his press officers if they should fail to get a piece of coverage in *The Scotsman* every Monday without fail. 'Used to put me in a terrible position,' grins Wright; and the Edinburgh Central Library cuttings file does indeed show a terrific volume and variety of coverage during Rudman's directorship. Unlike some other Traverse directors, he likewise exploited without question the traditional London bias of British theatrical life, seeking and achieving regular London transfers of Traverse productions; he allowed the Traverse season to remain firmly focused on the Festival, with its maximum opportunities for exposure in the national press (and also introduced some hugely successful Festival innovations, such as the Traverse Tattoo in the courtyard which acted as a showcase for all sorts of Fringe shows); and he specialised, with one or two exceptions, in new English and American plays, acted by well known English actors, rather than seeking the kind of local Scottish material and acting style which later, in Chris Parr's time, caused the

Traverse to lose coverage and prominence in the London press.

In fact according to Rudman himself, he thought when he came to the Traverse that the fact that it was in Scotland was 'a joke – a very good joke, but a joke; and that half its success was that it was the least Scottish thing in Scotland.' It wasn't until 1972 – towards the end of his time in Edinburgh – that he began to realise that there was a serious demand for the Traverse to function as part of the Scottish theatre scene rather than a northern outpost of the English circuit. In that year, he directed C.P. Taylor's *Black and White Minstrels* – a play about wife-swapping in the Glasgow 'bohemoisie' ('all about wanting to bed people all the time, and talk about art and socialism – it had the Traverse audience screaming with self-recognition . . .') – and a strange extravaganza called *Tell Charlie Thanks for the Truss*, which featured an all-Scottish cast and music by Tom McGrath, and came to be seen by many as the precursor of the famous *Great Northern Welly Boot Show* of that year, which set Billy Connolly and many others on the path to stardom. But by and large, Rudman avoided the Scottish dimension in his major Traverse productions, and he continued to receive extensive and respectful coverage in the UK and international press; Michael Billington remembers meeting him in the courtyard one Festival, trying anxiously to spot the face of the doyen of New York critics Clive Barnes among the approaching crowd.

Throughout his time in Edinburgh, he also campaigned relentlessly for Edinburgh Corporation (the local authority) to increase its tiny £350-a-year grant to the theatre. He held successful Traverse Trials on contemporary political issues, partly with the motive of attracting young, ambitious politicians – John Smith, Malcolm Rifkind, Robin Cook – into the place and enlisting their loyalty and support; and in 1971 this policy paid off brilliantly when Rifkind, then a young city councillor in Edinburgh, was instrumental in persuading the Corporation to increase the grant, first to £1,000, and then, in a noisy debate of the full Council which overruled a sub-committee decision, to £2,000. This five-fold increase in local authority support was of more than simple cash value to the Traverse. Even though Rudman specifically refused to give the Councillors assurances on the 'decency' of future productions, and had to listen to a fair amount of reflex barracking from those Councillors who had made opposition to the Traverse part of their stock in trade (one described the Traverse staff as 'a load of layabouts who should be in industry'), it signified that the theatre had in some sense been accepted by the city establishment; and that fact in turn impressed the Scottish Arts Council out of all proportion to the amounts involved, paving the way for massive increases in public funding in the mid-70's.

And while he was agitating for big public money, Rudman did not make the mistake of ignoring the cumulative effect and psychological importance of internal fund-raising. Despite his interest in broadening the theatre's appeal and maximising audiences, Rudman cherished, appreciated and was hugely entertained by his relationship with the Club and Committee; and although there was a major row when he tried, after the Festival of 1971, to raise the wages of his talented Assistant Nick Kent by unilateral decree – and he certainly never saw eye to eye with the radically-minded Traverse traditionalist Joe Gerber, who replaced Nicky Fairbairn as Chairman in 1972 – he kept his Committee in good spirits almost throughout his three years at the Traverse, encouraging all sorts of strange and lively fund-raising events like art auctions, parties, an open day at Nicky Fairbairn's Fordell Castle in Fife, and a barbecue on Cramond Island in the Forth, which Neil Primrose – later the Earl of Rosebery – happened to own. 'By and large,' he says, 'if you're doing OK at the box office, any Board will leave you alone . . .'; and at the Traverse box-office Rudman did better than OK.

In January 1973 – in a particularly apt farewell gesture, again designed to establish the theatre as a fixture in the public mind – Rudman organised a 10th Anniversary Gala for the Traverse at the King's Theatre in Edinburgh, featuring Lindsay Kemp, Jim Haynes, Fenella Fielding and many other Traverse stars. The event raised over £2,000 towards the wiping out of the theatre's debt, and by the time Rudman left in March – to become Artistic Director of Hampstead Theatre Club – the total accumulated deficit of the Traverse had actually been reduced from £12,000 to £1,500 – and that, Rudman remembers, was an interest-free loan from Tom Mitchell, with payment indefinitely deferred. Apart from this astonishing financial achievement, the theatre itself was in good heart, its reputation was high, it had as many full members as at any time in its history, and it was in good odour with its major funding bodies, the Arts Council and the local authority; as Allen Wright says, the Traverse 'was a good-going place all through Rudman's time, and I admired what he did very much – so much so that I wondered how they'd manage when he left.'

In almost every way, then, Michael Rudman's period at the Traverse was an unalloyed triumph. He established the theatre in its new home, and brought the building alive with warmth and activity and strong professional productions. He made it a welcoming centre for poetry and jazz and folk music and cabaret as well as for playwrights and actors; he fought for its future with passion and energy, and left it as well-provided as he could. And yet his legacy to the Traverse was not, in the end, an unmixed blessing. What Rudman had done, in setting the new Grassmarket theatre on a firm organisational and financial base, was to move the Traverse decisively into the world of 'proper theatre', into the world of proper wages, proper overtime, conventional administrative structures. '*Admit* that the place was established?' he says, in answer to a suggestion in Alistair Moffat's study of the Fringe. 'I positively tried to *sell* the idea that it was established, in order to shore up the funding. But I never could see why 'established' had to mean 'establishment'.

And there was the rub; because the Traverse had been founded, and run throughout its early years, by people who could see exactly why. The Traverse had been created out of an instinctive understanding that the birth of new kinds of theatre required new structures – a constant rethinking of the physical, social and psychological relationship between stage and audience, a revolution in the geography and organisation of theatre itself. The early Traverse therefore existed right on the edge of existing definitions of theatre, on the boundary of theatre and life; it was from this knife-edge position, from its ability to face the questions why theatre? why plays? why not poems or happenings or something else instead? that it had drawn its extraordinary vitality. But when it began – gradually at first, and then more definitely as the 70's wore on – to carry a substantial technical and administrative staff, and when that staff began to depend on the theatre for a reasonable livelihood, those vital to-be-or-not-to-be questions came to sound frivolous and cruel; as with any established institution, the survival of the organisation itself became a goal, and the absolute value of the theatre's work (as opposed to its relative value compared with other theatres – i.e., 'we are the only new-play theatre in Scotland') was discussed less and less.

It's not, of course, that Michael Rudman consciously set the theatre on a more conservative path. Given the new building, the larger auditorium, the growing establishment needed to support it and supply it with 'product', the move towards a more orthodox style of theatre organisation must have seemed entirely natural and desirable. It was simply that unlike Stafford-Clark, Rudman had not been through the process of the early Traverse, and had no ideological reason to resist the inevitable pressures towards a more conventional operation. What's more, any negative effect of the changes was well masked during his time at the Traverse, partly because he and Penny Richardson were adept at controlling costs, partly because of his own near-genius for balancing and reconciling the various pressures on the organisation – from those who wanted experimental theatre and those who wanted more accessible new plays, from writers, from touring companies, from funding bodies, from Club members, from the different strands of opinion in the Committee – and partly because of external factors well beyond Rudman's control, which he tends to refer to, engagingly, as 'luck'.

For even today, Rudman himself is almost superstitiously reluctant to take much credit for his achievements at the Traverse. He pronounces himself proud of his productions of *Pantagleise*, of Tom Mallin's *Curtains*, of Eveling's *Caravaggio Buddy*, pleased with any help he may have given to the playwright Cecil Taylor through the successful production of *The Black and White Minstrels* (Taylor's first play after a long absence from the stage), happy with his success in keeping the Traverse alive and giving it a new sense of momentum; but he is acutely aware, particularly when claiming a role in the early career of a gifted writer or actor, that someone else might have spotted the talent just as well. In his Artistic Director's report to the 1971 AGM of the Traverse – the year of the great £3,000 surplus – he spoke about the insecurity that flickers across the theatre professional's face as soon as you congratulate him on anything, the fear that success can turn to failure in no time; and a touch of that insecurity hangs about Rudman still, even after five successful years at Hampstead and a decade as a National Theatre Associate. At that AGM, he listed six reasons for that year's excellent performance, none of them related to his own skill. The sixth was 'luck' – 'because we were lucky in our choice of plays and players; and anyone who doesn't believe in luck in the theatre doesn't believe in luck in love or in the stock market.'

But Rudman's luck extended beyond the intangibles of audience approval. In his first year, he benefitted from the tail end of the tradition that people would work at the Traverse for next to nothing simply to feel the thrill of it; Equity put a stop to that during the early 70's. He benefitted from the continuing availability of fairly substantial public and private money; some £4,000 of the amount wiped off the Traverse deficit in Rudman's time came in the form of special government grants to organisations making progress in paying off their own debts, and private donations – particularly from the theatrical impresario Eddie Kulukundis, who has sat on the Traverse Board as a special friend and patron ever since Rudman first introduced him in 1970 – remained high throughout the period.

Rudman was lucky, too – perhaps luckier than he knew – in coming to the Traverse at a time when there was so much creative energy around in experimental touring theatre and, above all, in the Traverse Workshop. What Stafford-Clark had offered Rudman was 'simply my version of the kind of partnership that had worked so well between me and Gordon'; and whatever tensions the arrangement may have caused, there is no doubt that at very little extra cost to the Traverse (Stafford-Clark raised his own Arts Council backing), it generated one of the richest periods of production in the theatre's history. Without the wealth of exciting touring theatre available at the time, without the creative input of the Mecklers and the Marowitzes and the Stafford-Clarks, it would have been difficult for Rudman to justify his laid-back, open-door policy; and if the Traverse had been thrown back entirely on its own creative resources in the early 70's – on the work of Rudman and, say, his main associate Nick Kent – the overall programme would have been less exciting, and narrower in appeal. Half a decade later, Chris Parr was to find it almost impossible to fill his lengthening dark season with good touring product; but in the early 70's the product not only existed, but was intimately bound up with the atmosphere, the ideas and the history of the Traverse itself.

But this kind of luck could not last for ever; and once Rudman's big, warm, dominant personality had gone from the Traverse, and the financial climate began to deteriorate, the problems of the new-style organisation began to make themselves obvious. Basically, the Traverse was left with the beginnings of an infrastructure which it could only maintain – through the years of wage inflation in the mid-1970's – if it attracted ever-increasing public subsidy, or, alternatively, continued to expand its operation and increase its audience. One way or the other, the need to protect its own establishment increasingly forbade the theatre to be too silly and experimental, to ask really radical questions, and to play fast-and-loose with the tolerance of audiences and of an increasingly unsympathetic Arts Council; for significantly, Ronald Mavor, with what Max Stafford-Clark remembers as his 'passionate understanding' of the Traverse's work, had retired from his Arts Council post in 1971.

The Traverse story since 1973 is therefore, essentially, about a struggle – sometimes on the part of Artistic Directors, sometimes on the part of the Traverse Committee – to retain a sense of artistic freedom, and of the right to ask risky, fundamental questions about theatre, in the face of intense institutional pressures from within the Traverse, as well as from outside, towards a more rational, predictable and orthodox kind of operation. In a sense, it became a struggle between the reality of the Traverse's situation in the 70's and 80's – as a famous, well-established artistic institution – and the persistent dream of its origin as a tiny, idealistic, minimum-cost operation, dedicated without reservation to the utterly new, the totally surprising, and the by-definition uneconomic. As Michael Rudman himself observed, in a farewell piece he wrote for *Theatre '73*, it is a theatre that can never forget its beginnings, in all their tatty glamour. So it's perhaps not surprising, in the strange, dialectical history of the place, that the next Traverse director was no brash, expansionist whizz-kid, but a young man with every reason to remember and cherish the ideals of the Traverse's early years; and every intention, what's more, of trying to make them live again in the 1970's, changed circumstances or no.

CHAPTER 6
Mike Ockrent

Mike Ockrent first set eyes on the Traverse Theatre towards the end of 1965. He was a bright middle-class boy from London, in his second year as a physics student at Edinburgh University; he had directed a single student production – of a play called *They Couldn't Sleep* – at the University theatre in Adam House; and he had fallen in love with the idea of being a theatre director. 'We played it dead straight,' he recalls, with a kind of droll tolerance for his youthful self, 'and the audience *laughed* until they were *sick*. I thought it was wonderful. I couldn't wait to do something else . . .'.

The 'something else' he set his heart on was Peter Weiss's gruelling exposé of Nazi war crimes, *The Investigation*, which had just appeared in London; and when he contacted Weiss's agent about the possibility of performing the play, he discovered that Jim Haynes – then still in full flow up at the Traverse – had also expressed an interest in it. The agent suggested they get together, Haynes rang Ockrent, and in no time at all, he found himself drawn into the magic circle of Haynes' Traverse, sitting up late in the bar arguing the toss about art and life, seeing and loving shows like Jack Henry Moore's *The Fantastics*, and preparing his huge and successful pro-am production of *The Investigation*, which appeared – in the echoing spaces of St. Mark's Unitarian Church – in February 1966, with a whole range of unlikely Traverse luminaries, including the playwright Stanley Eveling, in the 24-strong cast. After Haynes left the Traverse, in June of that year, Ockrent's connection with the place tailed off rapidly. In 1967, under Gordon McDougall, he co-directed Paul Foster's *The Hessian Corporal*; but thereafter he made a vow to the Physics Department to concentrate on work, retreated back into university circles, and only emerged occasionally to direct the odd student show under the waggish pseudonym Warrender Parks.

All the same, his brief contact with the Jim Haynes Traverse had made the most profound impression on him. 'It never seemed grubby or tacky to me, in James Court,' he says. 'It was like a little, bright oasis suddenly as you went up those stairs, all polished wood, and to me it was a wildly intellectual place, wonderful and mysterious . . .' He remembered the conversations, the intellectual excitement, the easy-going internationalism. Above all he remembered the sense of an artistic community in the building; and when he became Artistic Director of the Traverse in March 1973, he set out to try to recreate some of that atmosphere in the Grassmarket.

Since his final graduation from Edinburgh in 1969, he had been working with Joan Knight at Perth Theatre, first as a trainee, then as an assistant, and finally as Associate Director; and the tough and detailed professional grounding he received there – directing eight or ten vastly varied productions a year in a lovely, intimate proscenium-arch auditorium, with barely ten days' rehearsal for each show – combined with his studio experience to make him one of the most accomplished stage directors ever to work at the Traverse. He had met Michael Rudman at a Scottish Television drama awards dinner in 1971, when

Ockrent's Perth production of *Hedda Gabler* ('all white like snow, with designs by Poppy Mitchell!') was nominated for a production award. Rudman immediately invited him back to the Traverse to direct, and over the next two years he was responsible for successful Traverse productions of Charles Dyer's *Staircase*, David Halliwell's *Little Malcolm And His Struggle Against The Eunuchs* ('a quite brilliant production' says Rudman), Edvardo Manet's *The Nuns* and C.P. Taylor's *Allergy*. By the Spring of 1973, he was very much the chosen successor. 'I felt the more sanguine about leaving the place,' says Rudman, 'because I knew Mike was so very good.'

Not, of course, that his appointment was a foregone conclusion. It was characteristic of Rudman's open regime at the Traverse that he had offered a platform to large numbers of young directors, including – as well as Ockrent – Chris Barlas, Nick Kent and Chris Parr. Parr, like Ockrent, was keen to take over the Traverse in 1973, and the Committee – riven as usual by mild ideological tensions – found it difficult to choose between them. On one hand, Parr offered a kind of natural progression of Rudman's popular new-plays policy, but with a strong Scottish input; on the other, Ockrent offered a stout re-commitment to an international and experimental vision of the Traverse, and in the end it was a pair of unrepentant Traverse traditionalists – Stanley Eveling and Joe Gerber, Chairman from 1972–73 – who forced the decision in Ockrent's favour; in a rare moment of organisational recognition for playwrights, Eveling had been co-opted to represent their interests on the selection committee.

Ockrent won the Traverse job with two clear commitments. The first was to restore the international dimension of the Traverse's work, which had receded into the background with Rudman's 'new British plays' policy; and the second was to introduce an element of serious professional design to all Traverse productions. Before 1973, Traverse design was generally a matter of discussion between the writer and the director, followed by ingenious improvisation, on a limited scale, by the stage management team. But Ockrent – after his experience of working with designers at Perth, where audiences are still inclined to applaud a decent set given half a chance – was convinced that the visual potential of the Traverse was not confined to a few variations on the colour of the back wall and the layout of the seating modules. He introduced first Diana Greenwood, and then Poppy Mitchell, as resident designers at the Traverse, and those who saw productions during that period often retain the most vivid memories of the effects they achieved – in productions like Strindberg's *Dream Play* and *To Damascus*, and in Stewart Conn's *Thistlewood* – by dramatic rearrangement of the auditorium, sometimes combined with ambitious set-building and decor. Sheila Harborth, then the Traverse Production Manager, remembers Joan Knight's production of *You'll Never Be Michelangelo* in July 1973 as 'entirely pink – pink walls, pink drapes, pink carpets', and for the 1975 production of *To Damascus*, the Traverse team actually built a long sloping road, running through the auditorium between two banks of seating.

But by the summer of 1973 – a few months after he took up the job – Ockrent had added a couple of fresh ideas to his agenda. Earlier in the year, just after his appointment, Ockrent had written around various embassies asking for information on new work and interesting developments in theatre across Europe; and one or two had responded by inviting him to come and see for himself. In Berlin, he had met Peter Stein's Schaubuhne company, and been tremendously impressed by them – 'not just by the show I saw, but by their whole method of working, the research, the work with the actors, the detail that went into everyone's understanding of the period and the piece and so on.' Ockrent came home determined – limited resources notwithstanding – to set up a permanent company at the Traverse, and to make another attempt, in a modified and perhaps more disciplined style, at the kind of collaborative approach that had interested Max Stafford-Clark, and was still strongly represented in the Traverse programme by visiting workshop companies like Paradise Foundry and Moving Being.

In fact, Ockrent never used the 60's word 'workshop' in relation to his company; he expected them to work faster and in a more businesslike style, to meet the demands of Traverse programming, and to tackle classics and translations as well as new work. But within the bounds of the Traverse structure, he tried – after early 1974, when the company finally took shape – to run the theatre in as democratic a style as possible, involving the company and staff in decisions about programming and policy, and, in one notable case, allowing the cast of *Schippel* – led by the astonishing Simon Callow, who later wrote at length about the incident in his book *Being an Actor* – to vote a complete re-casting of the production a week into rehearsal. The result, with Callow cast as the Prince, was one of the most successful Traverse productions ever, and one of the few to achieve a West End transfer.

Ockrent also tried to involve the established Traverse writers – Cecil Taylor and Stanley Eveling – in the working of his company, and he says that he felt committed, come what might, to producing any play they gave him. The contrast with Michael Rudman's safety-first approach to commissioning is obvious, and yet it's one of the ironies of the Traverse's position that the more committed an Artistic Director is to the specific writers with whom he works, the more he tends to be criticised for a lack of interest in new writing in general. Of the eight productions Ockrent directed during his two-year regime, three were new plays by Scottish-based writers (Eveling's *Union Jack and Bonzo* and *Dead of Night*, and Stewart Conn's *Thistlewood*), and another three – *Columba*, *Gynt!*, and the brilliant *Schippel* – were complete reworkings of classic texts by C.P. Taylor. But the fact that Ockrent was the only Traverse director to introduce no new writers to the theatre damaged his image with the playwrights' lobby, and most Scottish writers felt that the Traverse was relatively closed to them during this period.

Nor did Ockrent's idea of drawing a complete theatre community around him in the Grassmarket stop at the professionals. In an interview in July 1973, he told *The Scotsman*'s Allen Wright that he was 'anxious to strengthen relations between members of the Traverse and the people who work there.' 'After all,' he said, 'we all go out the same exit. There is no stage door. I want people to feel we are all in it together, and it is not just another theatre where a play is performed, and the audience can take it or leave it.' In essence, Ockrent was the last Traverse Director to believe strongly and positively in the idea of the Traverse as a Club, drawing strength, inspiration and a sense of artistic direction from its own peculiarly committed audience, a self-selected group of people with a special interest in new and experimental work. He introduced events like post-performance discussions and pre-performance talks, designed to involve the audience in the thinking behind the work. He resisted the suggestion – already beginning to make itself heard around the Traverse – that the Grassmarket auditorium was too small to generate a reasonable income ('Let's face it,' he says, 'we found it difficult enough to fill 100 seats a night, never mind 300. That's always been true of the Traverse – was in the 60's, was in my time, still is now'); and he battled royally – through the worst of Britain's mid-70's inflation crisis – for the subsidy that would enable it to survive in the form of an intimate theatre with a challenging, unfamiliar repertoire.

And from the point of view of those most closely involved in it – the company actors, the staff, the writers, regular and committed Traverse-goers – Ockrent's vigorous rearguard action against the pressures of the 70's seems to have been highly successful. Ockrent himself remembers it as an intense, stimulating period, full of intellectual camaraderie in the company, loud arguments in the bar, much bandying of Marx and Mao. His company – Janet Amsden, David Bedard, Simon Callow, Susan Carpenter, Roger Kemp, Roy Marsden and James Snell, in the summer of 1974 – had a strong radical bias, and wanted the work to be 'socially-conscious and class-conscious'. Ockrent suspects, with hindsight, that 'most of it was pretty wishy-washy', but the passion and idealism inspired by the company working-method produced powerful ensemble work, and to judge by contemporary reaction and today's recollection, some of Ockrent's shows – notably Strindberg's *Dream Play* and *Schippel*, both in 1974 – were amongst the finest single productions ever seen at the Traverse.

He kept his promise to restore an international dimension to the Traverse programme, presenting neglected work by writers like Brecht, Fassbinder, Strindberg, Handke, Kroetz and Sternheim, on whose expressionist comedy *Burger Schippel* the company's great hit was based; in 1974, he invited directors from Israel and Romania to work with his company, and Radu Penciulescu's Brecht double-bill of *The Exception and the Rule* and *The Measures Taken* was particularly admired. At the same time, he directed completely new plays by Stewart Conn and Stanley Eveling, and made room under the Traverse banner for new work by Brian Comport and Richard Crane. The theatre continued to play host to a dwindling, but still lively band of touring workshop companies, including Snoo Wilson's Paradise Foundry and the newly-formed Joint Stock; there were co-productions with Foco Novo and Theatre Unlimited.

Certainly, the Traverse audience during 1973–75 never quite hit the heights of the Mike Rudman period. Box office income dropped by about 10% in Ockrent's first year, and never recovered enough to compensate for the savage inflation that hit the theatre in 1974; by the end of 1975, membership had dwindled to around 1,600, the same level as at the end of Max Stafford-Clark's regime. But attendances seem to have stayed at a respectable level at least until the spring of 1975, when ticket price rises caused a slump; in all three of Mike Ockrent's Festivals at the Traverse, more than 5,000 people passed through the turnstile, equalling the record triumphantly set by Michael Rudman in 1970, and in 1974–75 the Scottish Arts Council reported a total Traverse attendance of 23,000, although that figure may be slightly inflated by audiences picked up by *Schippel* on its successful autumn tour to Belfast and the Open Space in London.

And yet there was something about Mike Ockrent's directorship that just failed to ring bells, strike sparks, create a buzz beyond the confines of the Traverse; unlike Jim Haynes or Mike Rudman, or, later, Chris Parr, Ockrent never became a well-known figure in Edinburgh life. Part of the problem was the predictable one of the strongly creative director trying, with the other hand, to run a prominent theatre institution. It's all very well for Traverse directors to talk about the collaborative nature of the theatrical process, and to seek to absorb themselves in it. But the nature of the theatre institution, and of the artistic director's job as we conceive it, fights them every inch of the way, in that the actual power they wield – in terms of their ability to employ writers, actors, other theatre professionals – is so great that their intense involvement with one group of artists causes resentment, bitterness, and powerful feelings of exclusion in the theatrical community at large; and it's interesting that Stafford-Clark, Ockrent and now Jenny Killick – perhaps the most personally gifted of all the Traverse directors in terms of creating theatre – have each voluntarily walked away from the job as it were in mid-term, deliberately surrendering it to someone of a more entrepreneurial cast of mind. It's as if they had suddenly seen that so far from offering an open platform for the director's own creativity, the Traverse eventually imposes responsibilities that make the direct exercise of that creativity extremely difficult.

And in Ockrent's case, that underlying problem was sharpened by the particular situation in which he found himself. The times were changing at breakneck speed in Scotland in the mid-70's. It was the age of the international oil price crisis, of raging inflation, of miners' strikes and the three-day week. It was also the age of Scotland's oil, the *Great Northern Welly Boot Show*, growing national consciousness and the push towards devolution; and for all his brilliance as a director, for all his understanding of the Traverse's past and his dedication to its ideals, Ockrent never got to grips with the basic task of tapping the new surge of creative energy all around him in Edinburgh. He considered, reasonably enough on the face of it, that the strong Scottish policy of the Royal Lyceum theatre at the time – with Bill Bryden directing in the main house, and Bill Pryde and Kenny Ireland at the Young Lyceum – left the Traverse free to take a more cosmopolitan line; the Pool lunchtime theatre in Hanover Street was also offering a regular outlet for new Scottish writing in the early 70's, and it seemed the Traverse's best strategy was to do something completely different.

But in fact, Ockrent had slightly misread the situation. With the Lyceum at the height of its success providing a mixed programme of Scottish plays and classics, Edinburgh was not as starved of good cosmopolitan theatre as it had been in the early 60's; fundamentally, there wasn't much to choose between a Scottish-accented production of Buchner's *Wozzeck* by the Young Lyceum Company and an English-accented production of Sternheim's *Schippel* at the Traverse. Perhaps the arts, internationally, had suddenly reached a point where it was more radical, and more imperative, to get to grips with your local culture before it disappeared, than to dabble in an increasingly institutionalised international arts scene; at any rate, all that happened was that the action, the focus of Edinburgh's cultural life, moved elsewhere, leaving the Traverse slightly out of the picture.

If Ockrent's ideas about the Traverse had translated perfectly into practice, then the membership, with whom he had sought to build a closer relationship, might have nudged him in the direction of the new generation of Scottish writers that were coming up behind the Evelings, the Taylors, the Conns; in June 1975, Ockrent told *The Scotsman* that his failure to discover new writers was 'his greatest disappointment'. But somehow that didn't happen, and the charge of 'elitism', unheard-of in the 1960's, began to stick to the Traverse membership for the first time in its history. The truth is that no-one objects to elites as long as they agree with them, or see them as representative of wider opinion; in the 1960's the Traverse had managed to thrive and to attract public subsidy despite its status as a private club, because its members seemed, in some way, to want the things that society itself wanted or needed at the time – an end to sexual hypocrisy, a new informality, a shake-up of structures, a recognition of the absurdity of things.

But by 1975, the Traverse membership had lost that representative edge, that sense of identity and direction; and insofar as Mike Ockrent had put his trust in the members – in their commitment, their insight, the quality of their response and advice – they failed to meet the challenge. From 1973–75 the Committee was chaired by the generous and energetic Lord Rosebery, whom Sheila Harborth remembers doing handstands in the bar, but it would be hard to say what its members had in common in real-life terms. Swithering between Ockrent and Parr, apparently unable to reconcile the ideas of internationalism and Scottishness, they allowed the artistic initiative to pass from them, and into the hands of an Arts Council – under Ronald Mavor's successor Sandy Dunbar and his influential Drama Director John Faulkner – which saw the way the political wind was blowing, and was increasingly interested not only in distinctively Scottish theatre, but in populist approaches designed to make the arts more accessible, and to broaden the social base of audiences.

Involved as he was, in 1975, in the work of his company, in the excitement of transferring *Schippel* to the West End (where it appeared under the title *The Plumber's Progress* at the Prince of Wales Theatre, with Harry Secombe in the title role) and in a titanic battle to persuade the two new local authorities, Edinburgh District Council and Lothian Regional Council, to part with enough money to see the Traverse through the terrible inflation of 1975–76, Mike Ockrent was only peripherally aware of these background pressures. So far as he was concerned, the main difficulties he had faced at the Traverse were of a more practical kind. In the first year, there had been the effort of establishing himself in a theatre which, following Rudman's footsteps, he saw as part of the British scene; as a director who had only ever worked in Scotland, he saw himself at a disadvantage through sheer lack of knowledge of English actors, and raced to make up for lost time.

He had also felt the pressure of inheriting – as a young and tentative Artistic Director – an existing administrative set-up, headed by Sheila Harborth as Production Manager, which he found quite 'set in its ways.' It's a measure of how much the Traverse atmosphere had changed since the move to the Grassmarket that such a feeling was remotely possible; it's hard to imagine anyone being intimidated by the motley collection of ambitious young transients – like Max Stafford-Clark, or Geoff Moore of Moving Being – who had been Traverse Stage Managers in the 60's, or by the unobtrusively dedicated Stage Director Bill Muir, who saw the Traverse through its years in James Court and left for the Mickery Theatre early in 1970. But the tussle to bend the Traverse to his company method of working took up considerable energy in Ockrent's first year, and he now firmly believes that a theatre's administration should change at least as often as its artistic direction, in an attempt to avoid the all-too-common situation in which administrators control and dominate the conditions of work, and artists – directors, designers, actors – have to pass through as transients, unable to break down and reform the structures to meet changing artistic needs.

But the main pressures on Ockrent throughout his directorship were financial. In 1973, he inherited a Traverse which – solvent and vigorous though it had become under Mike Rudman – was already on its way to a much higher cost-base than before. In 1973, moved by consistent protests from the staff about low wage levels by comparison with other theatres, a deputation from the Traverse Committee – led by Joe Gerber and Kate Eveling – had gone to the Arts Council and extracted a huge 45% increase in the basic revenue grant in order to boost salaries. The Artistic Director's weekly pay shot up from just over £20 to just over £30, and the stage management found themselves elevated from £12 or £15 a week to more than £20; and that was the year – as the Chairman dolefully informed the 1974 AGM – when public subsidy from the Arts Council and local authorities first represented more than half of the Traverse's total turnover. It was in this vulnerable condition – with a massive voluntary increase in fixed costs and dependence on subsidy just tucked under its belt – that the Traverse had to face not only the roaring inflation of 1974–76, when the general price index in Britain rose by more than 50% in two years, but also a series of swingeing additional increases in Equity minimum rates. Just before Mike Ockrent left, the Traverse's bill for actors' wages increased by more than 40% in a single year, and the operating deficit on the Traverse's theatre work – including the bulk of staff salaries – rocketed from £17,000 in 1972–73 to £52,000 three years later.

By and large, the Traverse's income actually kept up with these frightening cost increases. The Arts Council's total commitment to the Traverse – made up of a complex patchwork of grants for revenue purposes, visiting companies, new writing and building work – almost trebled in the same three-year period, but the pressures and uncertainties caused by cost increases on such a scale placed a terrific strain on the organisation, and in the summer of 1975 – with audiences hit by ticket price rises and costs still soaring – Ockrent projected that the Traverse would end the 1975–76 financial year with a deficit of more than £20,000; for the first time in the theatre's history, it was decided that there would be no Traverse productions after the Festival, and staff were issued with redundancy notices. In the run-up to the Festival, Ockrent staged a well-orchestrated press outcry about the threatened closure, and with the help of Bill Taylor – a dynamic Labour Councillor and brilliant advocate, who later became Traverse Chairman – managed to extract a £7,500 grant from the new Regional Council, which was used to lift the redundancy threat from the staff. The Arts Council came through with a supplementary grant to bail the Traverse out, and the organisation (but, ominously, not the autumn productions; there were only seven Traverse productions in 1975, compared with averages of over 20 in the mid-60's) survived to fight another day.

How much this constant financial strain had to do with Mike Ockrent's departure from the Traverse is hard to say. Characteristically, the moment of decision he remembers had to do with a much more personal and artistic impulse; he says that he was sitting one spring day on the set of *To Damascus*, looking at Poppy Mitchell's long winding road wandering off out of the little auditorium, and he suddenly realised that the scale of his work at the Traverse had got out of hand. 'I thought, I have to leave. This is ridiculous. This is not what the Traverse should be doing, and clearly if I'm thinking of expanding, I ought to start working on bigger stages, and it's probably about time that I did . . . so I went.' Perhaps the two problems – financial and artistic – were not entirely unrelated; ironically, Ockrent's design policy, with the extra labour it entailed, had been one factor in the Traverse's soaring costs, and perhaps he sensed that the Traverse – which had flourished in James Court on a low cost/low income/moderate subsidy basis – couldn't take much more of this high cost/low income/huge subsidy mode of operation without sustaining serious spiritual damage.

At any rate, by the summer of '75 he had decided to take a year's sabbatical from September; and – in a curious echo of the situation following Max Stafford-Clark's part-withdrawal from the theatre, which likewise opened the way for a strongly contrasting successor – the Committee accepted that the best man to replace him, on a temporary basis, would be his rival of two years before, Chris Parr.

Ockrent's frustration with the tiny scale of the Traverse stage proved strangely prophetic; in 1988, he is one of the most successful commercial stage directors of his generation, growing rich on the London and New York earnings of smash-hit (and award-winning) shows like *Me and My Girl* and Stephen Sondheim's *Follies*. Caught up in the hit-and-run world of large-scale commercial production, he still cherishes the role of small theatres in promoting new work, and like Michael Rudman, he insists that the sense of detail and concentration he learned in the confined spaces of the Traverse has stood him in good stead in producing strong, credible productions in some of the largest auditoriums in the country; above all, he retains a powerful nostalgia for the company atmosphere, the sense of comradeship and community he was able to draw around himself in Edinburgh, and has hardly had time to experience since.

With hindsight, it's hard not to see Mike Ockrent's time at the Traverse as a romantic interlude, a breathing-space in the push towards a bigger, brighter, more populist Traverse that characterised the theatre's development in the 70's. But at the height of Ockrent's achievement there, in the autumn of 1974, with *Schippel* playing to capacity audiences and Simon Callow laying the foundations of a glittering career nightly in the Grassmarket, I doubt whether many Traverse-goers would have swapped the experience for an entire bill of new Scottish mini-plays. Stanley Eveling, who worked with every Traverse director up to and including Ockrent, says that despite all the talk about writers and workshops and companies, and in spite of 'all the *life* kerfuffle that went on around the place, the idea that it was changing everyone's life . . .', all that has ever happened at the Traverse, objectively speaking, is that talented young directors have had an opportunity to learn their craft in a situation of low costs and high visibility. The exceptionally glittering careers of ex-directors like Mike Ockrent suggest a grain of truth in what he says; but those who saw his work at the Traverse between 1973 and 1975 would probably agree that there are worse things, for an audience and for a theatre, than being experimented upon by a director of Mike Ockrent's calibre.

CHAPTER 7
Chris Parr

Chris Parr moved into the Traverse, in the autumn of 1975, with all the decisive energy of a man who knows the times are on his side. His expressed policy was to present plays which were 'public, accessible and relevant, and written by people born in the United Kingdom,' his intention was to make sure that the Traverse presented more new Scottish work than ever before; and although the abrupt change of style he brought to the organisation provoked some mutterings of dissent among the Committee and membership, the protests were remarkably muted.

The truth was that by 1975, the Traverse had no option but to face up to its underlying situation. Its main patron was no longer the Traverse membership nor any coalition of members, wealthy donors, and local authority supporters; it was the Scottish Arts Council – now the sole source of more than half of the Traverse's income – and the opinion of the Scottish theatrical world as mediated through the Drama Panel of that Council. The Traverse had therefore reached a point where it had to justify itself not only in terms of audience appreciation and international recognition, but also in terms of the rest of Scottish theatre; it had to find a role within the Scottish scene which would justify its exceptional level of subsidy, and there is no doubt that in the climate of 1975, what was wanted from the Traverse was that it should bring its expertise and its high standards of production to bear on Scottish writing.

The spirit of the moment was not only Scottish but 'anti-elitist'. In 1977, the Arts Council formally adopted a drama policy aimed at increasing audiences for drama in 'numbers, social width and commitment', and the ideas behind that policy were already current in 1975. For the next decade, the idea of an experimental theatre club, supported by the interest of a committed but limited audience, was out of fashion with a vengeance, and despite occasional flurries of protest when constitutional changes were proposed, the Traverse membership – which remained around the 1500–2000 mark throughout the late 70's – showed little interest in regaining the artistic and organisational initiative. What's more, the prevailing trend of opinion against the exclusive Club idea had strong support inside the Traverse itself, where some of the staff of the post-Rudman era – trained up in more orthodox theatres – were beginning to feel irked by their position as employees of a Committee whom they regarded as a bunch of amateurs. On the back of a staff copy of some Committee minutes for late 1975, there is a delicious doodle which reads, 'We want really nice people on the Committee who will 1) put their hands in their pockets 2) give us a lot of nice dinner parties 3) fund-raise successfully 4) leave us to do our jobs 5) leave us to play at theatre 6) go and play at Committee meetings in someone else's house'.

On the whole, the Traverse's professional staff – now led by Sheila Harborth, the Production Manager, who was made Administrator in 1977 – tended to reject the idea that the Traverse needed a small, unorthodox and democratic structure in order to produce small-scale, flexible, experimental theatre. Like Michael Rudman, they couldn't see the connection between being established and being 'establishment'; their whole instinct was towards a bigger, more securely-based Traverse, able to generate higher income, attract sponsorship, and offer 'prestige' pay-offs to classy patrons and rich Board members. For that reason they tended to support both the idea of 'going public' (i.e. abolishing the Club), and the idea – increasingly canvassed throughout the late 70's – that the Traverse should expand into a larger theatre space; and as it happened, their impulse to expand the Traverse operation received a powerful impetus in the summer of 1975, when Dr. Butterworth, the owner of the West Bow property, abruptly decided to sell up.

The Committee decided that the only way to secure the Traverse's future was to try to buy the building, which occupies three sides of an ancient Old Town courtyard; and Lord Rosebery, then just about to retire as Chairman, not only promptly solved the immediate problem by buying up the property on the Traverse's behalf (for about £40,000), but after a stout fund-raising effort from the Committee and some help from the Arts Council, also guaranteed the substantial bank loan they needed to help buy it back into the ownership of the Club. Paradoxically, though, this magnificent gesture of old-style private generosity to the Traverse plunged it the more decisively into a new, expansionist age; for better or worse, for the next four years – first under the Chairmanship of the Glasgow surveyor Tom Laurie, and then of Councillor Bill Taylor – the Committee minutes seethed with references to building works, to acquisitions of stray corners of the premises, to the removal of other tenants and to plans for the comprehensive redevelopment of the whole courtyard.

Chris Parr therefore came into his inheritance at a time when powerful practical and political considerations were urging the kind of popular Scottish policy he adopted; but the point about Parr – and the key to his unique achievement at the Traverse – is that he did not adopt it for cynical or pragmatic reasons. He was absolutely in tune with the mood of the mid-70's in Scotland, helping to create it as well as responding to it; he believed in the power of specific, local experience to illuminate broader issues, he believed passionately that there was a rich new seam of Scottish writing talent which the Traverse must encourage, and he believed in more accessible theatre for a more broadly-based audience. The Traverse has never had a working-class director, but Parr – as a hard-up meritocrat from the outer fringes of London, who won his way into Oxford on brain-power alone – was the nearest it ever came to it; and his whole career, both before the Traverse and since, has been marked by a strong cultural antipathy to the British establishment, and its metropolitan values, that sets him apart from the Traverse tradition. At Bradford University – where he was the first fellow in theatre in the early 70's – and later at Scottish Television in Glasgow and at the BBC in Belfast and Birmingham, his abiding obsession has been the finding and nurturing of local, regional writers, of what he called, in taking up the Traverse job, 'the talent on the doorstep'. Whatever other career ambitions he may have had, he was fundamentally indifferent to London, to its theatre scene, and to the opinions of metropolitan critics;

no other Traverse director, however brave or experimental, has been able to lay claim to that particular – and in the Scottish context crucial – kind of integrity.

When Parr arrived at the Traverse, he already had some clear ideas about new Scottish writers. He had directed two or three shows at the little Pool lunchtime theatre in Hanover Street, where many of the writers he later presented at the Traverse had been given a showing; in England, he had seen and read a battered script of an embryonic play about Laurel and Hardy by Tom McGrath, Glasgow underground poet and jazz musician, and founder-director of the city's Third Eye Centre. In his first few months in Edinburgh – in the aftermath of Mike Ockrent's epic financial battle – Parr had to sit out a long winter season of visiting productions, which he described to the Committee as 'extremely unsatisfactory'; but at the end of the year, he came through with a strong general policy statement affirming his commitment to new British playwrights and 'accessible' themes, and outlining a season of eight productions including three new Scottish plays, three new English ones, a 'rockatorio' by Chris Judge Smith, and a bill of three or four short plays by Scottish writers to run in repertoire.

The plays which emerged – in the sensational spring-summer season of 1976 – were Tom Gallacher's *Sea Change* (a play about North Sea oil based on *The Tempest*), Hector MacMillan's smash-hit comedy *The Gay Gorbals* (about an attempt to set up a gay organisation in the prickly heartland of Glasgow machismo), McGrath's *Laurel and Hardy*, and half a dozen short Scottish plays including a double-bill about movies by Campbell Black and Robert Walke. In the English 'half' of the programme there was Robert Holman's Orwell play *Outside the Whale*, and Judge Smith's *The Kibbo Kift*, with music by J. Maxwell Hutchinson. By the end of the 1976 Festival, the Traverse had also mounted productions of David Edgar's *Saigon Rose*, Richard Crane's *Nero and the Golden House* (Edgar, Holman and Crane were all protégés of Parr's from his days in Bradford) and Howard Barker's *Wax*; and Parr was beginning to develop and refine his policy.

At the Club AGM in June 1976, he produced a series of audience-figures for 1974–5 and 1975–6 which showed quite clearly that Traverse productions did better than visiting shows, and Traverse productions of new Scottish plays did best of all; for the October-May period audiences were up by more than 30% on the previous year, and one of the conclusions of Parr's report to the membership was that 'Scottish plays should have a regular place in the repertoire.' He also argued that the Traverse must 'widen its function and terms of reference', perhaps by touring some of its work; that box office considerations would have to loom larger in future, since the right to fail was being diminished by economic pressures; and that the Traverse would have to mount a volume of activity that 'split the seams' of the present building if it were to seem serious in its need for a larger auditorium.

The seam-splitting duly started in the 1976 Edinburgh Festival, when the Traverse transferred its most successful show, *Laurel and Hardy*, to the Old Chaplaincy Centre in Forrest Road, where it played in a strong Scottish-based Other Traverse porogramme with The Heretics'

production of Donald Campbell's *The Jesuit*, and Borderline Theatre's *An'
Me wi' a Bad Leg Tae* by Billy Connolly; and the success of the Other
Traverse – which played to almost 8,000 people during the three weeks
of the Festival – confirmed the direction of Parr's policy. In September,
when it became apparent that Mike Ockrent had decided not to return
after his sabbatical year, Parr was confirmed by the Committee as
Artistic Director for 1976–77. Like Max Stafford-Clark, he was a strong
and persuasive writer of memos to his Committee, in a style more
powerful and economical, less impetuous and engaging; and he
responded to his appointment with a brisk policy statement detailing his
intention to place a stronger emphasis on Scottish work (although he
made it clear that he would like to continue to 'hold a torch' for English
writing at the Traverse), to develop a touring function for the theatre,
and to 'continue attempting to demonstrate that the Traverse can fill the
new, enlarged role envisaged for it.'

In April – encouraged by the Traverse's relatively secure financial
situation – Parr and Sheila Harborth drew up a discussion document for
the Committee, suggesting two lines of future development for the
Traverse. It could, they suggested, either resolve to remain a Club
indefinitely, in which case it had better try to find ways of making itself
more financially self-sufficient; or it could adopt the 'development plan'
(sketches of which were apparently already on view in the foyer of the
theatre), which allowed for a second and much larger public theatre-
space in the ground floor of the Grassmarket building. This would
maximise box-office income, and meet Arts Council and local authority
reservations about giving large subsidies to a private association. The
document was a sophisticated and well-balanced piece of work, which
acknowledged that the second option would raise the 'whole question of
the future identity of the Traverse'; but Parr and his Administrator
clearly believed that it offered the best chance of escape from the high-
cost-low-income-unreliable-subsidy trap in which the Traverse found
itself. In fact, the Committee never seem to have been quite as
enthusiastic about the development plan – and the massive fund-raising
effort it would inevitably involve – as Parr and Harborth would have
wished; but in May they decided to go ahead with the building project
(while remaining a Club for the time being). For the rest of the year, Parr
and Harborth continued to refine their plans for a new 200-seat public
Traverse downstairs, backed by a studio for experimental and project
work in the existing theatre, and the scheme remained officially on the
Traverse agenda into the 1980's.

Of course, there was some unhappiness among members and
supporters about this radical change of approach and identity. Some of
Parr's attitudes might have been calculated to annoy more traditional
Traverse members. Many, like Allen Wright, were dismayed by his
relative indifference to the international dimension of the Traverse's
work, which they had prized as evidence of Edinburgh's survival as
something more than a provincial city, and upset by his summary
dismissal of the two established Traverse playwrights C.P. Taylor and
Stanley Eveling, on whom he felt the theatre relied too heavily (in fact
Taylor cheerfully won his way back into the programme within a year,

although Eveling stayed away until 1983). He must also have jangled sensitive nerves among Edinburgh's carefully anglicised middle-class with his enthusiastic endorsement of a kind of working-class drama (full of titles like *Next Time Bring a Wee Something Tae Drink, Son*) that was both alien, and uncomfortably close to home. In September 1976 – following Parr's confirmation as Artistic Director – the former Chairman and doughty Traverse traditionalist Joe Gerber resigned from the Committee, declaring that he was 'tired of being in a minority of one.' He left behind him a sharp and disgruntled letter to all Committee members, protesting mildly about Parr's plans to form a touring company (which he felt would impose a choice of productions unsuitable for the Traverse and its audience), moderately about the plans for the building (which he felt would create an unnecessary financial strain so soon after the purchase of the property), and much more strongly about the increasing domination of the Traverse organisation by professional staff who, he said, often treated members of the elected Committee with 'undisguised contempt'.

But by and large, the Traverse organisation was in what Parr remembers as a 'bullish' mood, rushing to embrace the idea of an expanded theatre and an expanded role; and it is quite clear from the tone of Parr's policy documents that for all his talk of box-office pressures and limitations on the right to fail, he was actually fascinated, at least to begin with, by the project of finding a bigger, wider-ranging audience for the Traverse. According to Parr, all Traverse directors tend to prefigure their future careers in their policy for the theatre, and certainly his preoccupation with wider audiences and the mainstream of British experience can be traced through into his work as a television drama producer in Belfast and the Midlands; to him the little Grassmarket theatre was simply a base for a much bigger and more populist operation, and he concedes, with hindsight, that for a Traverse Director he was perhaps 'a little too excited' by big spaces and big audiences.

For the time being, though, the Parr bandwagon rolled on unchallenged, into three years of remarkable work that came close to establishing a complete new repertoire for modern Scottish drama. In the autumn of 1976, he and his quiet Assistant Director Peter Lichtenfels – who had been appointed by Mike Ochrent in the summer of 1975, and directed almost as many productions as Parr himself in this period – produced another two Traverse shows, Michael Ondaatje's *The Collected Works of Billy the Kid* (directed by Lichtenfels) and George Byatt's *The Silver Land*. Then in spring 1977 – after the now obligatory season of visiting companies – they launched another strong series of Scottish plays, including, in Tom McGrath and Jimmy Boyle's *The Hardman*, one of the most successful Traverse productions ever, a strong, searing, intensely theatrical account, based on Boyle's own story, of the life of a Glasgow street-fighter and 'enforcer' face to face with the Scottish criminal justice system.

And it was with *The Hardman* – directed in that first production by Peter Lichtenfels – that Parr's artistic policy really began to hit its stride. More than for any other artistic director (except possibly Jim Haynes, with his famous interest in 'pelvic regions'), it's possible to detect a single, powerful theme in Parr's directorship; what he had done – and a mere glance down the list of Scottish plays performed during his first three years, the titles like *The Hardman, Street Fighting Man, Next Time Bring a Wee Somethin' Tae Drink, Son*, demonstrates the point – was to open the middle-class doors of the Traverse to a whole area of male working-class experience in Scotland and particularly in Glasgow, a high-energy, strongly physical culture with a powerful undercurrent of aggression and suppressed tenderness.

Peter Lichtenfels, standing on the sidelines at rehearsals early in the Parr era, remembers feeling pure shock at the kind of undisciplined macho behaviour in which some Scottish actors felt they had to indulge in order to prove their manhood. But Parr was willing to ride this out in order to get at the wellsprings of energy underlying it; and through plays like *The Hardman*, which dealt specifically with the culture of violence, and later John Byrne's magnificent *Slab Boys* trilogy, the best of his writers began to work their way through this kind of fierce, competitive, exhibitionist male experience into a much more rounded sense of humanity. To compare the theatrical pyrotechnics of Byrne's original *Slab Boys* (1978) with the rich texture of the final trilogy play *Still Life* (1982), is to catch some sense of the emotional journey involved, and there's no doubt that Parr's single-minded support for a group of gifted Scottish writers in the late 70's opened the way to a shift and a maturing of Scottish self-images that has had a profound impact on the nation's cultural life, including the popular culture of rock music and TV drama.

Of course, there were other strands of drama – from England, from the East Coast, from a more gentle kind of Scottish experience – in Parr's regime, and it should be said that he directed very few of those famous Scottish productions himself; all the John Byrne plays were originally directed by David Hayman, *The Hardman* by Peter Lichtenfels, McGrath's 1978 play *The Android Circuit* by Robin Lefevre. But in 1977 Parr directed a much-admired double-bill of C.P. Taylor's *Walter* plays, *Getting By* and *Going Home*; in the magnificently productive year of 1978 (probably one of the best in Traverse history for quantity and quality) there were fine Parr productions of Tom Gallacher's *Mr Joyce is Leaving Paris* and Robert Holman's *Rooting* alongside *The Slab Boys, The Android Circuit*, John Bett's *Street Fighting Man* and Donald Campbell's *Somerville the Soldier*, some of which transferred once again to the Other Traverse during the Festival. In 1979, Parr directed Michael Wilcox's *Rents* – a rare and powerful play about the gay scene in Edinburgh by an Englishman from Northumberland – and in 1980 he moved on to a belated commitment to women writers, promoting Traverse productions of Marcella Evaristi's *Hard to Get* and Alison Watson's *Moving In*, and himself directing Kate Collingwood's *Tea Tent Talk*, an exercise in total naturalism – referred to by one critic of his policy as the 'Great Bridge Roll Disaster of 1980' – which involved the buttering and mashed-boiled-egging of several hundred filled rolls in front of the audience every night of the week. At the end of that year, one of Parr's final gestures at the Traverse was another stylish play about the Edinburgh middle classes, John Hale's account of the real-life *Case of David Anderson QC*, about an Edinburgh

QC whose career was destroyed by unproven allegations of a sexual scandal.

But in the end, it was the working-out of those themes of aggression and violence and male display that was most memorable about Parr's Traverse regime, and in that sense it reached its climax at the Edinburgh Festival of 1979, when Tom McGrath's great ape-drama *Animal* – based on the idea that the catharsis of human violence through theatre has its equivalents in the rituals of ape behaviour – was presented at Moray House Gymnasium as part of the official Festival programme, and attracted international acclaim. At that point, the Traverse had reached an unparalleled peak of subsidy and recognition in Scotland, and was beginning to break through once again – but this time with a distinctive Scottish voice – into the international drama scene. Between 1975–76 and 1979–80, its total grant from the Scottish Arts Council had increased by more than 45% *in real terms*, with its local authority funding also rocketing from only £3,000 in 1975 to more than £40,000 in 1980; and although attendances in the Grassmarket were not spectacularly high (no-one has ever quite equalled Michael Rudman's 1972 figure of 25,000 paying customers there) the total Traverse audience in Edinburgh, including the Other Traverse, reached heights of almost 35,000 in 1978 and 1979.

As matters turned out, it might have been a far, far better thing for Chris Parr to have quit on this four-year peak of achievement than to try to sustain his Traverse directorship into the 80's; for from the autumn of 1979 things suddenly began to turn sour, and some of the old unresolved tensions about the future of the Traverse began to reassert themselves. As usual money was the immediate cause of the problem; towards the end of 1979, the Traverse (which had overestimated its probable grant for the year from both Arts Council and local authorities) ran into severe budgetary difficulties, and had to announce an unprecedented 'dark' period of almost three months over Christmas. What seems to have been happening, with hindsight, is that the Arts Council was beginning to signal a change of attitude to the Traverse. Over the years from 1975 to 1980, the theatre (like the Council itself) had had an average annual grant increase of 25%, but by 1980, with the advent of the Conservative government, the atmosphere was changing, while the growth of interest in new Scottish drama (ironically partly encouraged by the Traverse itself) – meant that the demand on Arts Council funds was increasing. Chris Parr was frankly dismayed, in particular, by the project for a new Glasgow Theatre Club at the Tron; if the Arts Council could barely afford one expensive new-play theatre, he reasoned, how on earth was it going to afford two?

At any rate, this sense of a slight cooling-off in relations between the Traverse and its major funding body found the organisation, for all its recent success, remarkably ill-equipped to face such a crisis. All through the late 70's, the Traverse staff, led by Parr, had been pressing for the implementation of the theatre's expansion plans, arguing that the success of Parr's popular policy provided the ideal springboard for the move to a larger public operation; in 1978, the development plan for a large downstairs theatre was confidently announced to the press, *The*

Scotsman printing the story under the headline 'Extension of theatre will double seating'.

But somehow, the move to make this ambitious scheme a reality never gathered momentum. Perhaps the Committee was a shade ambivalent in its attitude; perhaps there was a lingering reluctance, somewhere in the heart of the organisation, to move yet further from the tiny, nurturing, hothouse auditorium in which it had been born. As Max Stafford-Clark points out, an audience for a new play which looks respectable and supportive in a 100-seat theatre can look very forlorn indeed in a 250-seater; at any rate, nothing materialised from the building project during Chris Parr's time except a new Downstairs Bar, which, given the radical change in Scottish licensing laws which wiped out the Traverse's traditional club advantages as a drinking-place, was something of a financial disaster.

What all this talk of a larger building had done, though, was to set the organisation ever more firmly on an expansionist path, with an increasing cost-base which, in the absence of a new theatre, could only be met by ever-increasing grants. As Parr puts it, his answer to escalating costs was always to 'dance higher' on the ladder of subsidy, and to try to attract more box-office income; and when neither of those was forthcoming, he had no option but to cut productions and go dark. He never tackled the question of cutting back the Traverse's cost-base to a more sustainable level. For one thing, he was deeply uninterested in administrative detail; for another, the idea that the Traverse should start slimming itself back into its Grassmarket premises, becoming, in the phrase of the day, 'leaner and fitter', would have been a betrayal of the whole mood of his directorship, which had been to expand the Traverse organisation into something with a much wider scope.

To make matters worse, the Traverse faced this difficult moment in its affairs quite disunited, with serious bad feeling between the staff and the Committee, and particularly between Chris Parr and his Chairman, Bill Taylor. Throughout the Chris Parr era, there had been an underlying tension between the staff and the Committee, made almost inevitable by the explicit rejection of the old Club concept of the Traverse – and therefore of the Club's elected representatives – that was in the air. Sheila Harborth was openly embarrassed by what she felt was the 'low calibre' of Traverse Committee members during the period (they were lawyers, architects, schoolteachers); she despaired of their indecision, their financial timidity, their lack of commercial know-how, their inability to carry out the effective fund-raising which she felt to be their proper function. In fact, the Committee had always been a fairly mixed group of professionals with a few co-opted 'angels' to add weight and clout; but whether Harborth's assessment of the Committee members was accurate or not, the fact that these divisions existed and were strongly felt within the Traverse hardly encouraged constructive discussion of its future.

At any rate, during 1980 relations inside the organisation were increasingly strained. Faced with financial pressures, the staff were inclined to blame the Committee for weakness and indecision in missing the chances of the late 70's, and failing to put the Traverse on the road to a bigger and more viable operation; the Committee, in turn, were increasingly baffled and alarmed by the fact that the Traverse, with the highest real-terms income in its history, was somehow unable to keep its doors open and sustain the size and number of its own productions. As the Secretary Susie Raeburn dolefully put it in the Committee minutes for October 1980, 'Chris Parr circulated a report throughout which it was emphasised that the Traverse is "bleeding to death"'; and this kind of exaggerated gloom continued throughout the year, with a series of downbeat newspaper headlines along the lines of 'Trouble at the Traverse' and 'Traverse in Travail.'

In fact, many of the events of 1980 bespeak a total exhaustion with the Traverse and its problems on Parr's part. In 1976, fresh into the job and with a programme of new plays straining at the starting-gate, he might scarcely have noticed such a minor financial crisis. But by 1980, with the effects of the abortive 1979 referendum beginning to cast a deep gloom over the Scottish scene, and with the 'ebb and flow' of theatrical energy (as Parr put it in a letter to *The Scotsman*) drifting away from the Traverse a little, he simply lacked the energy and chutzpah to run up deficits, pay them off, and snatch the initiative in determining the scope of his operation back from the Charlotte Square bureaucrats of the Arts Council. By the end of 1980, even the Arts Council Drama Director Tony Wraight was dropping hints about the need for a more adventurous approach; but Parr had let the pressures grind him down, and the tone of his discourse became more and more petulant, and less and less persuasive. What the situation required was some creative lateral thinking about how to extract the maximum use from the Traverse resources; after five years and nine years in their respective organisational niches, Parr and Harborth were the last people to provide it, and the messy end of Chris Parr's reign at the Traverse provides a perfect illustration of the truth of Mike Ockrent's maxim that neither a director nor an administrator should stay in the job for much more than four years. 'After that, you get institutionalised,' says Ockrent. 'And the Traverse has to be a revolutionary institution. If it's not overstretching itself, it's nothing.'

At the end of the year – during the successful run of *David Anderson QC* – Parr and the Committee fell to arguing about various directing commitments he wanted to undertake outside the Traverse, and the atmosphere deteriorated further. But the final row, when it came in January 1981, was actually over one of the most unorthodox aspects of his policy, namely his lack of interest in making a big splash for the international audience and the London critics over the Festival. According to Peter Lichtenfels, to whom it fell to report the matter to the 1981 AGM, Parr was faced, in mid-1980, with a choice between dropping his autumn productions – notably *David Anderson QC* – or making do with a thin Festival programme of only four shows, Evaristi's *Hard to Get*, John Anderson's *Snapshots*, Andrew Dallmeyer's *Yobs and Snobs* and a production of Barry Collins' monologue *The Ice Chimney* from the Lyric, Hammersmith. He chose to continue with the autumn programme, but there was a general feeling – expressed by Bill Taylor in the letter to the Committee that finally provoked Parr's resignation – that the Festival effort had been unnecessarily puny and had done the Traverse no credit.

Parr of course rejected the idea that he had sabotaged the Festival programme in order to emphasise the Traverse's plight, but what incensed him most of all was Bill Taylor's unwillingness, as Chairman, to give him the full and unreserved support he felt he needed. In a flurry of acrimonious letters he resigned, leaving behind a recommendation that Peter Lichtenfels should be made caretaker Director in his place.

Because of the sourness surrounding his departure – and the slackening of energy in the Traverse programme towards the end of his time – Chris Parr's reputation as a Traverse director probably stands less high than it should today. Scottish playwrights still look back with nostalgia, of course, to a time when the door of the Traverse seemed decisively open to them and their style; their house magazine *Scottish Theatre News* dubbed him 'St. Chris Parr of Blessed Memory', and always caricatured him with a little halo. But as if to compensate for this adulation, a kind of competing scepticism about the Parr era has grown up, a myth that it consisted of little more than a series of bad, boring, naturalistic plays by parochial writers set in Scottish living-rooms, totally untheatrical and fit for nothing but instant transfer to the small screen, if that.

In fact, the merest glance at what Parr actually produced at the Traverse shows that this is less than fair. The great Scottish successes of his period – *The Slab Boys*, *The Hardman*, *Animal*, McGrath's *1–2–3* trilogy in the spring of 1981 – were all in different ways deeply theatrical and formally challenging. John Byrne was a gifted artist who had developed a strong and sophisticated theatrical taste over years of play-going in London and Glasgow; Tom McGrath was an international writer and musician who had been around the Traverse since Jim Haynes' day; and *Animal* and *1–2–3*, both directed by Parr, were as innovative in style and technique as any new plays ever produced at the Traverse. It's not even true – although it is often said – that Parr was a better producer and script-editor than he was a director. Even when he was dealing with naturalistic material – as in *Anderson QC* or Michael Wilcox's *Rents* – his productions always had a polished, stylish look about them; and when he went for real naturalism, in *Tea Tent Talk* and in *Rooting*, which actually featured live pigs in the auditorium, he went so far over the top that the results were strangely intriguing. The worst that can be said of his programme is that it contained some dross (but every Traverse director has some atrocious productions to his credit), that there was a certain small-scale sameness of subject-matter towards the end, and that it ran out of steam in its final year; in other words, its only serious fault was that it all went on a little too long.

It's also said – to Parr's annoyance – that his policy was not experimental; that it was designed to be 'safe' and 'popular', and was therefore out of line with the Traverse tradition. But in fact, at its best, Parr's policy was that most exciting of theatrical events, a high-risk programme which *turns out* to be popular. His attitude was not fundamentally commercial, although he wasn't above playing on the box-office potential of his work; his policy was simply another kind of cultural gamble, beyond the 60's stereotypes implied in the phrase 'experimental theatre', and he can hardly be blamed for making it work.

His abiding fault and most conservative trait, as a Traverse director, was his failure to question and re-examine the underlying structures of the organisation he inherited; in allowing the pattern of rising establishment costs to go unchallenged, and failing to scotch the arrogant, divisive attitude that went with the expansionist mood, he weakened the organisation's ability to deal with the inevitable funding crisis when it came.

But in a sense, Parr's shortcomings as director of the Traverse operation – and the severe internal problems he bequeathed to his successor – are simply the negative side of his intense creative contribution to what was happening in Scotland in the 70's. His directorial style is difficult to place on the spectrum between entrepreneurship and active creation; he did contrive, in the best entrepreneurial tradition, to open the Traverse to a new wave of writers and actors. But at heart he was more of a creative director than he looked, happy to surrender administrative control to his staff, strong in his sense of what kind of work he wanted to do (he once described himself as 'a bit of a frustrated writer'), by common consent quite brilliant at finding and challenging new playwrights, and helping them to find a distinctive dramatic voice; and it's in the extraordinary development of Scottish theatrical language during the late 70's that the strength of his contribution can be traced. Alone among all the Traverse directors, he put his faith in the touchy, neglected culture he found around the theatre, and drew tremendous artistic energy from those immediate roots. As Max Stafford-Clark says, 'A theatre director – wherever he is – has to be humble, to keep his ear on the street and *listen.*' In his strange, arrogant way, Chris Parr had some of that cultural humility; it's Scotland's loss, and perhaps the Traverse's too, that so few of his colleagues have shared it.

CHAPTER 8
The Traverse in the 80's: Peter Lichtenfels and Jenny Killick

According to Mike Ockrent, directing the Traverse is such an intense experience that leaving it is 'like getting divorced. You know, people can't go back for four or five years; they have to wait for the emotions to subside . . .' The evidence suggests that he's right; Chris Parr could not go back with any equanimity until 1985, and Peter Lichtenfels, who left in 1985, hasn't been back yet. In that sense, the Lichtenfels directorship hasn't quite subsided into Traverse history, and final verdicts on it would be premature. What can be said, though, is that he reversed the usual pattern of Traverse directorships in a quiet but remarkable way. Where most of his colleagues have swept into the theatre on a surge of energy and creativity, and left a few years later in a state of exhaustion and mild burnout, Lichtenfels found the Traverse at an exceptionally low creative ebb, made a muted initial impact on it, and yet slowly nursed and cajoled and nourished it – through what were certainly the most difficult years in its history – back towards the impressive crescendo of artistic energy and success on which he left it, immediately after the Edinburgh Festival of 1985.

When Lichtenfels took the Traverse on in April 1981 (first as caretaker following Chris Parr's resignation, and then, after beating off competition from 81 other candidates, as Artistic Director in his own right), his declared policy was simple. He wanted to continue Chris Parr's commitment to new British writing, although his emphasis would be less Scottish; he wanted to encourage the work of women writers and directors, which seemed to him to be full of energy at that point; and he wanted to make the Traverse less insular again, to increase its international links, and to bring into the theatre the best international visiting companies he could find, as a point of comparison and stimulus for the Traverse's own work. So far, so predictable; and as Lichtenfels moved into the Traverse job, many were inclined to see him as a pale Chris Parr substitute in what one observer called 'shades of grey', incapable of giving the place the radical creative jolt into the 80's it obviously needed.

But there was a little more to Lichtenfels than that. Born in Canada in 1951, he was a tall, quiet, formidably stubborn young man who had crossed the Atlantic in the early 70's determined to find a niche in British theatre within two years, and had just made his deadline at Hampstead Theatre Club in 1975. Later that year, the departing Mike Ockrent appointed him Trainee Director at the Traverse; and throughout Chris Parr's regime – apart from a period as Associate at Liverpool Playhouse in 1980 – he had been working quietly around the theatre, directing major shows like *The Hardman*, reading scripts, watching, absorbing, learning. At Chris Parr's feet – or in the corner of Parr's tiny office, where he spent as much time as he could – he had acquired a certain skill in working with writers; but he had also been forming his own ideas about the running of the theatre, which interested him rather more than it did Parr. 'I remember,' he says, 'we both arrived on the same day in 1975, and I sat in Chris's office being quite aggressive and saying, "It's my right to learn about budgets, it's my right to know about all that . . ."'

So by the time Lichtenfels became Artistic Director, he had also built up a kind of hidden agenda for the job, beyond his public policy, and the cardinal point on it was a simple one; he was resolved that the Traverse would never, ever again, on any financial consideration, sacrifice its Festival programme as it had in 1980. Lichtenfels could see that the political climate in Scotland was turning against the Traverse. The Scottish Arts Council was short of cash and looking for cuts; the new Drama Director Bob Palmer, appointed at the beginning of 1981, was a former Edinburgh Theatre Workshop director with a strong community arts interest, who held no brief for the Traverse at all. The theatre's dwindling seasons and huge Arts Council subsidy (£200,000 in Lichtenfels' first year, or more than 65% of the total Traverse budget) were attracting increasing hostility from other arts organisations; the prospects for local authority funding – which had reached a peak of £50,000 in 1980–81, only to fall back to £30,000 three years later – were bleak and growing bleaker. Clearly, there were going to be battles to be fought; in order to fight them the Traverse needed to re-establish itself quickly, in the eyes of the influential London media, as a unique asset British theatre could not afford to lose, and the obvious way to do that was to restore the tradition of the big Traverse Festival splash.

The relationship between the Traverse and the Festival has always been fundamental to the nature of the place. Born out of the Edinburgh Festival Fringe, existing at the geographical heart of it, contributing to it, belonging to it, once its only late-night drinking club and still one of its great social and artistic centres, the Traverse depends on the Festival for a substantial slice of its income and most of its vitality. As Peter Lichtenfels puts it, 'the Festival is to the Traverse what the pantomime season is to other theatres'. In purely financial terms, the annual massive influx into the city brings a huge surge in audiences and in bar income; in the 1980's it has not been unusual for the Traverse to present a third of all its performances for the year, and to take a third of its total box-office income, during the three weeks of the Festival.

But what happens in the Festival is more than a matter of audience figures and box-office receipts. As Michael Rudman puts it, in these three August weeks, when the London 'season' is over and the arts establishment decamps en masse for the north, Edinburgh effectively becomes the greatest arts metropolis in the world, and the major centres of the Festival – including the Traverse – experience a concentrated attention and high-profile media exposure otherwise unknown outside London or New York. It's this guaranteed Festival exposure that makes the Traverse so different in atmosphere from other small theatres around Britain, that puts pressure on the work to achieve standards comparable with the best in the world, that attracts the brightest and most ambitious young directors to it. Michael Rudman, that sharpest of all observers of the politics of the Traverse, believes that this unique double advantage – in working all year in the low-profile, well-supported environment of the only studio theatre in what might be a big provincial city, and then suddenly enjoying the high visibility and intense public response of a metropolitan and international theatre centre – accounts almost entirely for the Traverse's special atmosphere, for its fame, for its success; and in their different ways, almost all the Traverse's directors seem to agree with him.

Except, of course, Chris Parr, to whom words like 'metropolitan' and 'national' (meaning London-based) were anathema. In his own phrase, he was 'ambivalent' about the Festival. 'I used to feel,' he says, 'that it was like living in a house that suddenly became horribly over-full, where people wouldn't go to bed, and kept you up talking till three, and had parties that you didn't want . . .' The whole thrust of his directorship had been towards a different set of values, a challenging of the idea that recognition in the *Sunday Times* is always a better thing than recognition in *The Scotsman*. He had successful Festivals certainly, particularly in 1978 when his Other Traverse programme won a Fringe First. But his orientation was Scottish, and by the end of 1980 Allen Wright was lamenting in *The Scotsman* that his policy 'attracted much less notice from the London critics' than the Traverse had traditionally enjoyed. 'This penalty I foresaw, and am personally prepared to pay', replied Parr with some dignity; the difficulty was that after the disappointment of the 1980 Festival, his Committee felt that they could not pay it any longer, and the fact that the Scottish Arts Council began to blow colder in its support for the great champion of Scottish playwrights perhaps indicates that the Committee's political instinct – to pander a little to the traditional support for the Traverse outside Scotland, and not to depend too heavily on one source of approval and finance – was a sound one.

At any rate, Lichtenfels shared that feeling to the full; and in fact by 1981 there were artistic, as well as political, reasons for the Traverse to look outward for inspiration. What exactly went wrong with the Traverse's new play programme in the early 80's is hard to say. Perhaps Lichtenfels was not quite as effective as Chris Parr in challenging writers into exciting, forward-looking work; perhaps the deadlocked administrative structure of the theatre – which had been set in the same organisational pattern since Michael Rudman's day – made its atmosphere less than magnetic to exciting new talent. Perhaps, as Lichtenfels' policy developed, his commitment to spending a higher proportion of Traverse resources on good visiting product (the visiting companies' budget rose from £6,000 to £30,000 over three years) began in itself to have an impact on the rest of the programme. Rod Graham of the BBC, then Chairman of the Scottish Arts Council Drama Panel, diagnosed a more general malaise, and was rash enough to hint in public that there was a 'fallow period' in new Scottish play-writing at the time, a suggestion which produced the obligatory howls of outrage from neglected writers everywhere. It was true, though, that the failure of the devolution referendum of 1979 had cast a strange pall of gloom over the Scottish scene, and over the hopes for a bright cultural renaissance that had gone with the political movements of the 70's; by 1980 many of the talented new generation of actors and directors who had dominated the 70's scene in Scotland – people like Alex Norton, Bill Paterson, Kenny Ireland, David Hayman, the inimitable Billy Connolly – had left for London, and it took time for Scottish theatre to recover its energy.

But whatever the reason, it seemed that the new plays at the Traverse in the early 80's never generated the challenging, exciting, assumption-jolting atmosphere that genuinely new work should, despite some worthwhile individual productions like Michael Wilcox's *Accounts* (1981), Liz Lochhead's first stage play *Blood and Ice* (1982), and the culmination of the *Slab Boys* trilogy in John Byrne's *Still Life* (also 1982); and throughout the period, Lichtenfels effectively used his strong Festival programmes not only as a source of publicity and coverage, but also as an engine for revitalising the Traverse artistically, for restoring the 'buzz' and energy and sense of occasion that brings a theatre to life and draws talent toward it.

Unlike Chris Parr – whose foreign contacts had been confined to a couple of quiet visits to Germany and Canada, where he toured *The Hardman* and *1–2–3* respectively – Lichtenfels was a dedicated hunter of good theatre, travelling tirelessly, trawling the auditoriums of Britain and Europe for shows that he felt would strike the mood of the moment; and his eye for quality was excellent. In 1981, he scored a triumph of good luck and good judgment when – searching for a replacement for Marcella Evaristi's play *Wedding Belles and Green Grasses*, delayed until the autumn season – he came across Claire Luckham's three-year-old *Trafford Tanzi*, a thumping, no-holds-barred theatre event telling the story of a modern marriage in terms of a wrestling match. The play had enjoyed a chequered career in pub/club venues around Liverpool and Leicester, but Lichtenfels' decision to bring Chris Bond's production to the Traverse propelled the show to national fame, and had audiences pouring into the theatre through the summer and during the Festival. Together with Traverse productions of Dusty Hughes' *Heaven and Hell* (a roistering costume drama about Boswell and Dr. Johnson, with splendid designs by John Byrne) and Wilcox's *Accounts*, it made a striking enough Festival programme to restore the Traverse's fortunes a little. Audiences during the Festival were 92% of capacity, with *Trafford Tanzi* playing to over 100%, and the Committee, almost audibly relieved, tacked a letter of thanks to staff for 'the quality of Festival "product"' (the Traverse Committee, to its credit, never used the word without quotation marks) onto the company noticeboard.

In 1982, Lichtenfels' great Festival triumph was the Barney Simon/Percy Mtwa hit *Woza Albert!*, the first of many tough, sweaty, hard-hitting South African shows that brought a new dimension of racial politics to the Festival in the middle 80's. Playing alongside Liz Lochhead's *Blood and Ice* and Lee Breuer's prestigious Mabou Mines group from New York, it placed the Traverse right in the centre of the Festival's international preoccupations; as a student director up for the Fringe, Jenny Killick squeezed in to see it from a precarious perch on the top corner of a seating module, and the ripples began to spread. In 1983 – with Killick now at the Traverse as an Arts Council trainee director – the whole Festival seemed to focus on the remarkable Wajda production of *Nastasia Filipovna* from Teatr Stary in Cracow, with Jerzy Radziwilowicz giving a performance of such force that the little Traverse space seemed to strain at the seams. In 1984, Emily Mann's post-Vietnam play *Still Life*, from New York, carried off the best reviews of the Festival;

the Market Theatre were back with *Black Dog*, and the whole three-week programme – 199 performances of thirteen shows, including seven of the Traverse's own productions – won a Fringe First award as an exceptional contribution to the Festival.

Lichtenfels' report on this Festival to the Board (which had by now become a Board as well as a Committee; in 1981 the Traverse had set up a nominal division between Club and Theatre Company in order to gain charitable status for its theatre work) reflects as much pride and relief and pure happiness as any document in the Traverse archive; but the road back to that point had been an appallingly difficult one. In Lichtenfels' first year, 1981–82, the theatre was closed for five winter months, from November until April, after Lothian Region was compelled to make swingeing cuts in its arts budget; the total number of performances was only 206 (compared with 400-plus in the mid-80's), and the number of people passing through the doors in the Grassmarket was barely over 13,000. In 1982–83, Lichtenfels managed to keep the theatre open through the autumn by involving himself with the Dance Umbrella programme; the number of performances crept up, and audience figures soared briefly when the Traverse presented the final play in John Byrne's *Slab Boys* trilogy, and then ran the whole trilogy in repertoire through the summer; but there was another four-month closure from December to April, and only five new Traverse productions in the year, the lowest figure ever. And in 1983–84, although the mood within the theatre was beginning to improve, the figures were even worse, showing only three Traverse productions of new plays (there were also productions of *Medea* and Tom McGrath's *The Innocent*), and an audience figure which, at less than 12,000, was actually lower than in the theatre's final year in James Court.

Not surprisingly, the organisation began to thrash around desperately in search of a way out of what seemed like a terminal decline. Following Bill Taylor's resignation in 1981, the Traverse Chairmanship passed from hand to hand like a suspect package, with four incumbents in two-and-a-half years. There were desperate, abortive marketing initiatives, 'marketing' being the Arts Council buzz-word of the day; in 1983, there was yet another attempt to escape from the low-income trap by moving to a new building, on the old Argyll Brewery site in the Cowgate. But by the end of that year the plan had fallen through for lack of any hope of raising adequate funds, and the membership had roused itself only enough to throw back in the teeth of the Board a strange plan to transfer ownership of the building from the Club to the Theatre Company, somehow related to the idea of getting rid of the Club and forming a proper, conventional theatre Board. Joe Gerber materialised at a Special General Meeting to make a fine speech about self-perpetuating oligarchies, and the elected Committee-cum-Board continued.

To make matters worse, this low ebb of performance and morale coincided with historically high levels of overall expenditure and Arts Council grant, and by late 1983 relations between the Traverse and the Council had reached total impasse, with the drama committee not only declaring that the Traverse operation was a hopelessly inefficient use of a large slice of its resources, but that the quality of the work was inadequate. They were strongly critical of the standard of direction and script development in that summer's three new plays, Rona Monro's *Fugue*, Alan Spence's *Space Invaders* and Stanley Eveling's *Buglar Boy*, and towards the end of the year there were explicit indications from Bob Palmer, the Drama Director, that the Council no longer wished to fund the Traverse in its present, expensive form. In the event – after the Administrator Sheila Harborth had literally collapsed under the various stresses of the situation – the immediate threat of closure was withdrawn, and funding continued at a level very slightly lower than before. But the Arts Council's displeasure continued throughout 1984, and at the end of the year there was more talk of 20%–30% reductions in grant; an Arts Council official told the *Glasgow Herald* that the Traverse in the 80's was 'neither very full, nor very solvent, nor very exciting', and – Festival time apart – it was difficult to contradict him.

But somehow, somewhere in the depths of the winter of 1983–84, the Traverse had turned a corner. The theatre experienced a small, unexpected windfall when it made a deal with a new brewery company, and used the money to shorten the winter 'dark' period from four months to two; and there was an immediate brightening of mood. It may have had something to do with the Chairmanship – which finally came to rest with Angela Wrapson, a determined and conscientious woman who saw it through into the Killick era – or with the Board's final decision to make the best of the building it had and forget expansion plans for the time being. It possibly had something to do with the change in the administration, which gave a new sense of freedom about different possible ways of using the theatre's resources; one of the items on Lichtenfels' private agenda for the job had been his determination to get the detail of the Traverse organisation – and particularly its budget – back under the control of the Artistic Director, and that tussle resolved itself, suddenly and unfortunately, when Sheila Harborth became ill in the winter of 1983–84 and eventually resigned, after an unparalleled 12 years at the Traverse. Her immense experience (for she had outlasted three Artistic Directors, first as a formidable Stage Manger and Production Manager, and finally as Administrator), and the key role she had played in building up the Traverse's reputation for professionalism and high production standards in fringe theatre, had given her a power and influence in the organisation no other administrator could rival, and in the middle 80's the Traverse administration has been a much more lithe and biddable affair. Most significantly, though, the change of mood had to do with the fruition of Lichtenfels' visiting companies programme, which, in the aftermath of *Nastasia Filipovna*, was generating new theatrical ideas both for Jenny Killick and for a completely new generation of writers; and of course, it had to with Killick herself.

Jenny Killick had arrived at the Traverse in the spring of 1983, fresh from college in London and a brief period as assistant to David Gothard at Riverside Studios. Gothard, now Peter Lichtenfels' Associate Director at Leicester Haymarket Theatre, is a kind of director-who-never-was of the Traverse. As Mike Ockrent's associate in 1974–5, he introduced his friend Peter Lichtenfels to the Traverse, and in the 80's he played a significant part in helping bring some of Lichtenfels' successful visiting productions to Britain. In 1983, he duly introduced Lichtenfels to Jenny Killick, and suggested that she try for the Traverse traineeship; and by early summer she had arrived in Edinburgh, 23 years old, bursting with talent, 'not knowing anything from anything' (as she puts it), and soaking up theatrical experience like a sponge. She brought with her into the Traverse orbit her partner Steve Unwin another brash and brilliant young director; and although she directed very little in her first year at the theatre – her first major venture was a fine student production of Tom McGrath's *The Innocent*, in March 1984 – she was learning, surveying the scene, and gathering around her a new group of writers, including John Clifford (from Edinburgh), Chris Hannan (from Glasgow via Oxford and Peter Lichtenfels), Peter Arnott (from Glasgow via Unwin's generation at Cambridge), and Simon Donald, a young Scottish actor/playwright of eccentric manner and great talent.

Nor was she simply hunting writers for the sake of it; she shared with all of these potential playwrights a clear artistic impulse, a frustration with the small-scale, quiet, detailed, personalised, social-observational drama into which the Traverse had been drifting since the end of the 70's. To a man (for initially they were all men) these playwrights were obsessed, at different levels, with large, sweeping political and social themes, with parables, allegories, epics, and historical parallels; and Killick was determined to release the Traverse space from its black box appearance and its literal sets, and to make theatrical life flow through it as if it represented the world itself.

This new mood in Scottish writing burst onto the Traverse stage in April 1984, when Killick co-directed a triple bill of short plays called *1984: Points of Departure* by Chris Hannan, Simon Donald, and another young Scot, Stuart Paterson; and it was clear that the theatre had found a younger, angrier, more fantastical – and, as it happened, strongly cosmopolitan – voice for the 80's. The 1984 plays toured to the Mickery Theatre in Amsterdam, and were rapturously received at the 'Fairground '84' event there. As Peter Lichtenfels says, 'When I came to the Traverse actors were still asking questions like, 'Have I just been to the toilet when I come on in this scene?' But in the 80's that went; we moved from observation to imagination, to a complete acceptance that what happens on stage is artificial. I suppose naturalism will come back at some point; but at the moment, it's decadent.'

In May, in an extraordinary gamble to maximise income and expand against the trend, the Traverse remodelled its ill-fated downstairs bar into a tiny low-ceilinged 60-seat theatre, rather similar, in dimensions if not in layout, to the original Traverse space in James Court; and with two auditoriums in operation, the cycle of decline was decisively broken. During the calendar year, Lichtenfels, Killick and Unwin between them produced 12 Traverse productions, including Chris Hannan's memorable first full-length play *Klimkov* (from Gorky's *Life of a Useless Man*) and Steve Unwin's much-admired production of Michel Tremblay's *Sandra/ Manon*; and in that year's Festival, the year of the Fringe First, the Traverse was able to line up seven shows which bore comparison not only with its foreign visiting companies, but with such bright British stars of the Traverse Festival programme as Susannah York in *The Human*

Voice and Simon Callow in *Melancholy Jacques*. The Traverse season continued into the autumn with John Byrne's *Candy Kisses*, the Christmas 'dark' period was reduced to only six weeks; and by Christmas, the Arts Council's renewed threats of deep cuts seemed to have lost their power to depress, although the total Arts Council commitment did in fact shrink slightly in cash terms, and as much as 15% in real terms, between 1984 and 1986.

At the beginning of 1985, Lichtenfels and Killick – now working effectively in tandem – reshaped the Traverse year to give a long, strong spring-summer run of productions with some carry-over of actors from one show to the next, a strong company feeling in the building for at least part of the year, ample chance for plays to increase their impact by resonating off one another, and a build-up of audience towards the Festival; and between them they planned the brilliant 1985 season – starting in April with Killick's production of Kroetz's *Through the Leaves*, and moving on through a season of eight Traverse shows to the striking new-play successes of Peter Arnott's *White Rose*, Hannan's *Elizabeth Gordon Quinn* and hit of the year *Losing Venice*, John Clifford's Spanish fantasy of declining empire – that allowed Lichtenfels to leave the Traverse that autumn with its international reputation higher than at any time since the early 70's.

What had happened in 1984 – beyond the change in administrative atmosphere, even beyond the impact of Lichtenfels' superb Festival programmes – was that the theatre had quietly reacquired one of those double leadership teams that suit it so well. Lichtenfels was a director firmly in the entrepreneurial tradition, better at spotting talent in others than at generating excitement himself. Like the most successful Traverse entrepreneur Michael Rudman, he liked to think of his theatre as an open space, in some ways a passive place, taking on the 'colouring' (as he put it in one of his policy documents) of whatever playwright or company was passing through. Like Rudman, he talked a good deal about 'serving' playwrights, and never wanted to restrict their work by running a permanent company; he also shared Rudman's acute understanding of the Traverse's political requirements in terms of public support.

But he lacked Rudman's commercial flair in mounting productions of popular, accessible new plays; and functioning in the colder climate of the 80's, he had to search and spend and travel the world to find the exciting touring product that was on the doorstep in the early 70's. Ask him what his proudest achievements were at the Traverse – apart from his great visiting companies – and he talks about writers like Michael Wilcox and Liz Lochhead, both of whom developed their play-writing careers through his interest and encouragement. But he mentions 'finding Jenny' in the same breath and with as much pride, and it's true that the generous artistic vision – and lack of petty ego – he showed in opening up the Traverse directorship to his clever, challenging young successor is one of Lichtenfels' greatest strengths.

Jenny Killick, on the other hand, could hardly have been a more different personality, a young director of immense talent but little experience with a great, driving, erratic and sometimes temperamental creativity of her own. Like Max Stafford-Clark, she arrived at the theatre barely more than a student, as what he called 'an unwritten-on-blackboard' and she calls 'a jelly, a blob, a blank, up for anything . . .' Like him, she carried with her no assumptions about what theatre should be. Like him she quickly developed, and retains to this day, an inclination to ask big, radical questions about theatrical form; why a studio theatre? why lights? why scenery? why this kind of organisation? why a permanent administration and temporary artists? why can't the administration *be* artists? who are the audience? why theatre at all? And just as Stafford-Clark's early relationship with Gordon McDougall allowed him to ask those questions in a relatively stable context, so Killick's relationship with Peter Lichtenfels gave her the same freedom. It was during her time as Lichtenfels' assistant that she produced her best directing work at the Traverse so far, the beautiful, rich-textured productions of Chris Hannan's *Klimkov* in 1984 and Kroetz's *Through the Leaves* in 1985; and when the Board appointed her Artistic Director from September that year – the first woman to hold the job, and the youngest director since Gordon McDougall – they were taking the same kind of chance as Nicky Fairbairn's Committee of 1967 on a young, unproved, exciting talent that had everything to learn in terms of artistic directorship.

And in fact – some great successes notwithstanding – her period as Director has been full of familiar stresses and strains. In terms of policy, she has continued the tradition of strong, international Festival programmes backed by a continuous Traverse season of new work in spring and summer; in the 1986 Festival she brought the memorable South African show *Bopha!* to the little Downstairs Theatre, and in 1987, at a disused washhouse in Abbeymount, the Traverse presented the wonderful *Le Lavoir* from Theatre de la Basoche in Amiens. She and Steve Unwin – formally appointed Associate Director in 1986 – have also struck a strong vein of new foreign work unperformed in Britain, and Unwin's productions of Mario Vargas Llosa's *Kathie and the Hippopotamus* and Manfred Karge's *Man to Man* have been the outstanding popular and critical successes of the '86 and '87 seasons.

But the quality of the Traverse's own new work has been affected by Killick's tremendous tussle to come to terms with the responsibilities of the Artistic Director's job, which she feels conflict constantly with her own development as a director. Under pressure, she tended to retreat slightly into a circle of vaguely Oxbridge-accented advisers; the rich dialogue between Scottish writing and acting and a whole series of cosmopolitan influences, which Killick seemed to be conducting in 1984–85, faded a little, and Scottish hackles rose. She pressed her historical-epical approach a season too far in 1987, when it began to look coy; and after half-a-decade of seasons powerfully focused on the Festival, it seemed as though it might be time for the Traverse to change the shape of its year once more, and re-establish itself with Edinburgh's theatre-going public by offering them a few winter hits. 'What I feel,' she says, 'is that I can see exactly what the Artistic Director's job is – the management, the planning, the fund-raising, the public role – and I'd love to do it. But if I'm going to direct, I haven't time. Or to put it the other way round, perhaps it's not wise to direct in the theatre you run. As a director, I like – need – to rock the boat; that's what you should be doing. But how can you rock it when it's your bloody boat? And people's jobs depend on you keeping it steady? You can't.' Indeed, when she announced her resignation from the Artistic Directorship – to take effect after the 1988 Festival – Killick said that her 'parting shot' to the Traverse was the thought that perhaps the next Artistic Director shouldn't be a director at all.

But Killick belongs to that experimental breed of Traverse directors whose experience of the place is all to do with rapid movement and learning. Running the Traverse in the hungry 80's – and there was another financial crisis, with more threats from the Arts Council, in 1987, when the Travese managed only five major productions – she has had to take on the public and political role, and learn to 'thump the table' with the best of them. She has become increasingly conscious of the receptive, facilitating aspects of the job; in 1988 only two out of eleven Traverse shows are Killick productions. 'The Director,' she says, 'has to make room for other people to play. You have to put your own development on hold, and that's why there's a limit to how long you can stay.' She has come back to a dialogue with Scotland; seven of the plays in the new Traverse season are by Scottish writers, and she feels that as London theatre becomes more internationally-minded – finding new foreign writers and shows before the Traverse can point the way as it did in the middle 80's – the development of a distinctive Scottish/avant-garde voice, rooted in the life around the theatre, is bound to be a key factor in sustaining the strength and originality of the Traverse's work into the 1990's.

So, in a sense, Jenny Killick's directorship has contained within it all the great interlocking tensions of the Traverse story. There is the tension between Edinburgh and the Festival, which is also the tension between the Traverse's Scottish roots and its national and international aspirations; there is the old Marowitz/Haynes tension between active creation of new work, and the very different job of making space for and welcoming the new when it appears from elsewhere. Above all, for Killick, there is the struggle to maintain the cutting edge of the Traverse's radicalism – its position at the outer limit of theatrical possibility – when it is, as she says, 'plugged in by every artery' to the conventional structures of British theatre, bound to act responsibly both as an employer and as a recipient of large amounnts of public money.

It's in the nature of an organisation like the Traverse that its past cannot – probably should not – tell us too much about its future; but one thing that is clear is that this last and greatest tension, between experimental freedom on one hand, and orthodox management and financial prudence on the other, has run through the length of the Traverse story, from the theatre's first great financial crisis in 1966 to the present day. The sources of the pressure towards sound conventional management have changed, of course, and so has the intensity of it. In the 60's, it came predominantly from Committee members and patrons worried about the abuse of their personal investment in the theatre. In the 70's it came from within, with staff and actors pressing for an end to the casual, low-wage employment policy the Traverse had operated in its early years. In the 80's it comes mainly from the funding bodies; and at every stage there has been a tendency to interpret the conflict as a unique crisis, a turning-point between some golden, halcyon past – where ther was plenty of money, an easy-going attitude, an uninhibited experimental freedom – and 'nowadays', which is seen as a grim period of financial restraint, institutional pressure, and, in the words of almost every Traverse director since Jim Haynes, 'the erosion of the right to fail'.

But in fact this kind of conflict – with the accompanying press brouhaha about 'Traverse closure threat' and 'Traverse in deficit crisis' – has recurred so often, and in such strikingly similar terms, that it's impossible to avoid the impression that it is in some way integral to the nature of the place. To be true to itself and its remit, the Traverse must always be making something new, making something where nothing was before; its whole existence depends on its ability to generate energy, brilliance, warmth, enthusiasm, and the resources which follow them, beyond what could possibly be calculated by any rational process. At every turning-point in its history – at its beginning, at the time of the move to the Grassmarket (when, as Nicky Fairbairn puts it in his autobiography, 'faith triumphed over caution, as it always should in matters of culture'), and in the crisis of 1983–84, when it went for broke on an expanding programme – the Traverse has had to gamble quite recklessly on its future, and it has won. In that sense Jim Haynes, with his irresponsible defiance of 'the rational calculation of economic means', has been proved right and right again; and his own reckless investment of any resources he could lay his hands on helped create an idea of the Traverse so powerful that it has easily survived these 25 years, passed on 'with passion', as Peter Lichtenfels puts it, from one Director to the next; so that when Jenny Killick was deciding whether to come to the Traverse, in 1983, David Gothard (who has ample reason to know better in every practical sense) simply told her, 'Ah, Jenny, the Traverse is the theatre where you do what you like.')

Of course, every Director eventually learns, in the dust and ashes of the committee room, that even at the Traverse freedom is limited; that well-subsidised though it traditionally is, this theatre too exists in the real world, where balance sheets have to be balanced and people row and grumble about overspending. But it's in the gap between that high expectation of freedom and the encroachment of harsh reality that Traverse directors traditionally pull off their unpredictable and death-defying feats of creativity; and it would be a fine thing, in its 25th anniversary year, if the Traverse were to celebrate by recognising, once and for all, that this conflict between artistic aspirations and financial prudence is not evidence of some catastrophic decline, nor, (despite the organisation's history of spectacular rows) a matter for personal blame, sackings and recriminations, but a creative tension that has to be accepted and lived with, year in and year out; as Mike Ockrent says, the Traverse is either overstretching itself, or it is nothing.

Every Traverse generation has had, of course, to work out its own way of maximising this freedom to experiment. In the 60's, Traverse directors relied on the free-wheeling mood of the time and the generosity of private patrons to bail them out; but neither could last for ever. In the 70's they threw themselves on the mercy of the Arts Council, and retained a sense of freedom by 'dancing ever higher', on the ladder of public subsidy. But the change in Arts Council attitudes in the 80's with tight advance budgeting and strict fiscal virtue at a premium, now mean that a theatre heavily dependent on subsidy has less freedom to gamble on its hunches than the average commercial company; which is why, in the late 80's – with the Traverse a little slimmer and fitter, administrative costs and overheads down, the Arts Council contribution back below 50% of total budget for the first time in a dozen years – Jenny Killick and the Traverse Board have become convinced that the way to maximise freedom is to rebuild the Traverse audience, to find a wider public, and to depend more on their direct response to the work than on the decisions of funding bodies.

In fact, it's indicative of how much the Traverse has changed since the early 70's (when Mike Rudman used to woo and study his audience, lapping up responses like 'I didn't like the play at all, Michael, but it's so well acted I'm coming again next week,') that Killick feels one of the main frustrations of the job is a lack of feedback. 'You yell out the work,' she says, 'and all you get in return is this little whisper . . .'. With hindsight, it seems as though the old Club audience ceased to function as an effective community, a source of coherent reaction to the work, sometime around the middle 70's; in 1982, Peter Lichtenfels told Scottish Theatre News quite categorically that 'we don't have a "Club" audience any more.' In the late 60's with the abolition of the Lord Chamberlain's Office, the Club had lost its usefulness as a protection against censorship. In the late 70's, it forfeited its last practical advantage with the change in Scottish licensing law. In the late 80's, the Labour District Council (now worth almost £40,000 a year to the Traverse, and never happy with the 'elitist' overtones of the Club idea) began to suggest that there would be distinct funding advantages to shaking off private status; and at the end of 1987 Killick, with her General Manager Anne Bonnar, and the new Chair of the Board, Sheena McDonald, had no difficulty in persuading the membership that the time had come to wind up the Club, to abolish the 'psychological barrier' to a wider audience, and to transform the Traverse into a public theatre at last. Once again, there's talk of a move to a bigger auditorium, this time in a new commercial development near the Usher Hall; and traditionalists who shrink from the thought of a 250-seat Traverse in a modern hotel complex might as well reflect that the place exists to blast assumptions about theatre, including the one that subsidy equals freedom, and bigger audiences necessarily mean a surrender to commercialism. Killick says that she, for one, is still 'mad enough and young enough and brave enough' to think she could do what she finds exciting and fill 250 seats a night. It certainly can't be taken for granted that the ideal Traverse for the 1990's would look anything like the little hot room in James Court, where actors and directors came together in the 60's to reaffirm the sweat and sex-appeal of live drama in the new television age; and there's even less reason why it should take the form of an infinitely flexible late-60's black box with cushioned seating modules. Throughout her time at the Traverse, Killick has waged a kind of one-woman war against the artificiality of the Traverse space, stripping it back to the stone walls and the window embrasures, revealing its true dimensions as a high, bright sailmaker's workshop, battling against the modules, asking why the audience can't just sit around on little stacking chairs; and she makes a powerful case – artistic, financial and political – for breaking out of the decaying 20-year-old closet of 'fringe' theatre, and returning, in a less exclusive and more populist style, to the close, immediate dependence on an Edinburgh audience that gave the Traverse its first great surge of vitality 25 years ago.

But one of the things that makes the Traverse special, in the end, is the fact that its audience cannot be defined simply by counting the people who see its shows in Edinburgh. What seems to have happened is that through a strange alchemy of events in its first three years – through the luck of being born at the right moment, through the passionate commitment of its first members, through the generous understanding of those with private and public cash to support it, through the strength of John Malcolm's basic idea that the place be dedicated to the interesting and uneconomic, and above all through the rare, free-flowing spirit of Jim Haynes who 'believed anything possible' – the Traverse somehow came to embody the notion of artistic freedom for the theatre professionals everywhere. It was the Fringe venue that got away, the crazy, youthful, one-off venture that somehow became a permanent theatre; and in that role, theatre people across the world – artists, critics, people who are interested in the theory and practice of the business – have taken it to their hearts, passed the idea of it on from one generation to the next, perpetuated its myth as though it were a symbol they needed.

What the Traverse has done with this inherited ideal of freedom has been to offer it, seven times since 1966, into the keeping of young, gifted theatre directors, and only *through* those directors to writers, actors and designers; this book has been about their response to that freedom, and its impact on them. And their success-story suggests that the experience works; that if you give bright young professionals a brief sense of freedom right at the start of their careers, put them in a position where there is no excuse not to lay themselves on the line and explain themsevles as artists – in Killick's words, 'to say what they really think about theatre'; in Mike Ockrent's 'to make an intellectual assessment of the work'; in Peter Lichtenfels' 'to think with a bit of heart, to think in terms of what's worth doing . . .' – then they will emerge with a stronger, clearer, better-worked out sense of what they're doing in the business of drama, and why it matters, that will give them a powerful edge over their contemporaries. Michael Rudman grasps the practicalities of the situation perfectly when he suggests that the Traverse will survive, as an institution, so long as there is a Scottish Arts Council to subsidise its year-round work, and an Edinburgh Festival to give it an international platform; I think it will also survive as an ideal and an image, so long as there is a market in British and world theatre for artists who have been free to face the ultimate questions about the value of what they're doing, and have survived to tell the tale.

But if the coalition of needs and interests that holds the Traverse together should finally fail; if the audience should at last dwindle beyond a joke, the Arts Council lose patience, the Festival fade from its international brilliance, the bright young directors drift elsewhere, then there need be no breast-beating over the death of the 'Traverse idea.' The Traverse has never been alone in cherishing the ideal of artistic freedom; there is no tension, no dilemma, no question in this story that is not faimilar, in modified and more complex forms, to every theatre company and arts organisation that ever looked beyond purely commercial values. It's simply that because of fate, because of circumstance, because of John Malcolm, because of Jim Haynes, the Traverse has been privileged, these 25 years, to play a special role in protecting and holding the dream. So if the old place finally goes – in a blaze of debt and glory, or in a whimper of cold prudence – then some damnfool artists, somewhere, will still be doing what John Malcolm and Terry Lane were doing in the autumn of 1962, clearing a space with their bare hands in which to create, in defiance of commonsense and every other rational law, the work they feel needs to be done; and in that place, the Traverse – or everything that matters about it – will live.

PART TWO
THE CHRONOLOGY

A Chronology of Traverse Theatre Productions 1963-1988
Compiled by John Carnegie

This chronology supersedes all previous published lists of Traverse productions. It has been compiled from research in the Traverse archives and newspapers and from interviews with people who have worked at the Traverse.

Owing to the nature of the Traverse, it has often been the case that productions of new work that have been announced in advance publicity are not mounted or – by the time that they are – have turned into something else. Therefore, although every effort has been made to make this list as accurate as possible, it has occasionally been necessary to make an informed guess over contradictory printed information or personal recollection.

Also, as the publicity staff of the Traverse throughout the years have always been grossly overworked, they have tended to give more priority to publicising the next production than to filing the details of the last one. As a result, many programmes are missing from the archives, and research has had to be concentrated on newspaper reviews and the (fading) memories of those present at the time. It is probable that details of some productions have disappeared irretrievably. If anyone can supply more accurate data, they should contact the Traverse or the publishers.

The compilation of a chronology such as this can give the opportunity for nostalgia and provide the fun of spotting the names of the famous before they became so. More seriously, it can provide the basis for academic research and enable journalists to tease out trends in theatrical fashion over the years.

However, perhaps the most important function this chronology could have is to remind theatre practioners of the quite phenomenal range of work the Traverse has donated to posterity. For those interested in statistics, the chronology includes 324 world professional stage premières and 106 British professional stage premières.

Of course, as is inevitably the case with an arts organisation concentrating on the new, some of the work has been mediocre or ephemeral but, as even a cursory glance through the chronology will confirm, the Traverse has produced much that is eminently worthy of revival. The compilation of this chronology will have been justified if it results in some of the plays it lists being once again brought to life.

Acknowledgements

Grateful thanks are due to the following people for the invaluable help they gave in compiling this chronology: Judy Aitken, Michael Almaz, Lynn Bains, Sally Bates, Amanda Belcham, John Binnie, Anne Bonnar, Dave Clarke, Stewart Conn, Andrew Dallmeyer, the staff of the Edinburgh Room in the Edinburgh Central Library, Bryan Elsley, Patrick Evans, Jeannie Fisher, Morag Fullarton, Mandy Gallacher, Isobel Gardner, Jon Gaunt, Hamish Glen, Val Govern, George Gunn, David Hamilton, Sheila Harborth, Nicholas Kent, Jenny Killick, Terry Lane (for the use of material from his detailed archive of 1963), Peter Lichtenfels, Christine Liddle, Liz Lochhead, Bob Macauley, Gordon McDougall, David McKail, Clunie MacKenzie, Joyce McMillan, Sue

Meek, Geoff Moore, the staff of the National Library of Scotland, Philip Osment, Kate Owen, Chris Parr, Robin Peoples, Alan Pollock, David Pounder, Bill Pryde, Roland Rees, Catherine Robins, Michael Rudman, Max Stafford-Clark, Andy Walker and Chahine Yavroyan.

I would also like to record the contribution made over the years by newspaper reviewers and arts editors (particularly Allen Wright of 'The Scotsman' and Richard Howe of the 'Edinburgh Evening News') in providing the kind of information in reviews and articles which has enabled the details of productions to be reconstructed.

Abbreviations

*	World Professional Stage Première	Dev.	Devised by
		Dir.	Directed by
†	British Professional Stage Première	Lgt.	Lighting designed by
		Lgt. & Sound	Lighting and sound designed by
A.D.	Assistant Director		
Adpt.	Adapted by	M.D.	Musical Director
a.k.a.	also known as	Mgt.	Producing management
Ass. Des.	Assistant Designer	Rev.	Revived on
assoc.	association	rpl.	replaced by
Chor.	Choreography by	Set.	Set designed by
Cos.	Costumes designed by	Trans.	Translated by
Des.	Set and costumes designed by		

The following points should be noted in using the chronology:

The chronology includes revue, dance, opera, music drama and multi-media performances as well as plays but excludes films, video, poetry readings. Talk-outs/Traverse Trials, games/happenings, music performances, cabaret and other non-dramatic events. Playreadings or 'action' readings given during a calendar year are listed separately at the end of the year. They are not counted as premières and no details of casts or directors are included.

The date given is that of the first performance at the Traverse – except in the case of the Traverse's own productions first performed elsewhere. In all cases, previews have been ignored and the date is that of the first press night. Details of cast and the creative production team are given where these are known. Prior to the beginning of Mike Ockrent's tenure as Artistic Director in 1973, it was the exception rather than the rule to have a designer on a production. (Up till then, any set was usually 'assembled' by the stage management team under the direction of the author and director.)

The title of the play is given in block capitals. When the performance consisted of a number of plays or events with an overall title, the latter is given first in inverted commas and individual items are listed in order of performance. Musicians are included at the end of cast lists after '– with'. Actors who only appear on tape or film are excluded (except for the production of 'Balls'). Details are also given of the appointment of Artistic and Associate Directors and (for the early years) of Board members.

The chronology includes not only productions mounted at the Old Traverse in the Lawnmarket and the present building in the Grassmarket but also other auditoriums managed by the Traverse in Edinburgh – usually at the time of the Edinburgh Festival. From the opening of the Downstairs Theatre in May 1984, all performances listed take place in the Upstairs Theatre unless otherwise indicated. In its time, the Traverse has produced four independent off-shoots; Traverse Festival Productions Ltd., The London Traverse, The Traverse Theatre Workshop and The Traverse Student Workshop. Except in the case of the former, only performances by these organisations which were seen on Traverse premises have been listed.

Productions fall into four categories: those mounted by the Traverse; those mounted by the Traverse in collaboration with other organisations; those given by visiting companies; and revivals. Entries are made as follows:

1. Traverse productions are in roman type, eg:
   ORISON by Fernando Arrabal. Trans. Barbara Wright. Cast: Rosamund Dickson, Clyde Pollitt.

2. Traverse productions in collaboration with other organisations are also in roman, with a note in brackets at the end indicating which company was involved, eg:
   A WHO'S WHO OF FLAPLAND by David Halliwell. Cast: James Garbutt, Russell Hunter. Dir. Michael Rudman. Lgt. Gerry Jenkinson for all three plays. (Traverse in assoc. with Quipu Productions.)

3. Productions by visiting companies are in italics, with a note in brackets at the end indicating which company was involved, eg:
   AN EVENING OF SAVAGERY AND DELIGHT – compiled from the work of Bertolt Brecht and his contemporaries by Agnes Bernelle. Cast: Agnes Bernelle with Michael Dress. (Mgt: Agnes Bernelle.)

In the case of visiting companies, only performances given on Traverse premises are noted. (During the Jim Haynes period – due to the nature of his policy – it is often difficult to define which productions were originated by the Traverse and which were simply done by ad hoc companies hosted by the Traverse.)

4. Revivals:

   4.1 Productions revived by the Traverse are in smaller roman type, eg:
   OVER THE TOP by Tom Buchan. Music by Robert Pettigrew. Cast: Russell Hunter, Tony Roper, Patience Tomlinson. Dir. Campbell Morrison. Des. Dermot Hayes. Lgt. Colin Scott. (Revival of the play premièred by the Traverse on 25 Apr. 1979.)

   4.2 Productions revived by other companies are in smaller italic type, eg:
   THE COCKROACH THAT ATE CINCINATTI by Alan Williams. (Revival of production which last opened at the Traverse on 25 May 1979.)

1962

20 Aug.   Cambridge Footlights open the 'Sphinx Nightclub' as a temporary late night revue venue on the Edinburgh Festival Fringe. It is situated in premises at 15 James Court in the Lawnmarket (owned by Tom Mitchell) which had been a brothel (variously known as 'Kelly's Paradise' and 'Hell's Kitchen'). The Footlights personnel include Tony Branch, Graham Chapman, John Cleese, Ian Lang, David Missen and Trevor Nunn.

Oct.   John Malcolm (as Director and Club Secretary) and Terry Lane (as his Associate Director and Club Treasurer) start to convert the temporary nightclub space into a permanent theatre club with 60 seats divided into two fixed seating banks facing each other. They name the theatre the Traverse after the 'traverse' style of staging.

20 Nov.   The first Traverse Theatre Club Committee of Management is formed. It consists of Tom Mitchell (President/Chairman), Jim Haynes, Terry Lane, John Malcolm and Andrew Muir. Prior to the opening of the theatre, they are joined by Sheila Colvin, Richard Demarco and John Martin. By December, John Martin (as Deputy President) has taken over the active role of Chairman from Tom Mitchell. Jim Haynes is in America from the end of November until 26 February 1963.

11 Dec.   John Malcolm leaves as the result of a disagreement and Terry Lane becomes 'Producer' (which title changes during 1963 to 'Resident Producer', then 'Director of Productions/ Theatre Manager' and finally 'Artistic Director').

1963

2 Jan.   Traverse manages to open with its first productions despite weather conditions described by the Met. Office as 'arctic'.

2 Jan.   † ORISON by Fernando Arrabal. Trans. Barbara Wright. Cast: Rosamund Dickson, Clyde Pollitt.
HUIS CLOS by Jean Paul Sartre. Trans. Stuart Gilbert. Cast: Rosamund Dickson, Terry Lane, Colette O'Neill (rpl. Peggy Martin from 4 January), Clyde Pollitt.
Both plays dir. Terry Lane.

23 Jan.   TWO FOR THE SEE-SAW by William Gibson. Cast: Rosamund Dickson, Clyde Pollitt. Dir. Terry Lane.

12 Feb.   FAIRY TALES OF NEW YORK by J. P. Donleavy. Cast: Rosamund Dickson, Tony Healey, Clyde Pollitt, Ian Trigger. Dir. Terry Lane.

24 Feb.   *AN EVENING OF SAVAGERY AND DELIGHT – compiled from the work of Bertolt Brecht and his contemporaries by Agnes Bernelle. Cast: Agnes Bernelle with Michael Dress. (Mgt: Agnes Bernelle.)*

26 Feb.   † PICNIC IN THE BATTLEFIELD by Fernando Arrabal. Trans. Barbara Wright. Cast: Rosamund Dickson, Richard Gill, Tony Healey, Clyde Pollit.
FANDO AND LIS by Fernando Arrabal. Trans. Barbara Wright. Cast: Rosamund Dickson, Richard Gill, Tony Healey, Terry Lane, Clyde Pollitt. Both plays dir. Terry Lane.

12 Mar.   DON JUAN IN HELL by George Bernard Shaw. Cast: Victor Carin, Richard Gill, Tony Healey, Jennifer Thorne. Dir. Rosamund Dickson.

2 Apr. † **UBU ROI** by Alfred Jarry. Trans. Barbara Wright. Cast: Rosamund Dickson, John Duncanson, Richard Gill, Tony Healey, Paul Kermack, Michael Lewin, Ian Trigger, Dir. Terry Lane. Cos. Jennifer Beach. (Rev. 13 Aug.)

15 Apr. **Jim Haynes is elected Chairman of the Committee of Management and Richard Demarco elected Vice-Chairman. Tom Mitchell remains as President.**

23 Apr. **A DOLL'S HOUSE** by Henrik Ibsen. Trans. R. Farquharson Sharp and Eleanor Marx-Aveling and revised by Torgrim and Linda Hannas. Cast: Rosamund Dickson, Margot Field, Richard Gill, Tony Healey, Jane Sharp, Frank Wylie. Dir. Terry Lane.

14 May. **THE LESSON** by Eugene Ionesco. Trans. Donald Watson. Cast: Annabel Barton, Rosamund Dickson, Tony Healey.
THE MAIDS by Jean Genet. Trans. Bernard Frechtman. Cast: Annabel Barton, Rosamund Dickson, Jane Sharp. Both plays dir. Terry Lane.

5 June **PRIVATE LIVES** by Noël Coward. Cast: Annabel Barton, Rosamund Dickson, Tony Healey, Grahame McPherson, Jane Sharp. Dir. Terry Lane.

25 June **REQUIEM FOR A NUN** by William Faulkner. Cast: Helen Fleming, Richard Gill, Tony Healey, Lillias Walker, Frank Wylie. Dir. Rosamund Dickson.

30 July *****THE BALACHITES** by Stanley Eveling. Cast: Rosamund Dickson, Richard Gill, Tony Healey, Keith Taylor, Ian Trigger. Dir. Terry Lane.

13 Aug. UBU ROI. Credits as before – except Kermack and Lewin rpl. Christopher Gilmore and David Quilter. (Revival of production first presented on 2 April.)

20 Aug. † **COMEDY, SATIRE, IRONY AND DEEPER MEANING** by Christian Dietrich-Grabbe in a version by Barbara Wright. Cast: Rosamund Dickson, John Duncanson, Richard Gill, Christopher Gilmore, Tony Healey, Dan McDonald, David Quilter, Hayne Ryan, Jane Sharp, Keith Taylor, Ian Trigger. Dir. Terry Lane.

24 Sept. **NEXT TIME I'LL SING TO YOU** by James Saunders. Cast: Pamela Craig, Michael Farnsworth, Tony Healey, Dan MacDonald, Ian Trigger, Dir. Rosamund Dickson. (Transfers on 28 Sept. to Ledlanet Nights Festival.)

15 Oct. † **THE DAYS AND NIGHTS OF BEEBEE FENSTERMAKER** by William Snyder. Cast: Mia Anderson, Pamela Craig, Rosamund Dickson, Michael Farnsworth, Tony Healey, Lucy Lowles, Dan MacDonald, Anne Raitt. Dir. Terry Lane.

5 Nov. **CANDIDA** by George Bernard Shaw. Cast: Mia Anderson, Roger Clissold, Pamela Craig, Michael Farnsworth, Tony Healey, Dan MacDonald. Dir. Terry Lane.

26 Nov. 'THREE MODERN NO PLAYS'. Trans. Donald Keene. Triple bill consisting of:
† **THE LADY AOI** by Yukio Mishima. Cast: Leslie Blackater, Pamela Craig, Rosamund Dickson, Michael Farnsworth. Dir. Tony Healey.
† **HANJO** by Yukio Mishima. Cast: Pamela Craig, Rosamund Dickson, Andrew Rimmer. Dir. Terry Lane.
† **THE DAMASK DRUM** by Yukio Mishima. Cast: Leslie Blackater, Pamela Craig, Rosamund Dickson, Michael Farnsworth, Tony Healey, Alec Monteath, Andrew Rimmer. Dir. Terry Lane.

24 Dec. **CRIME ON GOAT ISLAND** by Ugo Betti. Trans. Henry Reed.

Cast: Pamela Craig, Heather Canning, Rosamund Dickson, Michael Elwick, Alec Monteath. Dir. Terry Lane.

1964

4 Jan. **Terry Lane resigns as Artistic Director and leaves on 19 Jan. Callum Mill is appointed as caretaker Director.**

21 Jan. **THE STRONGER** by August Strindberg. Trans. Michael Meyer. Cast: Pamela Craig, Margaret Jordan, Alec Monteath.
PLAYING WITH FIRE by August Strindberg. Trans. Michael Meyer. Cast: Pamela Craig, Rosemary Davey, Philip Elimore, Michael Elwick, Margaret Jordan, Alec Monteath. Both plays dir. Callum Mill (who takes over rehearsals from Terry Lane).

11 Feb. **THE CARETAKER** by Harold Pinter. Cast: Michael Elwick, Callum Mill, John Shedden. Dir. Michael Geliot.

17 Mar. 'AN EVENING OF FARCE WITH CHEKHOV' – consisting of:
THE BEAR by Anton Chekhov. Trans. Elizaveta Fen. Cast: Roy Boucher, Louise Breslin, Callum Mill.
THE HARMFULNESS OF TOBACCO by Anton Chekhov. Trans. Eric Bentley. Cast: Roy Boucher.
SUMMER IN THE COUNTRY by Anton Chekhov. Trans. Eric Bentley. Cast: Roy Boucher, Callum Mill.
THE PROPOSAL by Anton Chekhov. Trans. Theodore Hoffman. Cast: Roy Boucher, Louise Breslin, Callum Mill.
SWAN SONG by Anton Chekhov. Trans. Theodore Hoffman. Cast: Roy Boucher, Callum Mill.

All five plays dir. Ann Stutfield. Songs by Bob Bauld.

14 Apr. † **HUGHIE** by Eugene O'Neill. Cast: Callum Mill, Clyde Pollitt. Dir. Brian Carey.
THE ZOO STORY by Edward Albee. Cast: Brian Carey, David McKail. Dir. Callum Mill. (Rev. 20 Apr. 1965.)

19 May **DEAD LETTER** by Robert Pinget. Trans. Barbara Bray. Cast: Brian Carey, Maxine Holden, Paul Kermack, David McKail. Dir. Callum Mill.

9 June † **THE DETOUR** by Martin Walser. Trans. Richard Grunberger. Cast: Brian Carey, Martin Heller, Maxine Holden (rpl. Isobel Black from 30 June), David McKail. Dir. Garry O'Connor.

7 July † **RED MAGIC** by Michael de Ghelderode. Trans. George Hauger. Cast: Isobel Black, Brian Carey, Martin Heller, Alex McAvoy, David McKail.
† **ESCORIAL** by Michael de Ghelderode. Trans. George Hauger. Cast: Alan Forbes, Alex McAvoy, David McKail. (Rev. 27 Aug.)
Both plays dir. Callum Mill.

11 Aug. † **GALLOWS HUMOUR** by Jack Richardson. Cast: Pamela Ann Davy, Roddy Maude Roxby, Barry Stanton. Dir. Charles Marowitz. Des. Susan Glanister.

14 Aug. † **HAPPY END** by Kurt Weill, Dorothy Lane and Bertolt Brecht in a version by Arnold Hinchcliffe and Monica Shelley. Lyrics trans. Michael Geliot. Cast: David Bauer, Christina Currie, Ros Drinkwater, Jon Farrell, Margaret Gould, Robert Henderson, Bettina Jonic, Chuck Julian, Paul Kermack, Tutte Lemkow, John Leishman, Michael McKevitt, Maureen McMahon, Marcella Markham, Ronald Muirhead,

Declan Mulholland, Frank Rennie, Charles Wade, Maria Warburg. Cast in London: Bauer, Beth Boyd, Currie, Otto Diamont, Drinkwater, Sylvia Gray, Roy Hanlon, Michael Heyland, Alan Hockey, Elric Hooper, Jonic, Julian, Kermack, Jon Laurimore, Jennifer MacNae, Markham, Joe Melia, Jane Murdoch, Warburg, Thick Wilson, Dir. Michael Geliot. Des. Ralph Koltai and Nadine Baylis. A.D. (in London): Gordon McDougall. (Traverse Festival Productions Ltd. at Pollock Hall, Edinburgh. Transfers to Royal Court, London on 11 Mar. 1965 presented by English Stage Company in assoc. with Peter Bridge and Traverse Festival Productions Ltd.)

18 Aug. † PHILIPP HOTZ'S FURY by Max Frisch. Trans. Michael Bullock. Cast: Isobel Black, Brian Carey, Tom Conti, Jan Hayton, Stuart Henry, David McKail, Isobel Nisbet. Dir. Callum Mill.

27 Aug. ESCORIAL. Credits as before – except Forbes rpl. Tom Conti. (Revival of production first presented on 7 July.)

28 Aug. † THE PARTY by Slawamir Mrozek. Trans. Nicholas Bethall. Cast: Tom Conti, Ken Jones, David McKail.
† THE ENCHANTED NIGHT by Slawamir Mrozek. Trans. Nicholas Bethall. Cast: Isobel Black, Brian Carey, Ken Jones. Both plays dir. Callum Mill.

Aug. Jim Haynes (while continuing as Chairman) replaces Callum Mill as Artistic Director.

22 Sept. * BIRDS, MARRIAGES AND DEATHS – A revue by Roger McGough. Cast: John Gorman, Michael McGear, Roger McGough. Dir. Joan Maitland. (Mgt: The Scaffold)

29 Sept. † THE WORK OUT by Albert Bermel. Cast: Annabelle Barton, Chuck Julian.
† THE RECOVERY by Albert Bermel. Cast: Annabelle Barton, Christopher Denham, Chuck Julian.
Both plays dir. Paul Kermack.

20 Oct. † THE MOTOR SHOW by Eugene Ionesco. Trans. Donald Watson. Cast: Annabelle Barton, Leonard Maguire, Declan Mulholland.
† THE OLD TUNE by Robert Pinget. Adapt. Samuel Beckett. Cast: Leonard Maguire, Declan Mulholland. (Rev. 5 Jan. 1965 prior to transfer to Theatre de Poche, Paris in Feb. 1965.)
THE LOVER by Harold Pinter. Cast: Annabelle Barton, Leonard Fenton, Declan Mulholland.
All three plays dir. Michael Geliot.

10 Nov. * YOU'LL COME TO LOVE YOUR SPERM TEST or 'You gave her a thorough examination, doctor?' by John Antrobus. Cast: John Antrobus, Rita Grenigault, Michael Hasted, Salubrious Lane, Michael McKevitt. Cast in London includes: Owen Hand. Dir. the author. (The production is then taken over by the Hampstead Theatre Club, London and opens there on 18 January 1965 before going on to London's West End.)

1 Dec. * BIRDS IN A WILDERNESS by Stewart Conn. Cast: Leonard Fenton, Stuart Henry, Monica Maugham, Helen Ryan, Paul Young.
* THE VOICE by John Calder. Cast: Leonard Fenton, Monica Maugham, Helen Ryan. Both plays dir. Jack Henry Moore.

22 Dec. A CHILD'S CHRISTMAS IN WALES by Lindsay Kemp and Jack Henry Moore – mimed to Dylan Thomas's recording of

his original. Music by Owen Hand. Cast: Lindsay Kemp – with Owen Hand. Dir. Lindsay Kemp.

1965

5 Jan. **THE OLD TUNE** by Robert Pinget. Cast as before. (Revival of production first presented on 20 Oct. 1964.)
THE DOCK BRIEF by John Mortimer. Cast: Leonard Maguire, Declan Mulholland. Both plays dir. Michael Geliot. (Double bill transfers to Theatre de Poche, Paris in Feb.)

25 Jan. * **THERE WAS A MAN** by Tom Wright. Cast: John Cairney. Dir. Gerald Slevin. Music arranged by Frank Spedding. (Rev. 20 Aug. at Morton Hall, Edinburgh after visit to Dundee Repertory. Transfers to Ledlanet Nights Festival on 7 Oct. Televised by BBC on 25 Jan. 1966. Rev. 11 June 1966 by Scottish Arts Council and Traverse Festival Productions at the Close Theatre Club, Glasgow with Victor Carin as Robert Burns. Rev. on 23 Aug. 1967 by Traverse Festival Productions in assoc. with John Martin at Palladium Theatre, Edinburgh with John Cairney back as Burns. (Then toured round world ad infinitum under the mgt. of John Cairney – including transfer to Arts Theatre Club, London on 13 Nov. 1967 – until he creates his own one man show about Burns in its place.)

2 Mar. * **SOME MEN AND ANIMALS** arranged by George Mully from the work of Franz Kafka. Cast: Kate Coleridge, Noel Collins, Tutte Lemkow. Dir. George Mully. (A long item from the programme, 'Report to an Academy', is rev. 7 Sept. prior to a transfer to Arts

Theatre Club, London, on 14 Sept. then – under the mgt. of Tutte Lemkow – televised by BBC and toured extensively round Europe.)

24 Mar. 'MORE THAN MEETS THE EYE' – Triple bill consisting of:
† **THE MAN WITH A FLOWER IN HIS MOUTH** by Luigi Pirandello. Trans. Frederick May. Cast: Charles Baptiste, Noel Collins. Music by Robin Williamson.
† **FROM NIGHT TO NIGHT** BY François Billetdoux. Trans. Mark Rudlin. Cast: Kate Coleridge, Noel Collins. Music by Bill Stronach and Amsg Glumly.
* **THE MASTER OF TWO SERVANTS** by George Mully with music by Bill Stronach and Amsg Glumly. Cast: Charles Baptiste, Kate Coleridge, Noel Collins, Frances Davidson.
All three plays dir. George Mully.

20 Apr. **THE ZOO STORY** By Edward Albee. Credits as before. (Revival of production first presented on 14 Apr. 1964.)
† **CHARLIE** by Slawomir Mrozek. Trans. by Nicholas Bethall. Cast: Brian Carey, David McKail, Stuart Mungall. Both plays dir. Callum Mill.

4 May. † **THE DIFFERENCE** by Peter Bergman. Cast: Colin Maitland, Gillian Watt.
* **A WEN** by Saul Bellow. Cast: Doreen Mantle, Harry Towb. Cast in London: Harry Towb and Miriam Karlin.
* **ORANGE SOUFFLÉ** by Saul Bellow. Cast: Doreen Mantle, Harry Towb. Cast in London: Harry Towb and Miriam Karlin. All three plays dir. Charles Marowitz. Des. Tony Carruthers (in Edinburgh). Des. Ralph Koltai (in London). ('A Wen' and 'Orange Soufflé'

later form bill entitled 'The Bellow Plays' which opens at the London Traverse at the Jeanetta Cochrane Theatre on 26 May 1966 before transferring to the Fortune Theatre, London on 26 June 1966.)

1 June † **A NIGHT WITH GUESTS** by Peter Weiss in a version by Laurence Dobie. Cast: Pricilla Benson, Christina Currie, Martin Heller, David Lloyd Meridith, Peter Porteous, Gordon Whiting.
* **SCLEROSIS** by Peter Barnes. Cast: Pricilla Benson, Martin Heller, Ian MacDonald, David Lloyd Meridith, Geoff Moore, Peter Porteous, Louis Vrakas, Gordon Whiting.
Both plays dir. Charles Marowitz. Des. Tony Carruthers. (Double bill transfers for single performance to Aldwych Theatre, London on 27 June.)

22 June **THE TYPISTS** by Murray Schisgal.
THE TIGER by Murray Schisgal.
Casts: Paul Kermack, Geraldine Newman. Both plays dir. Callum Mill.

2 July **DUBLIN FARE** – a revue by Mike Jones and Mike Newling. Music by Andrew Roberts and Jonathan Stafford-Clark. Cast: Irene Adams, Gill Hannan, Dinah Stabb, Constantin de Goguel, Mike Jones, Ian Milton, Mike Newling, Max Stafford-Clark. Dir. Max Stafford-Clark. (Dublin University Players in association with the Traverse. Reworked and revived under the title 'Stewed Irish' on 24 Aug. Transfers to Arts Th. Club, London on 5 Oct.)

13 July * **JOHNNY SO LONG** by Vivienne C. Welburn with music by John Foley. Cast: David Baxter, Eileen Colgan, Derek Green, Elizabeth Hop-

kins, Andrew McWhirter, Diane Saunders. Dir. Alan Simpson.

20 July * *AUTOMAN LOVES by John Frith. (Mgt: John Frith.)*

3 Aug. * **GREEN JULIA** by Paul Ableman. Cast: Jonathan Lynn, Philip Manikum. Dir. George Mully. Des. Tony Carruthers (in London). (Transfers to Arts Theatre Club, London on 2 Sept. then back to Traverse on 28 Sept.)

6 Aug. * **TWO** by Chor. Geoff Moore. Music by Bela Bartok. Cast: Eva McKay, Pamela Moore. Dir. Geoff Moore. Lgt. Jack Henry Moore. (Group One Ballet in assoc. with Traverse. Rev. 23 Aug. at Cathedral Hall, Albany Street, Edinburgh and on 17 Sept. at City Hall, Cardiff.)

17 Aug. * *OH GLORIA by Robert Shure. Music by Andrew Roberts and Jonathan Stafford-Clark. Cast: Irene Adams (rpl. Jill Hannah from 31 Aug.), Michael Mackenzie (not the Equity actor), Dinah Stabb, Max Stafford-Clark. Dir. Max Stafford-Clark. Des. Richard Demarco. (Mgt: Robert Shure.)*

20 Aug. THERE WAS A MAN by Tom Wright. Credits as before. (Traverse Festival Productions Ltd, at Morton Hall, Edinburgh. revival of production prem. 25 Jan.)

20 Aug. **ONE MAN'S SHOW** by Larry Adler. Cast: Larry Adler. Dir. George Mully. (Traverse Festival Productions Ltd. and Robert Paterson at Morton House, Edinburgh.)

23 Aug. **MACBETH** by William Shakespeare. Cast: Alex Allen, Jennifer Angus, Annabel Barton, Donald Bisset, Lees Borland, George Cormack, Charles Craig, Andrew Dallmeyer, Frederick Dally, Rosemary Davey, Betty Davis, James Dignam, James Fairley, Brigit Forsyth, Katy Gardiner, Harry Hughes,

Robert James, Robin John, Jonathan Kaye, David Kincaid, John Lancaster, Russel Laing, Alex McAvoy, Matt McGinn, Duncan MacRae, Leonard Maguire, Lee Menzies, Norman Morton, Meg Wynn Owen, Ian Paterson, Anne Raitt, David Robb, Andrew Ross, William Ross, Henry Stamper, Barbara Stuart, David Strong, Rosalind Thomas, Morton Ward, Ian Watson, Tom Wright, Jeremy Young. Dir. Michael Geliot. Associate Director: John Broome. Des. Annena Stubbs. Lgt. Francis Reid. Music by Guy Woolfenden. Sound Effects by David Collinson. (Traverse Festival Productions Ltd. and Edinburgh Festival Society at Assembly Hall, Edinburgh.)

23 Aug. 'DANCE PROGRAMME' – consisting of:
* BLUE AND GREEN VARIATIONS – Chor. Geoff Moore. Music by Ornette Coleman. Cast: Sean Collins.
* INSERT – Chor. Geoff Moore. Cast: Pamela Moore.
TWO. (See 6 Aug. for credits.) (Revival of ballet premièred at Traverse on 6 Aug.)
All three dir. Geoff Moore. Lgt. Jack Henry Moore. (Group One Ballet in assoc. with Traverse at Cathedral Hall, Albany Street, Edinburgh. Rev. 17 Sept. at City Hall, Cardiff in association with the Commonwealth Arts Festival and the Traverse.)

24 Aug. * HAPPY DAYS ARE HERE AGAIN by C. P. Taylor. Cast: John Barrard, Leonard Fenton, Bernard Goldman, Keith James, Edward Palmer, John Rapley, Leslie Scofield. Dir. Charles Marowitz. Des. Charles Marowitz (in Edinburgh). Des. Tony Carruthers (in London). (Transfers to Arts Theatre Club, London on 21 Aug.)

24 Aug. STEWED IRISH. Credits in Edinburgh as before – except without Milton. Cast in London includes: Christopher Serle, Des. Tony Carruthers (in London). (Dublin University Players in association with the Traverse. Reworked revival of production first presented on 2 July under the title 'Dublin Fare'. Transfers to Arts Theatre Club, London on 5 Oct.)

24 Aug. *BUBBLES* by Linday Kemp. Cast: Jack Birkett, Lindsay Kemp, Vivian Stanshall. Dir. the author. Cos. Richard Tredinnick. (Mgt: Lindsay Kemp Mime Theatre Troupe.)

31 Aug. * THE ART OF SAMUEL BECKETT – arranged by John Calder from the work of Beckett. Cast: David Baxter, Leonard Fenton, Michael Geliot. Dir. Michael Geliot. Des. Tony Carruthers (in London). (Transfers to Arts Theatre Club, London on 21 Sept. Rev. 19 October at Traverse.)

7 Sept. REPORT TO AN ACADEMY by Franz Kafka in a version by George Mully. Cast: Tutte Lemkow. (Revival of production first presented on 2 Mar.)
DIALOGUES by Paul Ableman. Cast: Paul Ableman, Penelope Lee. Both plays dir. George Mully. Des. Tony Carruthers (in London). (Double bill transfers to Arts Theatre Club, London on 14 Sept.)

10 Sept. **Jim Haynes is replaced as Chairman by Andrew Elliot but remains Artistic Director.**

14 Sept. * *SCAFFOLD* by Roger McGough, John Gorman and Michael McGear. Cast: John Gorman, Michael McGear, Roger McGough. Dir. John Lyndon. (Mgt: The Scaffold.)

16 Sept. * OF HOPE AND GLORY by C. P. Taylor. Cast includes: Helen Downing, Matt McGinn, Milton Savage. Dir. Jack Henry Moore. (Traverse in assoc. with Commonwealth Arts Festival and Jim Haynes at City Hall,

Cardiff. Closed after one performance. Disowned by the
author after his script had been
'cut to ribbons'.)

21 Sept. * THE ROAR OF THE KEELIE,
A TOUCH OF THE POOL –
An Entertainment by John Gor-
man and Matt McGinn. Cast:
John Gorman, Matt McGinn.

28 Sept. GREEN JULIA – Credits as before. (Rev.
of production first presented on 3 Aug.)

19 Oct. THE ART OF SAMUEL BECKETT –
arranged by John Calder from the work
of Beckett.
KRAPP'S LAST TAPE and
IMAGINATION DEAD
IMAGE by Samuel Beckett are
inserted into the revival of this
Beckett programme. Cast:
Leonard Fenton, Michael
Geliot. Whole programme dir.
Michael Geliot.

26 Oct. * FOCUS – a revue by Rosalind
Thomas, Kevin Smith and
Caroline Wiener. Cast: Kevin
Smith, Rosalind Thomas. Dir.
Caroline Wiener.

9 Nov. † ONKEL ONKEL by Gunter
Grass in a version by Ralph
Manheim and Johnny Speight.
Cast: David Baxter, Peter Bir-
rel, Lynette Chappel, Barry
Doan, Jill Richards, Eliza Ward.
Dir. Alan Simpson. Des. Tony
Carruthers. Music by Hum-
phrey Searle.

1 Dec. THE FANTASTICS by Tom
Jones and Harvey Schmidt.
Cast: Christopher Lethbridge
Baker, Wendy Brierley, Sean
Hewitt, Robert Hornery, Peter
Ellis Jones, Geoff Moore,
Pamela Moore, Henry Moxon,
Gordon Whiting. Dir. and des.
Jack Henry Moore.

7 Dec. * NO SHOW YES – assembled
by Geoff Moore. Cast includes:
Pamela Moore. Dir. Geoff Moore.
(Mgt: Geoff Moore.)

23 Dec. * THE ENCHANTED SQUARE
by Catherine Robins. Cast of the
nine includes: Gordon Whiting.

Dir. the author. (Mgt: Theatre
Workshop, Edinburgh.)

Dec. Max Stafford-Clark joins the
staff as Stage Manager.

1966

11 Jan. THE SCAFFOLD'S NEW
REVUE by the company. Cast:
John Gorman, Mike McGear,
Roger McGough. (Mgt: The Scaf-
fold.)

18 Jan. 'A MORAL EVENING' – Triple
bill consisting of:
† THE WOMAN TAKEN IN
ADULTERY – Anonymous.
Cast: Heinz Barnard, Kate Bin-
chy, Henry Moxon, John Shed-
den, Max Stafford-Clark, David
Strong.
† A DOOR SHOULD BE
OPEN OR SHUT by Alfred de
Musset. Cast: Heinz Barnard,
Kate Binchy.
* ALLERGY by C. P. Taylor.
Cast: Heinz Barnard, Kate Bin-
chy, David Strong. Cast in
London: Kate Binchy, Roy
Hanlon, Gordon Whiting.
All three plays dir. Michael
Geliot. Des. Ralph Koltai (in
London). ('Allergy' transfers to
London Traverse at the
Jeanetta Cochrane Theatre on
28 April.)

21 Jan. Jack Henry Moore (who had
been appointed by Jim Haynes
during the previous year as his
Assistant Director) is re-
allocated to the post of Stage
Manager by the Committee of
Management.

8 Feb. * MELTED ARCHITECTURE –
A serious revue with music by
Carl Davis and texts by Isaac
Babel, Bertolt Brecht, Lord
Byron, Gregory Corso, e. e.
cummings, Emily Dickinson,
Amsg Glumly, Langston
Hughes, Leo Lehman, Ezra
Pound and Steven Vinaver.
Cast: Carl Davis, Benjamin

Luxon, Glenda Russell, Christine Wilson. Dir. George Mully.

22 Feb. THE INVESTIGATION by Peter Weiss. Trans. Alexander Gross. Cast: Antony Aldgate, John Atkinson, Michael Christian, Stanley Eveling, Graeme Farnell, Harry Hankin, Tom Hutton, Eric Jenks, Peter Johnstone, Chris Knight, Russell Laing, Bob MacCauley, Jennifer MacKewn/Jenie Swartz, Rod MacLeod, Ian Mandleberg, Ken Murcott, Robin Mann, Matthew Pumphrey, Ian Robertson, John Rowley, Kenn Stafford, Robert Stafford, Joseph Zacchai, Mary Zuckerman. Directed by Mike Ockrent. (Traverse and Edinburgh University Dramatic Society at St. Mark's Unitarian Church, Edinburgh.)

1 Mar. 'TWO SIDES OF A COIN' – Double bill consisting of: THE DWARFS by Harold Pinter. Cast: Oliver Cotton, William Hoyland, Toby Salaman. * THE LOCAL STIGMATIC by Heathcote Williams. Cast: Oliver Cotton, Peter Hill, William Hoyland, Toby Salaman. Both plays dir. Peter Gill. ('The Dwarfs' was seen earlier on a tour of America with the same cast and director but was extensively rewritten by Pinter for the Traverse and re-directed. 'The Local Stigmatic' transfers to the Royal Court, London on 27 March. A new production by the Traverse – with many of the original cast – opens in Holland on 6 May.)

22 Mar. *THE MIRROR MAN by Brian Way. Dir. Ros Clark. (Mgt: Theatre Workshop, Edinburgh.)*

29 Mar. *THE PATERSON'S SHORTBREAD SHOW – a revue by Mike Newling and Mike Jones. Music by Charlotte Crichton. Cast: Charlotte Crichton, Con-

stantin de Goguel, Mike Newling, Max Stafford-Clark. Dir. Max Stafford-Clark.

29 Mar. 'ABOUT HUSBANDS BY WIVES' – Quadruple bill consisting of: THE WIFE OF BATH'S PROLOGUE by Geoffrey Chaucer. Adpt. Glen Walford. Cast: Glen Walford. THE STRONGER by August Strindberg. Cast: Caroline Fox, Jenie Swartz. A STREET AND A NUMBER by Ferenc Molnar. Cast: Eric Jenks, Glen Walford. BEFORE BREAKFAST by Eugene O'Neill. Cast: Jenie Swartz. All four plays dir. Glen Walford.

12 Apr. * SOMETIME NEVER by Roy Minton. Cast: John English, Rio Fanning, Pamela Miles, Jean Wynn Scott, Eliza Ward. Dir. Ande Anderson.

3 May THE SQUARE by Marguerite Duras. Trans. Barbara Bray. Cast: Paul Gillard, Amanda Reiss. † LA MUSICA by Marguerite Duras. Trans. Barbara Bray. Cast: John Thaw, Mary Yeomans. Cast in London: Sandor Eles, Joanna Dunham. Both plays dir. Milo Sperber. Des. Ian Knight (in London). (Double bill transfers to London Traverse at Jeanetta Cochrane Theatre on 25 Aug.)

6 May * ROOTED AND GROUNDED by Neil McLaughlan. Cast: Peter Hill, William Hoyland, Toby Salaman. THE LOCAL STIGMATIC by Heathcote Williams. Cast: Peter Hill, William Hoyland, Toby Salaman, Humphrey Taylor. Cast in London includes: Oliver Cotton, William Hoyland. Both plays dir. Jack Henry Moore. (Mickery Theatre,

Amsterdam in assoc. with the Traverse at the Mickery. Double bill transfers to Lantaarn Theater, Rotterdam later in the month. 'The Local Stigmatic' was a new production – although using many of the original cast – of the play first presented on 1 March. 'The Local Stigmatic' rev. 26 June for another performance at the Royal Court Theatre, London.)

6 June   **Jim Haynes' resignation as Artistic Director is accepted by the Committee of Management. Gordon McDougall is appointed as his successor at the end of July. Max Stafford-Clark (who had been working until 3 June as Stage Manager) joins him as Associate Director in Oct. and his policy takes effect from 27 Sept. after a period as General Manager.**

5 July   **SIX CHARACTERS IN SEARCH OF AN AUTHOR** by Luigi Pirandello. Trans. Frederick May. Cast: Gay Hamilton, Celia Hewitt, George Innes, Jim Macdonald, Roy Marsden, Max Stafford-Clark, Peter Townsend, Susan Williamson. Dir. Garry O'Connor. A.D. Georgette Illes.

2 Aug.   **RIDE A COCK HORSE** by David Mercer. Cast: David Burke, Zoe Hicks, Pamela Lane, Jeanette Muir, Judy Wilson. Dir. Stephen Frears.

23 Aug.   *UNDER MILK WOOD by Dylan Thomas. Cast: Brian D. Barnes. Dir. Brian D. Barnes. (Mgt: Brian D. Barnes.)*

23 Aug.   † **THE SWALLOWS** by Roland Dubillard. Trans. Barbara Wright. Cast: Catherine Finn, Tim Preece, Ewen Solon, Tessa Wyatt. Dir. Don Taylor. Des. Brian Vary (in London). (Transfers to Arts Theatre Club, London on 4 Oct.)

23 Aug.   * *THE SCAFFOLD PLUS ONE*

– a revue by Roger McGough. Cast: Wendy Brierley, John Gorman, Michael McGear, Roger McGough. (Mgt: The Scaffold.)

25 Aug.   * **DOUBLE DOUBLE** by James Saunders. Cast: George Innes, Brian Osborne, Toby Salaman, Heather Stoney, Susan Williamson. Dir. Max Stafford-Clark. Set. Nick Heppel.

6 Sept.   * **LORCA** by Bettina Jonic. Music by Harrison Birtwhistle. Cast: Tony Beckley, Nicholas Chagrin, John English, Michael Henderson, Christian Hughes, Bettina Jonic, Margaret Lesley, Pamela Miles, Joseph Morris, David Strong, Shane Younger – with James Christie, Alan Hacker, George Kirsch, A. McCree, Judith Pearce. Dir. Ande Anderson. Des. Tom Lingwood. Lgt. John Hall. (Traverse Festival Productions Ltd. and Edinburgh Festival Society at Gateway Theatre, Edinburgh.)

6 Sept.   * **THE LITTLE WOMAN** by John Hall. Cast: Wendy Brierley, Bill Johnson, Charles Lewsen, Julie Martin, James Watts, June Watts. Dir. Alan Vaughan Williams.

6 Sept.   *'IMPROMPTUS' – Quadruple bill consisting of:*
† *THE LATE by Rene de Obaldia.*
† *THE HANGMAN'S SACRIFICE by Rene de Obaldia.*
† *THE TWINKLING TWINS by Rene de Obaldia.*
† *SALUTATIONS by Eugene Ionesco.*
Casts: Paul Harman, Hildegard Neil, Gloria Parkinson, Brian Walton. All four plays dir. Peter James. (Mgt: Liverpool Everyman Theatre.)

6 Sept.   *THE SCAFFOLD PLUS TWO – a revue by the company. Cast of 5 includes: John Gorman, Michael McGear, Roger McGough. Dir. Michael Rigg. (Mgt: The Scaffold.)*

20 Sept. **RED NOSES FOR ME** by *Charles Lewsen. Cast: Charles Lewsen – with Bernard Sumner. Dir. the author. (Mgt: Charles Lewsen. Production seen again at the Traverse on 4 May 1967.)*

27 Sept. **INADMISSIBLE EVIDENCE** by John Osborne. Cast: Brian Carey, Saam Dastoor, Marian Diamond, John Fraser, Kathy McGregor, Miriam Margolyes, Valerie Sarruf. Dir. Gordon McDougall. (Transfers to YMCA Theatre, Edinburgh on 24 Oct.)

6 Oct. **LOOK BACK IN ANGER** by John Osborne. Cast: Brian Carey, Saam Dastoor, Marian Diamond, John Fraser, Valerie Sarruf. Dir. Gordon McDougall. (Transfers to YMCA Theatre, Edinburgh on 25 Oct.)

1 Nov. † **THE MAN OUTSIDE** by Wolfgang Borchert. Trans. David Porter. Cast: Saam Dastoor, Marian Diamond, Miriam Margoyles, Declan Mulholland, Sam Walters. Dir. Max Stafford-Clark. Des. Hamish Henderson. Lgt. Paul Miller.

11 Nov. * **REPORT FROM THE GAL-LOWS** *by Ian Mandleberg. Dir. the author. (Mgt: Edinburgh University Dramatic Society.)*

15 Nov. **THE DANCERS** By David Cregan. Cast: Saam Dastoor, Miriam Margoyles, Corinna Marlowe, Declan Mulholland, Mike Newling, Sam Walters. Dir. Gordon McDougall and Max Stafford-Clark. (Rev. 16 Dec.)

22 Nov. * **THE RESTORATION OF ARNOLD MIDDLETON** by David Storey. Cast: David Collings, Marian Diamond, Ann Holloway, Rosemary McHale, June Watson, Paul Williamson. Dir. Gordon McDougall. Des. Denzil Walker. Lgt. Paul Miller.

25 Nov. **THE SANDBOX** by *Edward Albee.*

THE WASTELAND by *T. S. Eliot. (Mgt: Edinburgh University Dramatic Society.)*

13 Dec. * **CALEDONIAN 6895** – a revue by Michael Jones and Michael Newling. Cast: Richard Howard, Michael Jones, Rosemary McHale, Miriam Margoyles, Michael Newling. Dir. Max Stafford-Clark.

16 Dec. **THE DANCERS.** Credits as before. (Revival of production first presented on 15 Nov.)

20 Dec. * **THE TIME FISHER** – improvised by the company from an idea by Catherine Robins. Cast: Michael Barry, Jim MacDonald, Rosemary McHale, Nancy Mitchell, Matthew O'Sullivan, Matthew Pumphrey. Dir. Catherine Robins. Set. Andrew Sanders. Cos. Ros Clark.

28 Dec. * **THE VIETNAM HEARINGS** – compiled from documentary sources by Gordon Mac-Dougall. Dir. Gordon McDougall.

30 Dec. * **BOSWELL IN SCOTLAND** – adapted by David Wright from James Boswell's Journals. Cast: Richard Howard, Mike Jones, Miriam Margoyles. Dir. Gordon McDougall.

1967

17 Jan. * **THE DAUGHTER-IN-LAW** by D. H. Lawrence. Cast: Betty Hardy, Richard Howard, Rosemary McHale, Lennox Milne, Brian Smith. Dir. Gordon McDougall. Cos. Cathy McGregor. Lgt. Paul Miller.

27 Jan. * **THE DENNING REPORT ON THE PROFUMO AFFAIR** – Adpt. Gordon McDougall. Cast: Nicholas Fairburn, Richard Howard, Rosemary McHale, Ian Milton, Brian Smith, Max Stafford-Clark, Clare Welch, Paul Williamson.

Dir. Gordon McDougall.

14 Feb. 'DEAD AND BURIED' – Triple
bill consisting of:
† **THE RECLUSE** by Paul Fos-
ter. Cast: Zoe Hicks.
† **BALLS** by Paul Foster. Cast
(on tape): Zoe Hicks, Richard
Howard, Callum Mill, Rosem-
ary McHale, Ian Milton, Sarah
Rivington, Tony Rohr, Paul
Williamson.
† **HURRAH FOR THE
BRIDGE** by Paul Foster. Cast:
Peter Conway, Christopher
Hill, Callum Mill, Ian Milton,
Sarah Rivington, Tony Rohr.
All three plays dir. Max
Stafford-Clark. Cos. Cathy
McGregor. Lgt. Paul Miller.
(Triple Bill transfers to Bristol
Arts Centre on 6 Mar. 'Balls'
rev. 20 Aug. as part of 'Mini
Plays' bill.)

14 Feb. * **THE HESSIAN CORPORAL**
by Paul Foster. Cast: John
Hunt, Sarah Kidd, Martin
Meade, Elizabeth Moore, Jane
Ogilvie, Bill Oliver, Elizabeth
Patterson, Sheena Smith, Kay
Walker, Elizabeth White, Oliver
Zeise, Mary Zuckerman. Dir.
Ian Mandleberg and Mike Ock-
rent. Supervised by Gordon
McDougall. A. D.'s: John Pick-
ering, Andrew Richardson,
Cos. Cathy McGregor. Lgt.
Paul Miller.
(Traverse in assoc. with Edin-
burgh University Dramatic
Society and Edinburgh College
of Speech and Drama. Re-
mounted in a professional pro-
duction by McDougall on 15
Aug.)

7 Mar. * **FANGHORN** by David Pin-
ner. Cast: Thelma Holt,
Edward Phillips, Heather Sto-
ney, Lesley Ward, Gordon
Whiting. Dir. Charles Maro-
witz. Lgt. Paul Miller.
(A production of the play by
Charles Marowitz with a diffe-

rent cast was presented by
Michael Codron and Michael
White at the Fortune Theatre,
London on 16 Nov.)

4 Apr. * *THE COMMISSION by Roger
McGough. Cast: Nadia Aitken,
George Camiller, Ian Collier, Pru-
dence Drage, Bill Stewart. Dir.
Peter James. (Mgt: Liverpool
Everyman Theatre.)*

12 Apr. * **A LIFE IN BEDROOMS** by
David Wright and David
Wood. Cast: Sheila Dawson,
Paul Hooper, Annabel Leven-
ton, Charles Lewsen, Ian Man-
dleberg, Corinna Marlowe,
Max Stafford-Clark, Kay Wal-
ker, David Wood. Dir. and
chor. Gordon McDougall. Des.
Cathy McGregor.

20 Apr. **TIMES ARE GETTING HARD
BOYS** by Keith Darvill. Dir.
Paul Tomlinson.

25 Apr. *HOW PLEASANT TO KNOW
MR LEAR by Charles Lewsen.
Cast: Charles Lewsen. Dir. the
author. (Mgt: Charles Lewsen.)*

4 May. RED NOSES FOR ME. Credits as
before. (Revival of production first presented at the Traverse on 20 Sept. 1966.)

9 May † *SUNSET IN LATE AUTUMN
by Friederick Durrenmatt. Trans.
Ulli Beir. Cast: Segun Olusala,
Segun Sofowote. Dir. Segun Olu-
sola.*
† *MORNING, NOON AND
NIGHT – dev. Segun Olusola.
Cast: Akin Euba, Segun Olusola,
Segun Sofowote. Dir. the author.
(Mgt: Mbari Mbayo Theatre Club,
Oshogbo, Nigeria.)*

10 May † *THE SUITCASE by Sebastian
Salazar Bundi. Adpt. Obotunde
Ijimore and the cast. Cast: Segun
Akinbola, Segun Olusola, Segun
Sofowote. Dir. Ijaolo. (Mgt: Mbari
Mbayo Theatre Club, Oshogbo,
Nigeria. Presented in double bill
with 'Morning, Noon and Night'.)*

23 May * **AN EXPEDITION TO PICK
MUSHROOMS** by Ranald Graham. Cast: Annabel Leventon.

* THE KING by Stewart Conn.
Cast: Peter Harlowe, Annabel
Leventon, Philip Manikum.
Both plays dir. Max Stafford-
Clark. ('The King' rev. 18 Aug.)

13 June *** GROUNDS FOR MAR-
RIAGE** by Don Taylor. Cast:
Peter Baldwin, Roderick
Brown, Ellen Dryden, Richard
Hampton, Barney Lawrence,
Pauline Letts, Lesley Nunner-
ley, Max Stafford-Clark. Dir.
the author.

27 June **MOURNING BECOMES
ELECTRA** by Eugene O'Neill.
Cast in London: Michael Bar-
rington, Judy Campbell, Saam
Dastoor, John Fraser, Peter
Harlowe, Gilly McIver, Corinna
Marlowe, Michael Murray,
Valerie Sarruf, Paul Tomlinson,
Judy Wilson, Thick Wilson.
Cast in Lebanon and Edin-
burgh: Campbell, Fraser, Sheila
Grant, Peter Harlowe, Robert
Harris, Marlowe, Gwynyth
Marshall-Jones, Murray, Sarruf,
William Simons, Richard Wil-
son, Thick Wilson. Dir. Gordon
McDougall. Lgt. Andre Tam-
mes (in Edinburgh). (Traverse
at Arts Theatre Club, London.
Production rev. on 22 Aug.
1968 at Baalbeck Festival, Leba-
non before transferring to
Churchill Theatre, Edinburgh
on 2 Sept. in assoc. with Edin-
burgh Festival Society, Gordon
McDougall and Traverse Festival Productions Ltd.

30 June *** THE STILL LIFE STORY** *Dir.
Ivor Davies and Ian Mandleberg.
Lgt. Andre Tammes. (Mgt: Edin-
burgh Experimental Group.)*

12 July *** COME AND BE KILLED** by
Stanley Eveling. Cast: Francesca Annis, Annabel Leventon, Robert Morris, Tim Seely.
Dir. Milo Sperber. (Rev. 31
Aug. in a new production with
the same cast.)

19 July *** A HOUSING SHORTAGE** by

John Antrobus. Cast: Annabel
Leventon, Brian Walton. Dir.
Paul Tomlinson.
THE PEDAGOGUE by James
Saunders. Cast: Tim Seely. Dir.
Ian Milton.
THE LATE by Rene de Obal-
dia. Cast: Francesca Annis,
Annabel Leventon. Dir. Paul
Tomlinson.
('The Pedagogue' and 'The
Late' rev. 20 Aug. as part of
the bill of 'Mini Plays'.)

15 Aug. **THE HESSIAN CORPORAL** by
Paul Foster. Cast: Peter Har-
lowe, Rosemary McHale,
Miriam Margoyles, Robert Mor-
ris, Hildegard Neil, Tim Seely,
Ian Trigger, William Simons,
Brian Walton. Dir. Gordon
McDougall. Des. Moira Mait-
land. Lgt. Paul Miller. Songs by
Ian Mandleberg and Gordon
MacDougall. (New production
of the play first presented by
the Traverse on 14 Feb.)
THE PERSIANS BY Aeschylus.
Cast: Peter Harlowe, Ian Man-
dleberg, Robert Morris, Hilde-
gard Neil, Toby Salaman, Tim
Seely, William Simons, Ian
Trigger, Brian Walton. Dir.
Gordon McDougall. Des. Moira
Maitland. Lgt. Paul Miller.
Music by Ian Mandleberg.

18 Aug. **THE KING.** Credits as before – plus
Lgt. Paul Miller. (Revival of production
first presented on 23 May.)

20 Aug. 'MINI PLAYS' – a selection of
very short plays given in continuous performance with the
audience free to come and go
between each like a cartoon
cinema. Daily programme
selected from the following:
BALLS. Credits as before. (Revival of
production first presented on 14 Feb.)
* COVER STORY by Michael
Jones. Cast: Rosemary McHale,
Philip Manikum, Christopher
Searle. Dir. Max Stafford-Clark.
† FREDDY by Patsy Southgate.
Cast: Annabel Leventon, Philip

117

Manikum. Dir. Max Stafford-Clark.

* EDINBURGH IMPROMPTU by Rene de Obaldia. Cast: Philip Manikum, Christopher Searle. Dir. Paul Tomlinson.

* GEOFFREY by Stanley Eveling. Cast: Brian Walton. Dir. Max Stafford-Clark.

THE LATE. Credits as before. (Revival of production first presented on 19 July.)

* NATURAL CAUSES by Ellen Dryden. Cast: Rosemary McHale, Philip Manikum. Dir. Paul Tomlinson.

THE PEDAGOGUE. Credits as before. (Revival of production first presented on 19 July.)

* THE SWORD by Steward Conn. Cast: Philip Manikum, Toby Salaman. Dir. Max Stafford-Clark.

Lgt. Andre Tammes for all nine plays.

('Cover Story' and 'Natural Causes' [in a new production] are rev. on 19 Oct. in a 'New Bill of Mini Plays' at Mickery Theatre, Amsterdam prior to transferring to Traverse on 31 Oct.)

21 Aug. † *FUTZ* by Rochelle Owens. Music by Tom O'Horgan. Cast: Seth Allen, John Bakos, Mari-Claire Charba, Peter Craig, Claris Erikson, Victor Lipari, Beth Porter, Michael Warren Powell, Marilyn Roberts, Rob Thirkfield. Dir. Tom O'Horgan. Lgt. Laura Rambaldi. (Mgt: La Mama Experimental Theatre Company, New York at Barrie Halls, Edinburgh.)

21 Aug. † *TIMES SQUARE* by Leonard Melfi. Music by Tom O'Horgan. Cast: John Bakos, Mari-Claire Charba, Jerry Cunliffe, Claris Erikson, Kevin O'Connor, Beth Porter, Marilyn Roberts. Dir. Tom O'Horgan. Lgt. Laura Rambaldi. (Mgt: La Mama Experimental Theatre Company, New York at Barrie Halls, Edinburgh.)

21 Aug. *** CONTRATYPE III** by Tarak Hassan, Sebastian Bergman, Peter Avery and Mike Simpson. Cast: Peter Avery, Pam Brighton, Martin Edis, Sarah Hunter, Mike Simpson. Dir. Sebastian Bergman. (Mgt: London University Dramatic Society at Barrie Halls, Edinburgh.)

22 Aug. † *MELODRAMA PLAY* by Sam Shepard. Music by Tom O'Horgan. Cast: Seth Allen, John Bakos, Mari-Claire Charba, Peter Craig, Jerry Cunliffe, Claris Erikson, Victor Lipari, Kevin O'Connor, Beth Porter, Michael Warren Powell, Rob Thirkfield, Dir. Tom O'Horgan. Lgt. Laura Rambaldi. (Mgt: La Mama Experimental Theatre Company, New York at Barrie Halls, Edinburgh.)

22 Aug. † *UNTITLED PLAY* by Lanford Wilson. Cast: Seth Allen, John Bakos, Mari-Claire Charba, Peter Craig, Jerry Cunliffe, Claris Erikson, Victor Lipari, Kevin O'Connor, Beth Porter, Michael Warren Powell, Marilyn Roberts, Rob Thirkfield. Dir. Tom O'Horgan. Lgt. Laura Rambaldi. (Mgt: La Mama Experimental Theatre Company, New York at Barrie Halls, Edinburgh.)

23 Aug. THERE WAS A MAN. Credits as before. (Revival by Traverse Festival Productions in association with John Martin at Palladium Theatre, Edinburgh of play premièred by Traverse on 25 Jan. 1965.)

31 Aug. COME AND BE KILLED by Stanley Eveling. Cast: Francesca Annis, Annabel Leventon, Robert Morris, Tim Seely. Dir. Max Stafford-Clark. (New production with original cast of play premièred by Traverse on 11 July. Transfers to open new York Arts Centre on 16 Sept.)

31 Aug. *** SANCTITY** by Robert Head. Cast: Lorenzo Adams J., Tony Cyrus, Gary Files. Dir. Arthur C. Stubbs. Cos. Christine MacKay. Chor. Lorenzo Adams J. (Mgt:

International Theatre Club.)

31 Aug. **THE MESSINGKAUF DIA-LOGUES** *by Bertolt Brecht. Dir. Lee Breuer. (Mgt: Studio Theatre, Paris, at Barrie Halls, Edinburgh.)*

1 Sept. † **UBU IN CHAINS** by Alfred Jarry. Trans. Simon Watson Taylor. Cast: Ian Mandleberg, Miriam Margoyles, Hildegard Neil, Toby Salaman, Christopher Serle, William Simons, Ian Trigger, Brian Walton, David Wood. Dir. Gordon McDougall. Des. Gerald Scarfe. Lgt. Andre Tammes. Music by The Soft Machine. Effects by Ivor Davies. (Traverse at Barrie Halls, Edinburgh.)

4 Sept. * **TOM PAINE** by Paul Foster. Cast in Edinburgh: Seth Allen, John Bakos, Mari-Claire Charba, Peter Craig, Jerry Cunliffe, Claris Erickson, Victor Lipari, Kevin O'Connor, Beth Porter, Michael Warren Powell, Marilyn Roberts, Robert Thirkield. Cast in London: Allen rep. Beverley Atkinson. Dir. Tom O'Horgan. Des. Hamish Henderson. Lgt. Laura Rambaldi (in Edinburgh). Lgt. Francis Reid (in London). (La Mama Experimental Theatre Company, New York and Traverse Festival Productions Ltd. in assoc. with Edinburgh Festival Society at Churchill Theatre, Edinburgh. In assoc. with Michael White and the Traverse, transfers to Vaudeville Theatre, London on 17 Oct. The first half of the play had previously been 'workshopped' at the La Mama Theatre in New York.)

4 Oct. † **A SEASON IN HELL** by Pat Hooker. Cast: Paul Harman, Robert Morris. Dir. Gordon McDougall.

19 Oct. 'NEW BILL OF MINI PLAYS' consisting of:

* **TRIO** by James Saunders. Cast: Ronald Falk, Karin MacCarthy, Philip Manikum.
* **THE GYMNASIUM** by Olwen Wymark. Cast: Ronald Falk, Philip Manikum.
COVER STORY by Michael Jones. Cast: Ronald Falk, Karin MacCarthy, Philip Manikum. (Revival of production first presented on 20 Aug.)
NATURAL CAUSES by Ellen Dryden. Cast: Karin MacCarthy, Philip Manikum. (New production of play premièred by Traverse on 20 Aug.)
* **TWENTY-SIX EFFORTS AT PORNOGRAPHY** by Carey Harrison. Cast: Ronald Falk, Nicholas Young.
All five plays dir. Max Stafford-Clark. (Traverse at Mickery Theatre, Amsterdam. Quintuple bill then tours to Gronigen and Rotterdam in Holland before transferring to Traverse on 31 Oct.)

24 Oct. **LOVE TO KILL** – *A programme of Songs and Drama devised by Sally Miles. Cast: Sally Miles – with Les Thatcher, David Whyte. (Mgt: Sally Miles. This production was later developed into a show called 'The Ruined Maid'.)*

31 Oct. 'NEW BILL OF MINI PLAYS' consisting of:
TRIO by James Saunders.
THE GYMNASIUM by Olwen Wymark.
COVER STORY by Michael Jones.
NATURAL CAUSES by Ellen Dryden.
TWENTY-SIX EFFORTS AT PORNOGRAPHY by Carey Harrison.
Credits as before. (Transfer of quintuple bill presented at Mickery Theatre, Amsterdam on 19 Oct.)

21 Nov. **A DRUNK MAN LOOKS AT THE THISTLE** *by Hugh MacDiarmid. Cast: Tom Fleming. (Mgt: Tom Fleming. Revived on 20 Aug. 1968.)*

1 Dec. † **LUDLOW FAIR** by Lanford Wilson. Cast: Marian Diamond, Gwyneth Marshall Jones. Dir. Gordon McDougall.
* **THE INERT** by Brian McMaster. Cast: Paul Harper,

Philip Manikum. Dir. Max Stafford-Clark.

Gordon McDougall resigns as Artistic Director and Max Stafford-Clark is appointed in his place. Stafford-Clark's programme takes effect from 9 May 1968.

19 Dec. *** THE LOLLIPOP TREE** – dev. Ros Clark. Cast: Judith Carne, Rosemary Davey, Patrick Dickson, Donald Pepper, Emil Wolk. Dir. the author. Des. Richard Hamlet and Ann Kirby. (Theatre Workshop, Edinburgh in assoc. with the Traverse.)

22 Dec. **WAITING FOR GODOT** by Samuel Beckett. Cast: Clive d'urban, Michael Harrigan, Philip Manikum, John Shedden, Richard Wilson. Dir. Gordon McDougall.

1968

6 Jan. *** PLEASE RENEW YOUR MEMBERSHIP** – A Revue. Cast includes: Philip Manikum, Gwynyth Marshall-Jones, Richard Wilson.

23 Jan. *** ABERFAN** or 'How the Abnormally High Welsh Rainfalls and The Amazingly High Scottish Wind Pressures Brought About a Dislocation of Scottish and Welsh Responsibilities' by Ranald Graham. Cast: Ros Clark and children from Theatre Workshop: Charles Birnie, Martin Flett, Gregor Graham, Tamsin Haggis, Gervas Huxley, Nanette Lassers, Cecilia McPheely, Michael McPheely, David Neustein, Julie Neustein, Malcolm Reading, Ann Robertson, Winnifred Ross, Jenny Skinner, Stephen Thomson, Julie Whitelaw. Dir. Gordon McDougall. A.D. Max

Stafford-Clark. (Traverse in association with Theatre Workshop, Edinburgh.)

2 Feb. *** *MASS IN F.*** *Dir. Ivor Davies. (Mgt: Edinburgh Experimental Group.)*

7 Feb. *** F IN MASS** by Nicholas Fairbairn and Gordon McDougall. Cast includes: Nicholas Fairbairn, Gordon McDougall. (Traverse management's answer to public criticism of 'Mass in F'.)

13 Feb. **THE PEOPLE SHOW NO. 3: THE EXAMINATION** *by Jeff Nuttall and the company. Cast: John Darling, Laura Gilbert, Mark Long, Syd Palmer – with the People Band. (Mgt: The People Show.)*

14 Feb. *** *THE PEOPLE SHOW NO. 11: SHEET/SOMETHING ELSE*** *by the company. Cast: John Darling, Muriel England, Laura Gilbert, Mark Long, Syd Palmer – with the People Band. (Mgt: The People Show.)*

21 Feb. **WOMEN BEWARE WOMEN** by Thomas Middleton. Cast: Lesley Bennun, Anthony Haygarth, Zoe Hicks, Richard Howard, Gwynyth Marshall-Jones, John Nettles, Matthew O'Sullivan, Valerie Sarruf, Brian Smith, Richard Wilson, Emil Wolk. Dir. Gordon McDougall. Des. Margo Samuel. Lgt. Andre Tammes. Chor. Marjorie Middleton. Music by Joyce Nettles.

19 Mar. *** WOULD YOU LOOK AT THEM SMASHING ALL THE LOVELY WINDOWS** by David Wright. Cast: Anthony Haygarth, Richard Howard, Gwynyth Marshall-Jones, John Nettles, Matthew O'Sullivan, Valerie Sarruf, Brian Smith, Richard Wilson, Emil Wolk. Dir. Gordon McDougall. Lgt. Andre Tammes.

11 Apr. **BOX AND COX** by J. Maddi-

son Morton. Cast: Anthony Haygarth, Matthew O'Sullivan, Emil Wolk. Dir. John Downie. (Rev. 28 Jan. 1969 at Traverse in a new production with one of the same cast.)

16 Apr. **UNCLE VANYA** by Anton Chekhov. Cast: Pamela Craig, John Downie, Richard Howard, John Nettles, Joan Knowles, Natasha Pyne, Valerie Sarruf, Brian Smith, Richard Wilson. Dir. Gordon McDougall. Lgt. Andre Tammes. Music by Joyce Nettles.

9 May *HOME FREE by Lanford Wilson.* Cast: Claris Erikson, Michael Warren Powell.
THE MADNESS OF LADY BRIGHT by Lanford Wilson. Cast: Claris Erikson, David Groh, Charles Stanley. Dir. and Des. Marshall W. Mason. (Mgt: American Theatre Project.)

28 May **ANGELS (OVER YOUR GRAVE) AND GEESE (OVER MINE)** by David Benedictus. Cast: Pamela Farbrother, Angela Galbraith, Anthony Haygarth, Anna Michaels, Derrick O'Connor. Dir. the author.

19 May † **COMINGS AND GOINGS** by Megan Terry. Cast selected from: Claris Erikson, Pamela Farbrother, Anthony Haygarth, Colin McCormack, Derrick O'Connor. Dir. Max Stafford-Clark. (Rev. 22 Aug. and 18 Oct. Transfers to Mickery theatre, Amsterdam in Nov.)

25 June * **THEME AND VARIATIONS** by Robert Phillips. Cast: William Cordery, Libby Glen. Dir. John Downie.

28 June *THE RUFFIAN ON THE STAIR by Joe Orton.* Dir. Daniel Morgan. (Mgt. Edinburgh University Dramatic Society.)

23 July * **THE LUNATIC, THE SECRET SPORTSMAN AND THE WOMAN NEXT DOOR** by Stanley Eveling. Cast: Angela Galbraith, Anthony Haygarth, Pamela Moiseiwitsch, Derrick O'Connor. Dir. Max Stafford-Clark. Set. Derrick O'Connor. Cos. Claris Erikson. Lgt. Andre Tammes. (During run at Traverse, production transfers on 6 Aug. to Spingold Theater, Brandeis University Interact Festival, Boston, USA Rev. on 10 Oct. at Traverse. Then transfers to Mickery Theatre, Amsterdam in Nov. prior to transferring to Open Space Theatre, London on 3 Dec.)

20 Aug. *A DRUNK MAN LOOKS AT THE THISTLE.* Credits as before. *(Revival of production which last opened at the Traverse on 21 Nov. 1967.)*

20 Aug. * *THE PEOPLE SHOW NO. 20: THE RAILINGS IN THE PARK by Jeff Nuttall.* Cast: John Darling, Muriel England, Laura Gilbert, Mark Long, Roland Miller, Syd Palmer. (Mgt: The People Show.)

21 Aug. * **ANNA-LUSE** by David Mowat. Cast: Claris Erikson, Pamela Farbrother, Angela Galbraith, Anthony Haygarth, Sara Kidd, Max Stafford-Clark, Derrick O'Connor. Dir. Max Stafford-Clark and (uncredited when Stafford-Clark had to take over from an actor who fell ill) the author. (Rev. 1 Oct. prior to transfer to Mickery Theatre, Amsterdam in Nov.)

23 Aug. **COMINGS AND GOINGS** by Megan Terry. Cast selected from: Erikson, Farbrother, Angela Galbraith, Haygarth, Sara Kidd, O'Connor, Max Stafford-Clark, Emil Wolk. Dir. Stafford-Clark. (Revival of production first presented on 13 May.)

24 Aug. * *THE PEOPLE SHOW NO. 21: SHOP, MRS BUTTERWORTH by Jeff Nuttall and the company.* Cast: John Darling, Muriel England, Laura Gilbert, Mark Long, Roland Miller, Syd Palmer. (Mgt: The People Show.)

27 Aug. *KEEP TIGHTLY CLOSED IN A COOL DRY PLACE by*

Megan Terry. Cast: Joseph Capone, Davis Hall, Roger Hendricks Simon. Dir. Roger Hendricks Simon. (Mgt: Yale University Theatre Group in assoc. with Open Space Theatre, London.)

27 Aug.   **THE PEOPLE SHOW NO. 8: EVIDENCE** by *Jeff Nuttall and the company.* Cast: *John Darling, Muriel England, Laura Gilbert, Mark Long, Roland Miller, Syd Palmer. (Mgt: The People Show.)*

30 Aug.   **THE PEOPLE SHOW NO. 19: THESE FOOLISH THINGS** by *Jeff Nuttall and the company. Cast: John Darling, Muriel England, Laura Gilbert, Mark Long, Roland Miller, Syd Palmer. (Mgt: The People Show.)*

1 Oct.   ANNA-LUSE by David Mowat. Cast: Erikson, Farbrother, Haygarth, Della Mathieson, Pamela Moiseiwitsch, Derrick O'Connor. Dir. Max Stafford-Clark only this time. (Revival of production first seen at Traverse on 21 Aug.)
NATURAL CAUSES by Ellen Dryden. Cast: Colin McCormack, Pamela Moiseiwitsch. Dir. John Downie. (New production of play premièred by Traverse on 20 Aug. 1967.)

10 Oct.   THE LUNATIC, THE SECRET SPORTSMAN AND THE WOMAN NEXT DOOR. Credits as before – except Galbraith rpl. Claris Erickson. (Revival of play premièred at Traverse on 23 July.)

18 Oct.   COMINGS AND GOINGS by Megan Terry. Cast selected from: Erickson, Farbrother, Haygarth, McCormack, Pamela Moiseiwitsch, O'Connor. Dir. Stafford-Clark. (Revival of production first presented on 13 May and last rev. 22 Aug.)

20 Nov.   † WAR by Jean Claude van Itallie. Cast: Michael Elphick, Richard Howard, Rosamund Nelson.
† MUZEEKA by John Guare. Cast: Lesley Brennan, Pavel Douglas, Michael Elphick, Richard Howard, Sall Insull, Rosamund Nelson. Both plays dir. Roger Hendricks Simon. Des. Mildred Hendricks. Lgt. Andre Tammes.

10 Dec.   * **CLOWN** – devised by Emil Wolk. Cast: Judith Carey, Jon Carfrae, Rosemary Davey, Ian Halliburton, Richard Love. Dir. Ros Clark. Cos. Berenice Sidney. (Mgt: Theatre Workshop, Edinburgh.)

11 Dec.   **THE PARTY** by *Slawomir Mrozek.* Dir. John Adams. (Mgt: Edinburgh Combination. New production of play given its British première by Traverse on 28 Aug. 1964.)

27 Dec.   * **THE LINE OF LEAST EXISTENCE** by Rosalyn Drexler. Music by Skin. Cast: Claris Erikson, Pamela Farbrother, Anthony Haygarth, Colin McCormack, Toby Salaman – with Gillies Buchan, Colin Hay, Bill Johnston, Ed Jones. Dir. Max Stafford-Clark. Des. John Downie and Catriona MacTavish. Lgt. Gerry Jenkinson. M.D. Bernard Sumner. (Rev. 19 Mar. 1969 at Liverpool University Arts Festival and transfers to Stables Theatre Club, Manchester on 23 Mar.)

1969

28 Jan.   **BROCHE** by *Stewart Conn. Cast: Jane Aldgate, Harry Gribbin, John Hunt, John King, Ken Langdon. Dir. Tony Aldgate. Des. Charles Alty. (Mgt: Edinburgh University Dramatic Society.)*

28 Jan.   **BOX AND COX** by J. Madison Morton. Cast: Anthony Haygarth, Colin McCormack, Toby Salaman. Dir. Anthony Haygarth. (New production – with one of the same cast – of the play which last opened at the Traverse on 11 Apr. 1968.)

4 Feb.   **THE PEOPLE SHOW NO. 24: WALTER** by *Jeff Nuttall. Cast: Laura Gilbert, Mark Long, Roland Miller. (Mgt: The People Show.)*

5 Feb.   **THE PEOPLE SHOW NO. 23: TENNIS** by *Jeff Nuttall and the*

company. *Cast: Laura Gilbert, Mark Long, Roland Miller. (Mgt: The People Show.)*

18 Feb. *** DRACULA** by John Downie, Claris Erikson, Stanley Eveling, Alan Jackson, David Mowat, Robert Nye, Bill Watson and the company from a scenario by John Downie and Max Stafford-Clark. *Cast: Susan Carpenter, Anthony Haygarth, Sue Lefton, Colin McCormack, Toby Salaman. Dir. Max Stafford-Clark and John Downie. (Transfers to Close Theatre Club, Glasgow on 11 Mar. Transfers to Ledlanet Nights Festival in summer. Rev. 24 Aug. at New Traverse. Transfers to Mickery Theatre, Amsterdam on 7 Oct.)*

28 Feb. *THE LOVER by Harold Pinter. (Mgt: Edinburgh University Dramatic Society. New production of play which last opened at Traverse on 20 Oct. 1964.)*

11 Mar. **†** *THE SUCCESSFUL LIFE OF 3 by Marie Irene Forness. Cast: Neil Johnstone, Stephen Rea, Dinah Stabb.*
ALTERNATIVES by the Company. Music by Hugh Portnow. Cast: Maurice Colbourne, Neil Johnstone, Nancy Meckler, Pauline Kelly, Hugh Portnow, Stephen Rea, Tony Sibbald, Dinah Stabb.
Both plays dir. Nancy Meckler. Cos. Claire Sorrell. (Mgt: The Freehold.)

14 Mar. *MR JELLO by George Birimisa. Music by Hugh Portnow. Cast: Maurice Colbourne, Nancy Meckler, Stephen Rea, Tony Sibbald, Dinah Stabb. Dir. Nancy Meckler. Cos. Claire Sorrell. (Mgt: The Freehold.)*

27 Mar. **IN A COTTAGE HOSPITAL** by Carey Harrison. Cast Raymond Bowers, Joyce Donaldson, Annette Kerr, Amanda Murray, Adam Ver-

ney, Gordon Whiting. Dir. Guy Slater.

1 Apr. *HOW BROPHY MADE GOOD by David Hare. Cast: Hilary Charlton, Moris Fahri, William Hoyland, Nicholas Nachtal. Dir. the author. (Mgt: Portable Theatre.)*

11 Apr. *CLOWNS HOUR. Dir. Robin Lefevre. (Mgt: Robin Lefevre Mime Company.)*

16 Apr. *CHAMBER MUSIC by Arthur Kopit. Cast includes: Susan Huggins, Lanni McInnes, Gabrielle Rose.*
† *FRAGMENTS by Murray Schisgal. Cast includes: Norman Browning, Roxanne Erwin, Blain Fairman, Gordon Honey. Both plays dir. Tom Kerr. (Mgt: West Canadian Youth Theatre.)*

17 Apr. ** HOW DO YOU DO IT, CHARLIE WAGG by John Rudlin. Cast: Ian Charleson, Tim Stephen-Jones, John Marwick, Lesley Mitchell, Geoffrey O'Kane, Gordon Roberts, George Rubienski, John Watt. Dir. Tony Aldgate. Lgt. John Cumming. (Mgt: Edinburgh University Dramatic Society.)*

22 Apr. *'DARKNESS THEATRE' – Triple bill of 'radio experiences' for the theatre using live unscripted voice sources' consisting of:*
THE DREAM by Barry Bermange.
AMOR DEI by Barry Bermange.
THE EVENINGS OF CERTAIN LIVES by Barry Bermange.
(Mgt: Barry Bermange.)

25 Apr. *THE PUNY LITTLE LIFE SHOW by Roger McGough with John Gorman and Mike McGear. Cast: John Gorman, Mike McGear, Roger McGough. (Mgt: The Scaffold.)*

1 May *** ANOTHER TOWN** by Leo Lehmann. Cast: Sue Lefton, Ann Russell, Toby Salaman. Dir. Max Stafford-Clark.

PLAY by Samuel Beckett. Cast: Sue Lefton, Ann Russell, Toby Salaman. Dir. Max Stafford-Clark. Des. Neil Lumsden. Lgt. Gerry Jenkinson. ('Play' transfers to New Traverse on 29 Aug.)

8 May † **FREEDOM FOR CLEMENCE** by Tancred Dorst. Cast: Rosamund Birks, Michael Howarth, John Hunt. Dir. Laurence A. Ewashen.

21 May * **LIES ABOUT VIETNAM** by C. P. Taylor. Cast: Anthony Haygarth, Jonathon Holt, William Hoyland.
* **TRUTH ABOUT SARAJEVO** by C. P. Taylor. Cast: Jonathan Holt, William Hoyland, Maggie Jordan.
Both plays dir. Alan Dosser.

10 June **THE SPORT OF MY MAD MOTHER** by Ann Jellicoe. Cast: Susan Carpenter, Anthony Haygarth, Sue Lefton, Colin McCormack, Ann Russell, Toby Salaman, Max Stafford-Clark. Dir. Paul Tomlinson. Lgt. Gerry Jenkinson.

1 July * **DEAR JANET ROSENBERG, DEAR MR KOONING** by Stanley Eveling. Cast: Susan Carpenter, Anthony Haygarth. Dir. Max Stafford-Clark. (Transfers to New Traverse on 26 Aug. Subsequently transfers to Royal Court Theatre Upstairs on 17 Sept. Then tours to Mickery Theatre, Amsterdam on 4 Oct. and Jomfru Ane Teatret, Aalborn, Denmark on 13 Oct. before returning to Theatre Upstairs on 20 Oct. Filmed in Holland for Dutch TV. Traverse production broadcast on BBC Radio 4 Scotland on 27 Oct. with original cast – radio presentation by Stewart Conn.)

5 Aug. * **SAWNEY BEAN** by Robert Nye and Bill Watson. Cast: Susan Carpenter, Anthony Haygarth, Sue Lefton, Colin McCormack, Ann Russell, Toby Salaman. Dir. Max Stafford-Clark. (Transfers to New Theatre on 28 Aug.)

24 Aug. **Traverse Theatre Club moves from 60 fixed seat 'traverse' theatre in the Lawnmarket to flexible modular 100 seat theatre converted from a former sailmaker's loft at 112 West Bow in the Grassmarket. On 17 Sept. BBC Radio 4 Scotland broadcasts a programme in celebration produced by Stewart Conn entitled 'Traverse Theatre 2' which includes a recording of the part of the opening ceremony undertaken by the Arts Minister, Jennie Lee. The Old Traverse Theatre is then used as the home of the Traverse Workshop Company before eventual conversion to housing.**

24 Aug. **DRACULA.** Credits as before – except dir. Stafford-Clark only plus Lgt. Roland Miller. (Revival of production premièred at Old Traverse on 18 Feb.)

26 Aug. **DEAR JANET ROSENBERG, DEAR MR KOONING.** Credits as before. (Transfer of production premièred at Old Traverse on 1 July.)

26 Aug. *THE MAN WHO ALMOST KNEW EAMONN ANDREWS by John Heilpern. Cast: Doug Fisher. Dir. Robin Midgely. (Mgt: Doug Fisher.)*

28 Aug. **SAWNEY BEAN.** Credits as before. (Transfer of production premièred at Old Traverse on 5 Aug.)

29 Aug. **PLAY.** Credits as before. (Transfer of production first seen at Old Traverse on 1 May.)

1 Oct. *'PACKAGE' – Sextuple Bill from Off-Off-Broadway consisting of:*
***EX-MISS COOPER QUEEN ON A SET OF PILLS** by Megan Terry.*
***BIRDBATH** by Leonard Melfi.*
***THE HUNTER AND THE BIRD** by Jean-Claude van Itallie.*
***Play with unknown title** by Jean-Claude van Itallie.*

THE LOVELIEST AFTER-NOON OF THE YEAR by John Guare.
BOTTICELLI by Terence McNally.
Casts: Garrick Hagon, Chris Malcolm, Mildred Mayne, Lisa Ross. Dir. Roger Hendricks Simon. (Mgt: Open Space Theatre, London.)

4 Oct. * **WHITE PANTOMIME** – dev. Lindsay Kemp. Cast: Lindsay Kemp. (Mgt: Lindsay Kemp.)

14 Oct. **MONSIEUR ARTAUD** by Michael Almaz. Cast: Sarah Golding, Tony Mathews. Dir. Chris Parr.

25 Oct. **THE UNDERGROUND LOVERS** – adpt. Pip Simmons from the play by Jean Tardieu. (Mgt: Pip Simmons Theatre Group.)

28 Oct. * **DORABELLA** by David Selbourne. Cast: Doreen Mantle, Ursula Mohan, Drew Woods, Phil Woods. Dir. Peter James. Lgt. Gerry Jenkinson.

7 Nov. *'Three Plays for Fun and Laughter'* – adpt. Danielle Grunberg from originals by George Courteline. Dir. Danielle Grunberg. (Mgt: Danielle Grunberg.)

14 Nov. **AN EVENING WITH FANNY BURNEY** – devised by Annie Inglis from the diaries of Fanny Burney. Cast: Rose McBain. Dir. Annie Inglis. (Mgt: Annie Inglis.)

25 Nov. **BREAD AND BUTTER** by C. P. Taylor. Cast: Michael Harrigan, Maggie Jordan, Peter Lincoln, Eileen Nicholas. Dir. Roland Rees. Lgt. Gerry Jenkinson.

15 Dec. **Max Stafford-Clark resigns as Artistic Director in order to concentrate on setting up the new Traverse Workshop Company.**

26 Dec. **THE TECHNICIANS** by Olwen Wymark. Cast: Dallas Adams, Michael Harrigan, Antonia Pemberton, John Shedden, Ian White. (Version of the play

seen at the Traverse had been considerably re-written by its author since its première production.)
* **STAY WHERE YOU ARE** by Olwen Wymark. Cast: Louise Breslin, Michael Harrigan, Antonia Pemberton, Ian White. Both plays dir. Michael Meacham. Lgt. Gerry Jenkinson.

28 Dec.* **THE FOWL CHURKEN-DOOSE** – a mime show by the company. Cast: Harry Newman, Rivard, Emil Wolk. (Mgt: Theatre Workshop, Edinburgh.)

1970

29 Jan. **THE FOUR SEASONS** by Arnold Wesker. Cast: Michael Irving, Sue Lefton. Dir. Toby Salaman. Lgt. Gerry Jenkinson.

3 Feb. **Michael Rudman is appointed as Artistic Director and his programme takes effect from the end of April.**

5 Feb. **THEY ALONE KNOW** by Jean Tardieu. Cast: Charles Dawson, Elaine Dishington, Moira Johnson, Hilton McCrae, Giles Webster.
WHO GOES THERE? by Jean Tardieu. Cast: Elaine Dishington, Moira Johnson, Hilton McCrae, Gordon Roberts, Giles Webster.
CONVERSATION SYMPHONIETTA by Jean Tardieu. Cast: Ian Charleson, Charles Dawson, Elaine Dishington, John Hetherington, Hilton McCrae, Gordon Roberts, Ruth Sallon, Bernice Stegers, Giles Webster.
Dir. Ian Charleson. Lgt. John Cumming. (Mgt: Edinburgh University Dramatic Society.)

19 Feb. * **HUMAN SEXUAL RESPONSE PART II** by Karl Tunberg. Cast: Paul Gayman, Pamela Rowland.
NOW THERE'S JUST THE THREE OF US by Mike Weller. Cast: Clive Endersby, Paul

125

Gayman, Davis Hall, Peter Marinker, Pamela Rowland. Both plays dir. Roland Rees. Lgt. Gerry Jenkinson. (The production of 'Now There's Just The Three Of Us' was originally presented by the Open Space Theatre, London on 12 Aug. 1969 with Peter Marinker and Pamela Rowland in the cast.)

3 Mar. **QUO VADIS** by the company. (Mgt: Les Tretaux Libre de Geneve.)

5 Mar. **REQUIEM FOR ROMEO AND JULIET** by the company. (Mgt: Les Tretaux Libre de Geneve.)

10 Mar. **PERICLES** by William Shakespeare. Adpt. Snoo Wilson. Cast: Will Morgan, Tony Robinson, Chris Waite, Susan White. Dir. Snoo Wilson. (Mgt: Portable Theatre.)

12 Mar. **ELECTRA** by Euripides. Trans. David Thompson. Cast: Vivien Berry, Elaine Dishington, Freda Dowie, Greg Jarboe, Thalia Kouri, Jeanna L'Esty, Andrew McCulloch, Catriona McTavish, Fay McTavish, Terence Skelton, Ginny Thompson. Dir. and Des. Hovhannes I. Pilikian. Masks and Cos. Jennifer Heap and Claris Erikson. Lgt. Gerry Jenkinson. Original music by Phil Grieve.

19 Mar. **COLOURS** by Annie Stainer and Jack Birkett. Cast: Jack Birkett, Annie Stainer.
INSECT – dev. Annie Stainer. Chor. Annie Stainer and Jack Birkett. Cast: Jack Birkett, Annie Stainer.
Both plays dir. Annie Stainer. Des. Reg Bolton. (Mgt: Eclipse. 'Insect' rev. 8 June 1971 at Traverse.)

31 Mar. **THE DUCHESS OF MALFI** by John Webster. Adpt. the company. Cast: Maurice Colbourne, Neil Johnston, Nina Glass, Hugh Portnow, Stephen Rea, Dinah Stabb,

Tony Sibbald, Tim Thomas, Rowan Wylie. Dir. Nancy Mecker. Cos. Karen Roston. (Mgt: The Freehold.)

7 Apr. **DRUMS IN THE NIGHT** by Bertolt Brecht. Trans. Richard Beckley. Cast: Maurice Colbourne, Neil Johnston, Nina Glass, Hugh Portnow, Stephen Rea, Dinah Stabb, Tony Sibbald, Tim Thomas, Rowan Wylie. Dir. Nancy Meckler. (Mgt: The Freehold.)

14 Apr. **DUO** – Chor. Geoff Moore. Music by Edie Gormet, Thelonius Monk, The Rolling Stones and Frank Sinatra. Cast: Hilary Beckett, Brian Hibbard.
STRANDED – Chor. Geoff Moore. Music by Scott Joplin. Cast: George O'Brien.
BENEDICTION – Chor. Geoff Moore. Music by the Incredible String Band. Cast: John Carter (a.k.a. Cassidy), Robin Courbet, Suz Dobson, Pamela Moore, George O'Brien, Julie Whitford. All three pieces dir. Geoff Moore. Des. and Lgt. Peter Mumford. (Mgt: Moving Being.)

17 Apr. * **THREE PIECES** – Chor. Geoff Moore. Music by Igor Stravinsky. Cast: Robin Courbet, Suz Dobson, Julie Whitford.
TRIO – Chor. Geoff Moore. Text drawn from Proust and R. D. Laing. Music by J. S. Bach and Bob Dylan. Cast: John Carter (a.k.a. Cassidy), Pamela Moore, George O'Brien.
* **THIS MIX** – Chor. Geoff Moore.
All three pieces dir. Geoff Moore. Des. and Lgt. Peter Mumford. (Mgt: Moving Being.)

15 Apr. **UNDER MILK WOOD** by Dylan Thomas. (Mgt: Greg Jarboe.)

21 Apr. **COWBOYS NO. 2** by Sam Shepard. Cast: David Hayman, Anthony Trent.
ICARUS'S MOTHER by Sam Shepard. Cast: David Hayman,

Barrie Houghton, Carolyn Jones, Ann Mitchell, Anthony Trent. **THE ROCK GARDEN** by Sam Shepard. Cast: David Hayman, Barrie Houghton, Ann Mitchell. Dir. Robert Walker. Des. Bob Ringwood. Lgt. Ian Pygott. (Mgt: Close Theatre Club Ensemble, Glasgow.)

1 May   **THE AMERICAN DREAM** by Edward Albee. (Mgt: Edinburgh University Dramatic Society.)

5 May   **THE PEOPLE SHOW NO. 33: GLASS** by the company. Cast: John Darling, Laura Gilbert, Mark Long. (Mgt: The People Show.)

8 May   **THE PEOPLE SHOW NO. 32: BUTTER** by the company. Cast: John Darling, Laura Gilbert, Mark Long, Roland Miller. (Mgt: The People Show.)

14 May   * **MUCK FROM THREE ANGLES** by David Halliwell. Cast: Sheila Ballentine, Tina Packer, Jack Shepherd. Dir. Michael Wearing.
* **A DISCUSSION** by David Halliwell. Cast: Paul Freeman, Tina Packer. Dir. Michael Rudman.
A WHO'S WHO OF FLAPLAND by David Halliwell. Cast: James Garbutt, Russell Hunter. Dir. Michael Rudman. Lgt. Gerry Jenkinson for all three plays. (Traverse in assoc. with Quipu Productions.)

22 May   * **DRIVE-IN** by David Kranes. Cast: Paul Freeman, Tina Packer. Dir. Jack Shepherd. (Mgt: Jack Shepherd.)

4 June   **STAND FOR MY FATHER** – adpt. Mike Gwilym and Nigel Hawthorne (under the pen names John Hudson and Francis Coleridge) from Shakespeare's 'Henry IV' plays. Cast: Paul Freeman, Marilyn Fridjohn, James Garbutt, Mike Gwilym, Robert Hamilton, Nigel Hawthorne, Roland

Oliver, Tim Preece, Job Stewart. Dir. Michael Rudman. A.D. Jules Boardman. Lgt. Gerry Jenkinson.

12 June   * **THE NIGHT BEFORE PARIS** by Martin Sherman. Cast: Claris Erikson, Robert Hamilton. Dir. Job Stewart. Lgt. Gerry Jenkinson.

30 June   **COCKY** by Jack Ronder. Cast: Russell Hunter. Dir. Anthony Kearney. (Mgt: Russell Hunter.)

9 July   * **CURTAINS** by Tom Mallin. Cast: Nigel Hawthorne, Antonia Pemberton, Ursula Smith. Dir. Michael Rudman. Lgt. Gerry Jenkinson. (World professional première production. Previously produced by the amateur Tavistock Repertory Company at the Tower Theatre, Canonbury, London on 9 Jan 1970. Traverse production is rev. 25th Aug. Transfers to Open Space Theatre, London on 19 Jan. 1971.)

14 July   * **FLOWERS** – dev. Lindsay Kemp (assisted by Lindsay Levy) inspired by Jean Genet's 'Our Lady of the Flowers'. Original music by Andrew Wilson. Cast includes: Michael Garrett, Maggie Jordan, Lindsay Kemp, Giles Milinaire, The Incredible Orlando (formerly Jack Birkett), Annie Stainer, Christopher Thomson. Dir. and Des. Lindsay Kemp. Other music by Steve Reich. (Mgt: Lindsay Kemp Theatre Troupe. Revived at Traverse on 3 Nov. 1970 and 1 Aug. 1972.)

30 July   * **ULTRAMARINE** by David Brett. Cast: Annie Balfour, Penny Casdagli, Hugh Fraser, Toby Salaman – with Andrew Adie, Linda Goddard, Michael Harrigan, David McNiven, Angie Rew.
* **MOTHER EARTH** – music and lyrics by David McNiven (with assistance from Ian Brown). Cast: Annie Balfour, Penny Casdagli, Hugh Fraser, Linda God-

dard, Michael Harrigan, David McNiven, Angie Rew, Toby Salaman – with Andrew Adie. Both plays dir. Max Stafford-Clark. Lgt. Gerry Jenkinson. (Mgt: Traverse Workshop Company. Extracts from Traverse production of 'Ultramarine' broadcast on BBC Radio 4 Scotland on 16 Sept. with Balfour, Castagli, Fraser and Salaman from the original cast – presented and introduced by Stafford-Clark and produced for radio by Stewart Conn. 'Mother Earth' revived at Traverse on 2 Dec. 1971.)

31 July **CHRIST WAS A PEACE FREAK.** Cast of 10. Dir. Bill Patterson. (Mgt: Golliardi – Keele University Performance Group.)

20 Aug. * **STRAIGHT UP** by Syd Cheatle. Cast in Edinburgh: Doug Fisher, William Franklyn, Peter Halliday, Polly James, Antonia Pemberton, Tim Wylton. Cast for Leicester, tour and London: Peter Halliday rpl. Ronald Hines. Dir. Michael Rudman. Lgt. Gerry Jenkinson. Traverse by arrangement with David Aukin Associates. Revived in association with Eddie Kulukundis at Phoenix Theatre, Leicester in May 1971 before touring to Dublin, Birmingham, Southsea, Oxford and Leeds. Transfers to Piccadilly Theatre, London on 16 Aug. 1971.)

25 Aug. CURTAINS. Credits as before. (Revival of production premièred at Traverse on 9 July.)

25 Aug. * **STUFF** – a late night enigma dev. The Scaffold. Cast: John Gorman, Polly James, Michael McGear, Roger McGough. (Mgt: The Scaffold.)

26 Aug. **MICROCOSM** – pigment and light in movement with music. (Mgt: Kingsley Cook. Revived at Traverse on 18 June 1974.)

1 Sept. * **FRUIT** by Howard Brenton. Cast: Peter Brenner, Paul Brooke,

Hilary Charlton, Colin McCormack, William Morgan. Dir. David Hare. Des. Jenny Gaskin. (Mgt: Portable Theatre.)

9 Sept. * **UBU AND UBU ARE DEAD** – dev. Jules Boardman and Kevin Sim after the life and works of Alfred Jarry. Music by Bread, Love and Dreams and Michael Garrett. Cast: Doug Fisher, Nigel Hawthorne, Polly James – with Andrew Adie, Michael Garrett, David McNiven, Angie Rew. Dir. Jules Boardman and Kevin Sim. Film sequences by Michael Radford. Slides by Diane Tammes. Lgt. and Sound Gerry Jenkinson.

21 Oct. **THE CARETAKER** by Harold Pinter. Cast: Robert Hamilton, John Lyons, Derrick O'Connor. Dir. Job Stewart. Lgt. Nick Heppel. (Traverse at Aberdeen Arts Centre. Tours to Fort Augustus, Dingwall, Dundee University, Harbour Arts Centre in Irvine, Girvan Beach Pavilion, Solgirth Arts and Theatre Club in Kirkintilloch, Alloa, Greenock, Adam Smith Centre in Kirkcaldy and Peebles High School. Rev. 8 Dec. at Traverse. New production of play which last opened at the Old Traverse on 11 Feb. 1964.)

27 Oct. † **DISASTER STRIKES THE HOME** by Charles Dizenzo. Cast: Clive Endersby, Jane Fox, Ron House, Bernard Hopkins, Ursula Smith, Anthony Trent. Dir. Jack Shepherd. Lgt. Nick Heppel.

3 Nov. FLOWERS. Authorship and production credits as before. Cast includes: Lindsay Kemp, The Incredible Orlando. (Revival of production premièred at Traverse on 14 July. Revived at Traverse on 1 Aug. 1972.)

8 Nov. * **ONE POTATO, TWO POTATO** by Douglas Livingston. Cast: David Burke, Anna Calder-Marshall. Dir. the author. (Mgt: Royal Lyceum Theatre Company, Edinburgh.)

19 Nov.   *** A GAME CALLED ARTHUR**
by David Snodin. Cast:
Timothy Dalton, Edward Jews-
bury, Judy Loe. Dir. Michael
Rudman. (World Professional
Première Production. Pre-
viously produced by the amateur Oxford Theatre Group
with the author in the cast at
St. Mary's Hall, Edinburgh on
24 Aug. Traverse production
transfers to Royal Court
Theatre Upstairs, London on 23
Feb. 1971.)

20 Nov.   *** THE KING AND THE
QUEEN** *by F. W. Willetts. Dir.
Toby Salaman. (Mgt: Traverse
Workshop Company.)*

1 Dec.   **THE STORY OF GILGA-
MESH, KING OF URUK, HIS
FRIENDSHIP WITH ENKIDU,
THE DEATH OF ENKIDU,
AND THE KING'S SEARCH
FOR EVERLASTING LIFE** *by
Frederick Proud. Dir. the author.
Des. John Hale. (Mgt: Soho
Theatre.)*

8 Dec.   **THE CARETAKER.** Credits as before.
Transfer of the production which was
first seen at Aberdeen Arts Centre on 21
Oct.)

17 Dec.   **THE BALLAD OF THE MARI
LWYD** by Vernon Watkins.
Cast: Alun Armstrong, Robert
Hamilton, Bernard Hopkins,
Pauline Kelly, Barrie Smith.
Dir. Glen Walford. Lgt. Nick
Heppel.
THE SHEPHERD'S PLAY by
the Master of Wakefield. Adpt.
John Barton. Cast: Alun Arm-
strong, Robert Hamilton, Ber-
nard Hopkins, Pauline Kelly,
Barbara Kukso, Barrie Smith.
Dir. Glen Walford.

22 Dec.   *** TROLLS** *by Annie Stainer.
Cast: Reg Bolton and Annie
Stainer. Dir. the author. Des.
Linda Broda. (Mgt: Theatre
Workshop, Edinburgh.)*

1971

7 Jan.   *** OH STARLINGS** *by Stanley
Eveling. Music by David McNi-
ven. Cast: Hugh Fraser, Anthony
Haygarth. Dir. Toby Salaman.*
† SWEET ALICE *by Stanley
Eveling. Music by David McNi-
ven. Cast: Anthony Haygarth,
Ann Holloway. Dir. Max
Stafford-Clark.
Lgt. Nick Heppel for both plays.
(Mgt: Traverse Workshop Com-
pany. Double Bill revived at Tra-
verse on 28 Feb.)*

12 Jan.   *** OUR SUNDAY TIMES** *by
Stanley Eveling. Music by David
McNiven, Angie Rew and Hugh
Fraser. Cast: Hugh Fraser, Linda
Goddard, Amaryllis Garnett,
Anthony Haygarth (rpl. Ike Isaac-
son for first week of run), Ann
Holloway, Colin McCormack –
with Andrew Adie, David McNi-
ven, John Ramsay, Angie Rew.
Dir. Max Stafford-Clark. Lgt.
Nick Heppel. (Mgt: Traverse
Workshop Company.)*

12 Jan.   **SUPERMAN** *by Pip Simmons
and the company. Music by Chris
Jordan. Cast: Ben Bazell, Nicky
Edmett, Warren Hooper, Lu Jef-
frey, Chris Jordan, Eric Loeh,
Paddy O'Hagan. Dir. Pip Sim-
mons. (Mgt: Pip Simmons Theatre
Group.)*

23 Jan.   *** BOOTS** *by Victor Lewis. Cast:
Hugh Fraser, Anthony Haygarth.
Dir. Colin McCormack. (Mgt:
Traverse Workshop Company.)*

24 Jan.   **FACADE** *by Edith Sitwell. Music
by William Walton. Cast: Ros
Clark, Roger Savage – with Keith
Glossop, Philip Greene, George
Gwilt, Andrew Kinnear, Terence
Newcombe, Andrew Shiva. Con-
ducted by Edward Harper. (Mgt:
Theatre Workshop, Edinburgh.)*

26 Jan.   **EL COCA COLA GRANDE** *by
the company. Cast includes: Kevin
Costello, Ron House, Diz White.
Dir. Ron House. (Mgt: Low Moan*

Spectacular. Revived at Traverse on 23 Nov.)

4 Feb.   * **DO IT** by Pip Simmons and the company after Jerry Rubin's 'Scenarios of the Revolution'. Music by Chris Jordan. Cast: Ben Bazell, Nicky Edmett, Warren Hooper, Lu Jeffrey, Chris Jordan, Eric Loeb, Paddy O'Hagan. Dir. Pip Simmons. Des. Laura Crow and Paddy O'Hagan. Movement by Eric Loeb. (Pip Simmons Theatre Group and the Traverse. Production subsequently tours to Leicester, Sheffield, Southampton, Leicester again, Bristol, Berlin, Denmark, Nancy, Oval Theatre in London, Young Vic Theatre in London, Cardiff, Royal Court Theatre Upstairs in London, Belgrade, Southampton, Mickery Theatre in Amsterdam, Bordeaux and Denmark again.)

23 Feb.   *PIGNIGHT by Snoo Wilson. Cast: Peter Brenner, Paul Freeman, Darryl Kavann. Dir. the author. (Mgt: Portable Theatre.)*

2 Mar.   * **THE ONE TO ONE** by Alisdair Skinner. Cast: Debbie Levin, Michael McKevitt. Dir. Chris Barlas. (Mgt: Alisdair Skinner.)

9 Mar.   **THE FALL OF SAMSON MOROCCO** by John Grillo. *Cast: Christine Donaldson, Jane Girdham, Maxwell Hutcheon, John Melville, Robin Park, Mairi Stewart. Dir. Rosamund Birks. Lgt. John Cumming. Music by Robin Park. (Mgt: Edinburgh University Dramatic Society.)*

11 Mar.   † **PANTAGLEISE** by Michael de Ghelderode. Cast: Arwen Holm, Neil Johnstone, Hugh Portnow, Stephen Rea, Dinah Stabb, Emil Wolk, Rowan Wylie. Dir. Michael Rudman. Lgt. Nick Heppel. (The Freehold in assoc. with the Traverse. Production subsequently seen on tour – including Mickery Theatre in Amsterdam, Denmark, Sweden and London.)

23 Mar.   * **A DAY WITH MY SISTER** by Stephen Poliakoff. Cast: Carole Hayman, Nigel Planer, Patsy Reading, Laurence Terry, David Warren. Dir. David Halliwell.

30 Mar.   * **BORGES AND MYSELF** *by Charles Lewsen. Cast: Charles Lewsen. Dir. and Des. the author. (Mgt: Charles Lewsen.)*

1 Apr.   * **THE COWBOY MOUTH** *by Sam Shepard and Patti Smith. Cast: Brenda Smiley and Donald Sumpter. Dir. Gordon Stewart. (Mgt: Gordon Stewart.)*

8 Apr.   * **A NEW COMMUNION – FOR FREAKS, PROPHETS AND WITCHES** *by the company and Jane Arden. Cast: Sheila Allen, Jane Arden, Elizabeth Danciger, Susanka Frey, Carol Kane, Liz Kustow, Rosie Marcham, Sally Minford, Penelope Slinger. Dir. Jane Arden. Lgt. John Massara and Jack Bond. (Mgt: Holocaust, A Woman's Theatre in assoc. with the Traverse. Transfers to Open Space Theatre, London on 5 May and later tours to Wales before being made into a film.)*

20 Apr.   *ZONK by John Grillo. Cast: Maev Alexander, Hugh Armstrong, Christopher Biggins, Christopher Ravenscroft. Dir. Malcolm Griffiths. (Mgt: Portable Theatre.)*

28 Apr.   **NO ONE WAS SAVED** by Howard Barker. Cast: Richard Durden, Patricia Hodge, Boyd Mackenzie, Susan Sheers. Dir. Chris Barlas.

4 May   *SE HIZO CARNE – Choreographed by Iris Scaccheri. Music includes Beethoven, De Falla and Credence Clearwater Revival. Cast: Iris Scaccheri. (Mgt: Iris Scaccheri.)*

20 May   **HAVE YOU MET OUR RABBIT?** by Michael Stevens. Cast:

Patricia Hodge, Boyd Mackenzie, Susan Sheers. Dir. Richard Durden.
MOBY DICK or 'The White Whale' by Keith Johnstone. Cast: Richard Durden, Anthony Trent. Dir. Boyd Mackenzie. ('Moby Dick' rev. 11 Jan. 1972.)

27 May   'REVUE SKETCHES' by Harold Pinter consisting of: **TROUBLE IN THE WORKS, THE BLACK AND THE WHITE, REQUEST STOP, APPLICANT, NIGHT, LAST TO GO.**
NIGHT SCHOOL by Harold Pinter. Cast for both halves of programme: Paul Freeman, Christine Hargreaves, Derrick O'Connor, Sheila Reid, June Watson, Allan Zipsin. Both halves dir. Job Stewart. Lgt. Katy Bird.

June   **Nicholas Kent is appointed Associate Director.**

8 June   INSECT. *Credits as before – except that Jack Birkett has changed his name to The Incredible Orlando. (Re-worked revival of production which last opened at the Traverse on 19 Mar. 1970.)*

10 June   *PENGUINS – devised by Annie Stainer. Cast: Reg. Bolton, Jenny Donaldson, The Incredible Orlando, Annie Stainer. Dir. Annie Stainer. Des. Reg Bolton. (Mgt: Eclipse.)*

17 June   **STAIRCASE** by Charles Dyer. Cast: Philip Guard, Martin Heller, Andrew Porter. Dir. Mike Ockrent. Des. Constantinous Corouillas. Lgt. John Dee.

22 June   † *MARTIN EVENT by the company. Cast: Michael Brooks, Steven Chapman, Ann Crumb, Donald Habermas, Christine Lahti, Terence Lamunde, Rusty Russ, Clive Sykes, Janice Young. Dir. Paul Holtfreter. Des. Denzil Walker. Lgt. Greg Jarboe. (Mgt: Ann Arbour Mime Troupe.)*

8 July   * **AS TIME GOES BY** by Mustapha Matura. Cast: Robert Aitko, Robert Coleby, Alfred Fagon, Carole Hayman, Mona Hammond, Oscar James, Stefan Kalipha, Patricia Moseley, Corinne Skinner, George Webb (repl. Frank Singuineau from 24 Aug.), T-Bone Wilson. Dir. Roland Rees. Lgt. John Dee. (Traverse and the Royal Court Theatre Upstairs, London in assoc. with Michael White. Transfers to Theatre Upstairs on 14 Sept.)

27 July   **WOYZECK** by Georg Büchner. Cast: Annie Balfour, Morag Deyes, Stewart Forbes, Hugh Fraser, Richard Harboard, Lindsay Kemp, Bill McCabe, Hamish McDonald (a.k.a. Jamie Macdonald Reid), Irene Muir, The Incredible Orlando, Alan Ross, Laurance Rudic, David Stuart, Lauren Vitello. Dir. and Des. Lindsay Kemp. M.D. Hamish McDonald.

5 Aug.   * *IN THE HEART OF THE BRITISH MUSEUM by John Spurling. Music by David McNiven and Angie Rew. Cast: Kevin Costello, Sabin Epstein, Amaryllis Garnett, Linda Goddard, David McNiven, Angie Rew, Tony Rohr – with John Ramsay. Dir. Max Stafford-Clark. Chor. Linda Goddard. Des. Sabin Epstein. Lgt. Bill Muir. (Mgt: Traverse Workshop Company. Rev. 30 Nov.)*

19 Aug.   * *THE NOVELIST by Tom Mallin. Cast: Robin Bailey, Barbara Jefford, John Turner. Dir. Michael Rudman. Lgt. Peter Jeffries. (Traverse by arrangement with David Aukin.)*

24 Aug.   * **LAY BY** by Howard Brenton, Brian Clark, Trevor Griffiths, David Hare, Stephen Poliakoff, Hugh Stoddart and Snoo Wilson. (Peter Ransley left the writing team and took his name off the credits before the opening. However, some of the script as performed was by

131

him.) Cast: Meg Davies, Catherine Kessler, Graham Simpson, James Warrior, Mark York. Dir. Snoo Wilson. (Traverse and Portable Theatre. Transfers to Royal Court Theatre Upstairs, London on 26 Sept. and subsequently to the Open Space Theatre, London.)

25 Aug. *AFTER LIVERPOOL* by James Saunders.
GAMES by James Saunders. Casts: Jane Bond, Judy Monahan, Andrew Norton, Robert Walker. Both plays dir. Naftali Yavin.

4 Sept. *DYNAMO (A Second-Hand Experience)* by Chris Wilkinson. Cast: Andrew Carr, Anthea Cooper, Pat Ford, John Grillo, Malcolm Kaye, Catherine Kessler, Linda Marlowe, Derek Paget, Jenny Runacre. Dir. Howard Panter and Frederick Proud. (Mgt: The Soho Theatre.)

7 Sept. * *P. C. PLOD* – a revue by the Scaffold. Cast: John Gorman, Michael McGear, Roger McGough. (Mgt: The Scaffold.)

14 Oct. * *SPEAK NOW* by Olwen Wymark. Cast: Lorna Heilbron, Peter Howell, Pauline Jamieson, Bill Nighy, Tony Steedman. Dir. Nicholas Kent. Cos. Elaine Hill. Lgt. Peter Jeffries.

26 Oct. * *AND DID HE COME* by Sean Hignett. Cast: Sandra Buchan, Bill Nighy, Tony Steedman. Dir. Nicholas Kent. Lgt. Peter Jeffries.

2 Nov. *THE PEOPLE SHOW NO. 39: THE SAND SHOW* by the company. Cast: Mike Figgis, Laura Gilbert, Mark Long, José Nava. (Mgt: The People Show.)

3 Nov. * *KNOCK KNOX – IT'S THE REFORMATION SHUFFLE* by John Melville. Music by Gillies Buchan. Cast: Anne Anderson, Gillies Buchan, Gordon Cruikshank, Ed Jones, John McNairn, John Melville, John Nicolson, Fred Warder, John Watt. Dir. John Melville. Cos. Irene Melville. Lgt. John Cumming. (Mgt: The New Theatre.)

9 Nov. *AC/DC* by Heathcote Williams. Cast: Jonathan Bergman, John Grillo, Claudette Houchen, Pat Quinn, Henry Woolf. Dir. Nicholas Wright. Touring production supervised by Henry Woolf. Des. Douglas Heap. A.D. Harriet McLaren. (Mgt: Royal Court Theatre Upstairs.)

18 Nov. * *DOCTOR GALLI* by Conrad Bromberg. Cast: Henry Woolf. Dir. Saxon Logan. Lgt. Peter Jeffries. (Mgt: Henry Woolf. Revived at Traverse on 29 Nov. 1974.)

23 Nov. *EL COCA COLA GRANDE* by the company. Cast: House, Alan Sheanan, John Smith, White, Gabrielle Vieder. Dir. House. (Mgt: Low Moan Spectacular. Revival of production which last opened at Traverse on 26 Jan.)

30 Nov. *IN THE HEART OF THE BRITISH MUSEUM.* Credits as before. (Revival of production premièred at Traverse on 5 Aug.)

2 Dec. * *BLUBBER* by John Grillo. Cast: Kevin Costello, Amaryllis Garnett, Tony Rohr. Dir. Max Stafford-Clark. (Revived at Traverse on 10 Feb. 1972.)
MOTHER EARTH Author and production credits as before. (Revival of production premièred at Traverse on 30 July 1970.) (Mgt: Traverse Workshop Company.)

8 Dec. * *THE LOONEYS* by John Antrobus. Cast: Barbara Atkinson, Petronella Ford, Richard Franklin, Robert Hamilton, Ralph Nossek, Andrew Porter, John Shrapnel. Dir. Michael Rudman. Lgt. Pete Jeffries. (Traverse by arrangement with David Aukin.)

10 Dec. *THE REAL McGONAGALL* by John Cairney. Cast: John Cairney. Dir. the author. (Mgt: John Cairney.)

23 Dec. *OUTSIDE IN* – devised by Ros Clark. Cast: Mary Cunningham, Martin Curtis. Dir. the author. (Mgt: Theatre Workshop, Edinburgh.)

28 Dec. 'CHRISTMAS PRESENT' –
comprising of:
* **STILL THE SAME OLD
HARRY** by Pete Morgan. Cast:
Giles Block, Susan Carpenter,
Richard Durden, Veronica
Lang.
* **STRANGERS IN A CAFE-
TERIA** by John Antrobus. Cast:
Giles Block, Richard Durden,
Veronica Lang.
* **COT** by Tom Mallin. Cast:
Giles Block, Veronica Lang.
* **TIME FOR GIVING** by Philip
Guard. Cast: Giles Block,
Susan Carpenter.
* **THE HAMMER AND THE
HACKSAW** by John Grillo.
Cast: Giles Block, Susan Car-
penter, Richard Durden, Vero-
nica Lang.
* **HE USED TO PLAY FOR
HEARTS** by Stanley Eveling.
Cast: Giles Block, Susan Car-
penter, Richard Durden, Vero-
nica Lang.
* **AN AMOUR** by David Halli-
well. Cast: Susan Carpenter,
Richard Durden.
* **DEATHSHIELDS** by David
Hare. Cast: Giles Block, Susan
Carpenter, Richard Durden,
Veronica Lang.
* **PASSION PLAY** by C. P.
Taylor. Cast: Susan Carpenter,
Richard Durden.
All nine plays dir. Nicholas
Kent. Lgt. Pete Jeffries.

1972

11 Jan. * **REASON THE SUN KING**
by Snoo Wilson. Cast: Giles
Block, Susan Carpenter,
Richard Durden, Veronica
Lang. Dir. Nicholas Kent.
MOBY DICK or 'The White Whale' by
Keith Johnstone. Cast: Richard Durden,
Anthony Trent. Recreated from Boyd
McKenzie's original production by
Anthony Trent. (Revival of production
which opened at the Traverse on 20
May 1971.)

**WILL THE KING LEAVE THE
TEAPOT?** by John Grillo. Cast:
Giles Block, Susan Carpenter,
Richard Durden, Anthony
Trent. Dir. Chris Barlas.

20 Jan. * *HITLER DANCES* by Howard
*Brenton. Lyrics by David McNi-
ven. Music by David McNiven
and Angie Rew. Cast: Kevin Cos-
tello, Sabin Epstein, Amaryllis
Garnet, Linda Goddard, Carole
Hayman, David McNiven, John
Ramsay, Angie Rew, Tony Rohr.
Dir. Max Stafford-Clark. Lgt. Pete
Jeffries. (Mgt: Traverse Workshop
Company. Revived at Traverse on
4 July.)*

1 Feb. *BEGINNING TO END* by
*Michael Andrews. Cast: Gabrielle
Hamilton. Dir. Michael Andrews.
(Mgt: Gabrielle Hamilton.)*

10 Jan. *BLUBBER. Credits as before – plus: Des.
by Sabin Epstein. Lgt. Pete Jeffries. (Revival
of production premièred at Traverse on 2
Dec. 1971.)*

17 Feb. * **TELL CHARLIE THANKS
FOR THE TRUSS** by Tom
Buchan with improvisation by
the company. Music by Tom
McGrath. Lyrics by McGrath
and Buchan. Cast: Sandra
Buchan, Gavin Douglas,
Michael Harrigan, Ian (a.k.a.
Kenny) Ireland, Charles Kear-
ney, Anne Kidd, John Malcolm,
Sean McCarthy, Mark Penfold.
Dir. Michael Rudman. Lgt. Pete
Jeffries.

14 Mar. *GENESIS* by Roy Kift. Music by
*Carl Davis. Cast: Paula Dioni-
sotti, Peter Evans, Mike Harley,
Neil Johnston, Wolf Kahler,
Christopher Ravenscroft, Jennie
Stoller, Ruth Tansey. Dir. Nancy
Meckler. (Mgt: The Freehold.)*

14 Mar. *MARY, MARY by Koy Kift.
Cast: Marty Cruickshank, Paula
Dionisotti, Mike Harley, Neil
Johnston, Wolf Kahler, Christopher
Ravenscroft, Jennie Stoller, Ruth
Tansey. Dir. Nancy Mecker.
(Mgt: The Freehold.)*

22 Mar. **THE MAROWITZ HAMLET** – *adapted from Shakespeare by Charles Marowitz. Cast: Candida Fawsitt, Ian Flavin, Petronella Ford, Philip Marchant, Tony Milner, Richard Monette, Michael O'Donoughue, David Scofield, Malcolm Storry, Derek Woodward. Dir. the author. Des. by Robin Don. A.D.'s Walter Donohue, John Burgess. (Mgt: Open Space Theatre, London.)*

22 Mar. **HAM-OMLET** *by Charles Marowitz – exercises and improvisations derived from Shakespeare's 'Hamlet'. Cast: as for 'The Marowitz Hamlet'. Dir. Charles Marowitz. (Mgt: Open Space Theatre.)*

13 Apr. **LITTLE MALCOLM AND HIS STRUGGLE AGAINST THE EUNUCHS** by David Halliwell. Cast: Ron Bain, Kenneth Cranham, Ralph Cotterill, Catherine Kessler, Denis Lawson. Dir. Mike Ockrent. Set. by Sheila Ness and Caroline McCulloch. Lgt. John Dee.

15 Apr. **SITUATION VACANT** *by the company. Dir. Sue Birtwhistle. (Mgt: Royal Lyceum Theatre-in-Education Company.)*

25 Apr. **KHARTOUM** *by John Melville. Cast: Anne Anderson, Max Hutcheon, Admed Kass, Hilton McCrae, Ian Mandleberg, Jim Martin, Yusef Malik, David Peate, Kalid Suliman, Giles Webster. Dir. the author. Lgt. Sandy Neilson. (Mgt: The New Theatre.)*

2 May **OCCUPATIONS** *by Trevor Griffiths. Cast: Diana Chappel, Tamara Hinchco, John Joyce, Graham Lines, Gavin Richards, Peter Sproule. Dir. Roland Rees. Des. by Di Seymour. (Mgt: 7:84 Theatre Company, England.)*

11 May * **PRIVATE PARTS** by Howard Barker. Cast: Susannah (a.k.a. Susie) Blake, Robert Bridges, Anthony Corlan (a.k.a. Higgins), Philip Guard, Denise Hirst, Elizabeth Hughes, Oscar James, Catherine Kessler, Lewis Teasdale. Dir. Nicholas Kent. Lgt. John Dee.

21 May **PLAYS FOR RUBBER GO-GO GIRLS** *by Chris Wilkinson. Cast includes: Patricia Hodge, Paul Seed, Emma Thomson. Dir. Malcolm Griffiths. (Mgt: Portable Theatre.)*

30 May **THE PEOPLE SHOW NO. 44: THE FLYING SHOW** *by the company. Cast: Mike Figgis, Laura Gilbert, Mark Long, José Nava. (Mgt: The People Show.)*

3 June **FITS AND STITCHES** *by the company. Dir. Sue Birthwhistle. (Mgt: Royal Lyceum Theatre-in-Education Company.)*

16 June * **THE BLACK AND WHITE MINSTRELS** by C. P. Taylor. Cast: Taiwo Ajai, Tom Conti, Harry Hankin, Alan Howard, Elizabeth Hughes, Patti Love. Dir. Michael Rudman. Lgt. Paul Spaven. (Rev. 24 August. Transfers to Hampstead Theatre Club, London on 21 Jan. 1974.)

20 June **THE DEFORMED TRANSFORMED** *by Lord Byron. Adpt. Steve Rumbelow. Cast: Teresa d'Abrua, Paul O'Connor, Bronson Shaw, Dave Walsh, Nigel Watson. Dir. Steve Rumbelow. Des. by Rita Siddon. (Mgt: Triple Action Theatre.)*

4 July *FLOWERS. HITLER DANCES. Credits as before – except minus Sabin Epstein. (Revival of production premièred at Traverse on 20 Jan.)*

13 July **THE RELAPSE** by Sir John Vanbrugh. Adpt. Michael Rudman. Cast: Fenella Fielding, Philip Guard, Elizabeth Hughes, Malcolm Ingram, Michael Percival. Dir. Michael Rudman. Lgt. Paul Spaven. Music by Adrian Secchi.

13 July **YOUR HUMBLE SERVANT** – *dev. Robert Robertson. Cast: Robert Robertson. Dir. Brian Ellis. (Mgt: Robert Robertson.)*

1 Aug. *FLOWERS. Author credits as before. Cast: Robert Anthony, Mark Baldwin, Stuart*

Forbes, Linda Goddard, Lindsay Levy, Lindsay Kemp, Ian Oliver, The Incredible Orlando, Carling Paton, Brian Rudkin, Andrew Wilson. Dir. and Des. by Lindsay Kemp. A.D. Lindsay Levy. Other music by Steve Reich. (Mgt: Lindsay Kemp Theatre Troupe. Revival of production premièred at Traverse on 14 July 1970.)

10 Aug. * CARAVAGGIO BUDDY by Stanley Eveling. Cast: Taiwo Ajai, Janet Chappell, Richard Durden, Ian Holm, Elizabeth Hughes, Patti Love, Tim Wylton. Dir. Michael Rudman. Cos. Brigid Holm. Lgt. Paul Spaven. Music and sound by Iwan Williams.

15 Aug. * AMALFI by David Mowat from 'The Duchess of Malfi' by John Webster. Music by David McNiven, John Ramsay and Angie Rew. Cast: Kevin Costello, Amaryllis Garnett, Carole Hayman, Angie Rew, Tony Rohr, Philip Timmins – with David McNiven, John Ramsay. Dir. Max Stafford-Clark. Lgt. Bill Muir. Movement by Sue Lefton. (Mgt: Traverse Workshop Company.)

24 Aug. THE BLACK AND WHITE MINSTRELS. Credits as before – except Howard rpl. Julian Curry. Cast in London includes: Tom Conti, Alan Howard, Elizabeth Hughes, Patti Love. Des. John Halle (in London). (Revival of production premièred at Traverse on 16 June. Transfers to Hampstead Theatre Club, London on 21 Jan. 1974.)

26 Aug. † REPLIQUE by Josef Szajna. Cast: Taiwo Ajai, Susanna (a.k.a. Susie) Blake, Trena Jun, Antoni Pszoniak, Philip Timmins, Josef Wieckorek. Dir. the author. (Traverse in association with Richard Demarco Gallery.)

29 Aug. THE PEOPLE SHOW NO. 46: THE PARIS SHOW by the company. Cast: Mike Figgis, Laura Gilbert, Mark Long, José Nava, Derek Wilson. (Mgt: The People Show.)

5 Sept. † SLEEP by Jack Gelber. Cast: Elizabeth Adare, Janet Chappell, Michael Elphick, Ian (a.k.a.

Kenny) Ireland, Sue Lefton, Kevin O'Connor, Leslie Rainey. Dir. Gordon Stewart. (Mgt: Jack Temchin and Kelley Winter.)

12 Oct. SALOME by Oscar Wilde. Adpt. Lindsay Levy. Cast: Robert Anthony, Ray Arazma, Mark Baldwin, Annie Balfour, Christmas Brown, John Church, Les Davidson, Lindsay Kemp, Andy Munro, The Incredible Orlando, Jean Selkirk, Giles Webster. Dir. Lindsay Kemp. A.D. Lindsay Levy. Cos. by Stuart Forbes and Mark Baldwin. M.D. Les Davidson. (Mgt: Lindsay Kemp Theatre Troupe.)

13 Oct. * SIDESHOW – dev. Lindsay Kemp. Music by Mama Flyer. Cast: Robert Anthony, Mark Baldwin, Annie Balfour, Christmas Brown, John Church, Lindsay Kemp, Lindsay Levy, The Incredible Orlando, Giles Webster – with the Mama Flyer Band. Dir. and Des. Lindsay Kemp. (Mgt: Lindsay Kemp Theatre Troupe.)

2 Nov. * THE BLOOD STREAM by Richard Crane from an idea by Aeschylus. Cast: Charles Bolton, Diane Fletcher, Samantha Green, Roland Oliver, Guy Slater, Tamara Ustinov. Dir. Chris Parr. Lgt. Cameron Crosby.

21 Nov. METAMORPHOSIS by Franz Kafka. Adpt. Steven Berkoff. Cast: Steven Berkoff, Maggie Jordan, Denis Lawson, Stephen Williams, Sammie Winmill. Dir. Steven Berkoff. Lgt. Shane. (Mgt: London Theatre Group.)

30 Nov. COME AND BE KILLED by Stanley Eveling. Cast: Stuart Bevan, Derek Carpenter, Narissa Knights, Judy Leibert. Dir. Nicholas Kent. (New production of play premièred at Old Traverse on 11 July 1967. Slightly rewritten by the author for this revival.)

Dec. Nicholas Kent leaves the position of Associate Director.

135

19 Dec. *** DAUGHTER, DAUGHTER, FETCH THE WATER** – *dev. Annie Stainer. Cast: Dawn Archibald, Reg Bolton, Annie Stainer. Dir. and des. by Annie Stainer. (Mgt: Theatre Workshop, Edinburgh. Revived at Traverse on 11 Dec. 1973.)*

26 Dec. **SANDY WILSON THANKS THE LADIES** *by Sandy Wilson. Cast: Sandy Wilson. (Mgt. Sandy Wilson.)*

1973

2 Jan. *** THE PEOPLE SHOW NO. 48: JOSÉ'S PIGS/CATTLE SHOW** *by the company. Cast: Mike Figgis, Laura Gilbert, Mark Long, José Nava, Derek Wilson. (Mgt: The People Show.)*

18 Jan. **'Traverse Tenth Anniversary Programme'** recorded in auditorium with live audience by BBC 1's 'Current Account'.

21 Jan. **'TRAVERSE TENTH ANNIVERSARY GALA'.** Cast (in order of appearance): Nicholas Fairburn, 'Bread, Love and Dreams', Russell Hunter, Andrew Cruikshank, Marty Cruikshank, The Incredible Orlando, Lindsay Kemp, Alan Jackson, Bill Simpson, Ursula Smith, Michael Rudman, Jim Haynes, John Cairney, Fenella Fielding, Tom Fleming, Polly James, The Scaffold. Lgt. Gerry Jenkinson. Musical Director: Adrian Secchi. (Traverse at King's Theatre, Edinburgh.)

25 Jan. **THE NUNS** by Edvardo Manet. Trans. Robert Baldick. Cast: David Beddard, John Breslin, Patricia Healey, Ralph Nossek. Dir. Mike Ockrent. Lgt. Cameron Crosby.

31 Jan. *** THAT'S THE SHOW** *by Lindsay Kemp. Cast: Lindsay Kemp. Dir. and Des. the author. (Mgt: Lindsay Kemp Theatre Troupe.)*

13 Feb. **JANITRESS THRILLED BY PREHENSILE PENIS** *by David Halliwell. Cast includes: Sally Faulkner.*
BLEATS FROM A BRIGHOUSE PLEASURE GROUND *by David Halliwell. Cast: Noel Collins, Anthony Millan, Murray Noble. Both plays dir. the author. (Mgt: Quipu Productions.)*

14 Feb. **ONE LONG HUNT** *by Philip Martin. Dir. Alan Swales. (Mgt: Quipu Productions.)*

27 Feb. **THE ZOO STORY** *by Edward Albee. Cast includes: Steven Berkoff.*
MISS JULIE *by Steven Berkoff after the play by August Strindberg. Cast: Steven Berkoff, Carol Cleveland, Eliza Ward. Both plays dir. Steven Berkoff. (Mgt: London Theatre Group.)*

Mar. **Michael Rudman is succeeded as Artistic Director by Mike Ockrent. His programme starts from May with the appointment of the Traverse's first Resident Designer.**

20 Mar. **BEOWULF** – *Traditional poem freely adpt. by Liane Aukin. Cast: Marty Cruikshank, Michael Harley, Dorinda Hulton, Neil Johnston, Wolf Kahler, Christopher Ravenscroft, Dinah Stabb, Paddy Swanson, Rowan Wylie. Dir. Nancy Meckler. (Mgt: The Freehold.)*

27 Mar. **THE BEARD** *by Michael McLure. Cast: Hilary Harwood, Keith Sharp. Dir. Derek Lister. (Mgt: Derek Lister.)*

1 Apr. *** BIG J AND LITTLE D** – *improvised by Derek Carpenter and Tina Glover. Cast: Derek Carpenter, Tina Glover. Lgt. Cameron Crosby. (Mgt: Carpenter and Glover.)*

5 Apr. **'SCENES FROM RURAL LIFE'** – Double bill consisting of: **ALLERGY** by C. P. Taylor. Cast: Derek Anders, Peter Kelly, Kate Stark. Dir. Mike Ockrent. Lgt. Cameron Crosby.

(New production of the play premièred by Traverse on 18 Jan. 1966.)

* NEXT YEAR IN TEL AVIV by C. P. Taylor. Cast includes: Susan Carpenter, Eithne Dunne, Peter Kelly, Peter Lincoln. Dir. Nicholas Kent. Lgt. Cameron Crosby.

26 Apr. *** THE BOY** by Hugh Hastings. Cast: Christopher Guard, Douglas Storm, Angela Rooks. Dir. Chris Parr. Des. Lesley Lindsay. Lgt. Cameron Crosby.

24 May **KASPAR** by Peter Handke. Trans. Michael Roloff. Cast: Colin Higgins, Richard Ireson, John Sommerville, Virginia Stark, Gillian Wray. Dir. Mike Ockrent. Des. Diana Greenwood. Lgt. Cameron Crosby.

14 June *** PLAT DU JOUR** by Brian Comport. Cast: Peter Gordon, Philip Guard, Alison King. Dir. Tim Preece. Des. Diana Greenwood. Lgt. Cameron Crosby.

22 June *KING HEROD EXPLAINS by Conor Cruise O'Brien. Dir. Tony Aldgate. (Mgt: Ian Mandleberg.)*

3 July *VAMPIRE by Snoo Wilson. Cast: Nicholas Ball, Michael Harrigan, Anna Mottram, Diana Patrick, Mark Penfold, Pat Rossiter. Dir. Malcolm Griffiths. Cos. Miki Van Zwanenberg. (Mgt: Paradise Foundry.)*

12 July **YOU'LL NEVER BE MICHAELANGELO** by Rodger Milner. Cast includes: Susan Carpenter, Madeline Christie, Roger Hume, Edward Wilson. Dir. Joan Knight. Des. Diana Greenwood. Lgt. Cameron Crosby.

20 July *I AM A CABARET by Archie Hind. Cast: Peter Kelly. (Mgt: Peter Kelly.)*

3 Aug. *** UNION JACK (AND BONZO)** by Stanley Eveling. Cast in Edinburgh: Sarah Benfield, Susan Carpenter, Alan Hockey, Richard Ireson, Katy Manning, Roy Sampson, Adrian Shergold, Irene Sunters. Cast in Amsterdam: Hockney repl. by John Malcolm. Dir. Mike Ockrent. Des. Diana Greenwood. Lgt. Cameron Crosby. (Rev. 23 Oct. at Mickery Theatre, Amsterdam before returning to Traverse on 6 Nov. Transfers to Hampstead Theatre Club, London on 17 Dec.)

14 Aug. *** THE SLEEP OF REASON** by Jehane Markham with Eric Berger, Keith Dewhurst, Phillip Hopkins, David Leland, David Markham, Tara Prem, Jack Shepherd, Anthony Trent and the company from a scenario by Jack Shepherd. Songs by Tim Hart and Jehane Markham. Cast: Deborah Baxter, Anthony Haygarth, Malcolm Ingram, Merelina Kendall, Derrick O'Connor, Susan Tracy, Anthony Trent, Richard Vanstone. Dir. Jack Shepherd. Set. Richard Vanstone and Anthony Trent. Cos. by Rita Taylor and Merelina Kendall. Lgt. Cameron Crosby. (Traverse in association with Theatre Unlimited.)

21 Aug. **DRUMS IN THE NIGHT** by Bertolt Brecht. Adpt. C. P. Taylor. Cast: Petra Markham, Stephen Rea, Irene Bradshaw, William Hoyland, Tom Marshall, Christopher Martin, Linda Polan, Ken Morley. Dir. Roland Rees. Des. Moshe Mussman. Music by Andy Smith. (Traverse in assoc. with Foco Novo Productions and the Hampstead Theatre Club. Transfers to Hampstead Theatre Club, London in Sept.)

28 Aug. ** MRS ARGENT by Tom Mallin. Cast: Sylvia Coleridge. Dir. Maxwell Shaw. (Mgt: Sylvia Coleridge.)*

28 Aug. ** THE PEOPLE SHOW NO.*

52: THE OKLAHOMA SHOW by the company. Cast: Mike Figgis, Laura Gilbert, Mark Long, José Nava, Derek Wilson. (Mgt: The People Show.)

4 Sept. * **THE JAWS OF DEATH** – dev. Mike Leigh. Cast: Richard Ireson, Alison Steadman, Adrian Shergold. Dir. Mike Leigh. (Mgt: Mike Leigh.)

11 Oct. * **LEGENDS** by Lindsay Kemp. Cast: Robert Anthony, Lindsay Kemp, The Incredible Orlando. Dir., Des. and Lgt. by the author. (Mgt: Lindsay Kemp Theatre Troupe.)

23 Oct. **THE MAIDS** by Jean Genet. Trans. Bernard Frechtman. Cast: Lindsay Kemp, David Meyer, Tony Meyer. Dir., Des. and Lgt. by Lindsay Kemp. (Mgt: Lindsay Kemp Theatre Troupe. New production of play which last opened at Old Traverse on 14 May 1963.)

6 Nov. UNION JACK (AND BONZO). Edinburgh credits as in Amsterdam revival before. Cast in London: Manning rpl. Patti Love. (Revival of production premièred at Traverse on 3 Aug. Transfers to Hampstead Theatre Club, London on 17 Dec.)

12 Nov. * **SECRETS** by Richard Crane. Cast: Charles Bolton, Elaine Ives Cameron, Christopher Hancock. Dir. Chris Parr. Des. Nick Sommerville. Lgt. Cameron Crosby. (Traverse at Queens University Festival, Belfast. Tours to Newcastle and then transfers to Traverse on 21 Nov.)

21 Nov. SECRETS. Credits as before. (Transfer of production premièred at Queens University Festival, Belfast on 12 Nov.)

11 Dec. DAUGHTER, DAUGHTER, FETCH THE WATER – dev. Annie Stainer. Cast: Dawn Archibald, Reg Bolton, Annie Stainer. Dir. and Des. Annie Stainer. Puppets by Sheila Skinner. Masks by Jill Campbell. Lgt. Roderick Orr-Ewing. (Mgt: Theatre Workshop, Edinburgh. Revival of production premièred at Traverse on 19 Dec. 1972.)

20 Dec. * **COLUMBA** by C. P. Taylor. Music by Peter Russell Brewis. Cast: Derek Anders, Deborah Benzimra, Charles Bolton, Peter Russell Brewis, Christopher Burgess, G. W. Cobb, Lynda Colston, Ian Cutler, Stuart Hopps, Fionna McPhee, Larry McKinnon, Bob Stuckey. Production by Stuart Hopps, Frank Nealon and Mike Ockrent. Des. Geoffrey Scott. Lgt. Cameron Crosby. (Traverse in assoc. with Scottish Theatre Ballet's Movable Workshop and Scottish Television.)

22 Dec. * **SON, SON, GET THE GUN** – dev. Reg Bolton. Cast: Joseph Bolton, Reg Bolton, Annie Stainer. Dir. the author. Marionettes by Jill Campbell. Lgt. Cameron Crosby. (Mgt: Theatre Workshop, Edinburgh. Revived at the Traverse under the title 'The Suitcase Circus' by the Long Green Theatre Company on 14 December 1977.)

1974

15 Jan. * **OPERATION ISKRA** by David Edgar. Cast: Ian Banforth, Michael Harrigan, Anna Mottram, Diana Patrick, Mark Penfold, Pat Rossiter. Dir. Chris Parr. Des. Miki van Zwanenberg. (Mgt: Paradise Foundry.)

24 Jan. † BREMEN COFFEE – A cautionary tale for grown-ups by Rainer Werner Fassbinder. Trans. Anthony Vivis. Cast: Vivienne Burgess, Jonathan Burn, David Calder, Leonard Maguire, Linda Marlowe, Roy Marsden, Michael Richmond, Judy Wilson. Dir. Ronald Hayman. Des. Brenda Harthill Moores. A.D. Enid Stott. Lgt. Cameron Crosby. (Traverse and Hampstead Theatre Club. Transfers to Hampstead Theatre Club, London on 18 Feb.)

25 Jan. **TUTTE LEMKOW'S ONE MAN SHOW OF JEWISH**

MUSIC, MIME AND DANCES. Cast: *Tutte Lemkow.* (Mgt: Tutte Lemkow.)

12 Feb. **THE HILLS** by Claude Duneton. Adpt. Alan Drury. Cast: Noel Collins, Isobel Nisbet, Murray Noble. Dir. Alan Drury. (Mgt: Quipu Productions.)

19 Feb. † *WASTE OF TIME I* – dev. Will Spoor. Cast includes: Will Spoor. Dir. Will Spoor. (Mgt: Will Spoor Mime Theatre.)

28 Feb. † **THE SIGN IN SIDNEY BRUSTEIN'S WINDOW** by Lorraine Hansberry. Adpt. Robert Nemiroff and Charlotte Zaltberg. Cast: Scott Anthony, Carol Cleveland, Alan Collins, Patricia Healey, Jeffrey Kissoon, Paul McDowell, Nancy Wait, Peter Whitman. Dir. Frank Nealon. Des. Kate Owen. Lgt. Cameron Crosby.

19 Mar. **THE PEOPLE SHOW NO. 55: THE SEASIDE SHOW** by the company. Cast: Mike Figgis, Laura Gilbert, Mark Long, José Nava, Derek Wilson. (Mgt: The People Show.)

28 Mar. **DON QUIXOTE** by Annie Stainer, Emil Wolk and Reg Bolton. Cast: Reg Bolton, Annie Stainer, Emil Wolk. (Mgt: Long Green Theatre Company. Revived at Traverse on 13 Dec. 1977.)

2 Apr. * **HERO BOOLEE** by John Green. Music by Richard Cherns. Cast includes: Tina Glover, Paul Kirk. Dir. the author. (Mgt: Theatre Workshop, Edinburgh.)

11 Apr. * **SHIVVERS** by Stanley Eveling. Cast: Deirdre Costello, Anthony Haygarth, Bill Stewart. Dir. Max Stafford-Clark. Des. Poppy Mitchell. Lgt. Cameron Crosby. (Transfers to Royal Court Theatre Upstairs, London on 14 May.)

25 Apr. **WOMEN OF TRACHIS** by Ezra Pound after Sophocles. Dir. Bill Pryde. (Mgt: Traverse Student Workshop.)

2 May **A DREAM PLAY** by August Strindberg. Adpt. Ingmar Bergman. Trans. Michael Meyer. Cast: Janet Amsden, Simon Callow, Susan Carpenter, Maggie Jordan, Roger Kemp, Lyndy Lawson, Roy Marsden, James Snell, Richard Vanstone. Dir. Mike Ockrent. Des. Poppy Mitchell. Lgt. Cameron Crosby. (Rev. on 6 Aug. with an expanded cast.)

8 May * 'An Improvised Show' *created by the company.* Cast: John Attenborough, Clive Bell, William Lee Currie, Rosalind Davies, Hilton McRrae, Colin Wood. (Mgt: Ritual Theatre.)

22 May **ENDGAME** by Samuel Beckett. Cast: Richard Stewart (a.k.a. R. S. Bailey), Brenda Donnison, Laurence Held, Terry Garcia. Dir. Rick Cluchey. Des. Robbie McMillan (a.k.a. Coltrane). Lgt. Cameron Crosby. (Mgt: San Quentin Drama Workshop.)

7 June * **SCHIPPEL** by C. P. Taylor. Adapted from 'Burger Schippel' by Carl Sternheim (trans. Ruth Michaelis-Jena). Cast: Janet Amsden, David Bedard, Simon Callow, Susan Carpenter, Roger Kemp, Roy Marsden, James Snell. Cast for 'The Plumber's Progress': Callow Gordon Clyde, Patricia Heneghan, Kemp, Marsden, Priscilla Morgan, Harry Secombe. Dir. Mike Ockrent. Des. Poppy Mitchell. Lgt. by Cameron Crosby for 'Schippel'. Musical Advisor for 'Schippel': David Johnson. Lgt. Joe Davis for 'The Plumber's Progress'. Musical Advisor for 'The Plumber's Progress': John McCarthy. (Rev. 13 Aug. then tours to Open Space Theatre, London on 17 Oct. and Arts Theatre, Belfast in Nov. Traverse production broadcast on BBC Radio 4 on 13 and 19 Jan. 1975

with original cast – produced for radio by Stewart Conn. Stage production rev. on 8 Oct. 1975. with the new title 'The Plumber's Progress' under the mgt. of Bernard Delfont and Richard M. Mills with James Grafton at the Princes of Wales Theatre, London.)

11 June   'WOMAN'S OWN' – two plays and few songs (music by Robert Pettigrew and lyrics by Robin MacWhirter):
AFTER BIRTHDAY by Pam Gems.
MY WARREN by Pam Gems. Cast for both plays: Maggie Jordan. Dir. Ian (a.k.a. Kenny) Ireland. (Mgt: Maggie Jordan.)

18 June   MICROCOSM. Credits as before. (Revival of production which last opened at the Traverse on 26 Aug. 1970.)

4 July   † **HEFETZ** by Hanoch Levin. Trans. Julian Heltzer. Cast: Susan Carpenter, Simon Callow, Stafford Gordon, Paul Humpoletz, Lesley Joseph, Roger Kemp, Gracie Luck, Jim McManus. Dir. David Mouchtar-Samorai. Des. Poppy Mitchell. Lgt. Cameron Crosby. (Rev. 18 Aug.)

26 July   **THE EXCEPTION AND THE RULE** by Bertolt Brecht. Trans. Eric Bentley.
THE MEASURES TAKEN by Bertolt Brecht. Trans. Eric Bentley. Casts for both plays: Janet Amsden, David Bedard, Stafford Gordon, Philip Guard and Lyndy Lawson, Roy Marsden, James Snell – with Federico Triay. Both plays dir. Radu Penciulescu. A.D. Frank Nealon. Des. Poppy Mitchell. Lgt. Cameron Crosby. Music by Adrian Secchi.

6 Aug.   A DREAM PLAY. Credits as before except Jordan and Vanstone rpl. David Bedard, Stafford Gordon, Philip Guard and Lesley Joseph in an expanded cast. (Revival of production first seen on 2 May.)

13 Aug.   SCHIPPEL. Credits as before. (Revival of production premièred on 7 June.)

18 Aug.   HEFETZ. Credits as before. (Revival of production first seen on 4 July.)

20 Aug.   * *THE FALL OF THE HOUSE OF USHER by Edgar Allen Poe. Adpt. Steven Berkoff and Terry James. Music by David Ellis. Cast: Steven Berkoff, Shelley Lee, Alfred Michelson. Dir. Steven Berkoff. Lgt. Shane. (Mgt: London Theatre Group. Revived at Traverse on 29 Oct.)*

27 Aug.   *ONLY ON PAPER – adpt. Nancy Mitchell from the correspondence between George Bernard Shaw and Dame Ellen Terry. Cast: Nancy Mitchell. (Mgt: Nancy Mitchell in the Traverse Bar.)*

27 Aug.   *DOMINIC BEHAN'S ONE MAN SHOW. Cast: Dominic Behan – with Billy Davidson. Dir. David Dunn. (Mgt: Dominic Behan.)*

3 Sept.   * *I'LL SHOW YOU MINE IF YOU SHOW ME YOURS – a hoary late-night entertainment by John Gorman and Andy Roberts. Cast: John Gorman, Andy Roberts, Josephine Wood. Dir. Roger McGough. Lgt. Cameron Crosby. (Mgt: John Gorman and Andy Roberts.)*

8 Oct.   * *THE BUG by Rick Cluchey and R. S. Bailey (a.k.a. Richard Stewart). Cast: Rick Cluchey, Laurence Held, Robbie McMillan (a.k.a. Coltrane), Jo Wood. Dir. R. S. Bailey. Des. Marek Obtulowicz. Lgt. Neil Sandford. (Mgt: San Quentin Drama Workshop.)*

15 Oct.   * *FOURTH DAY LIKE FOUR LONG MONTHS OF ABSENCE by Colin Bennet. Cast: Carole Hayman, William Hoyland, Caroline Hutchison, Malcolm Ingram, Tony Rohr, Toby Salaman. Dir. Max Stafford-Clark. Des. Diana Greenwood. Lgt. White Light. (Mgt: Royal Court Theatre Upstairs and Joint Stock.)*

16 Oct. **TWENTY SIX EFFORTS AT PORNOGRAPHY** by Carey Harrison. Cast: James Beattie, William Relton. Dir. Hugh Thomas. Lgt. Neil Sandford. (Mgt: National Late Night Theatre – Actors from the National Theatre Company. New production of play premièred by the Traverse on 19 Oct. 1967.)

17 Oct. 'MEN'S TALK' – Quadruple Bill consisting of:
HARD SLOG by Mike Stott.
FIXTURES by Mike Stott.
THE FORCE by Mike Stott.
BOTTICELLI by Terence McNally.
Casts: Desmond Adams, Gawn Grainger, Mike Hayward. Dir. Sebastian Graham-Jones. Lgt. Neil Sandford. (Mgt: National Late Night Theatre – Actors from the National Theatre Company. 'Botticelli' is a new production of the play which last opened at the Traverse on 1 Oct. 1969.)

22 Oct. **THE FOUR TWINS** by Copi. Trans. Anni Lee Taylor. Cast: Anita Dobson, Avril Marsh, Murray Salem, Cornelius Garrett.
EVA PERON by Copi. Trans. Anni Lee Taylor. Cast: Patrick Collingham, Anita Dobson, Avril Marsh, Murray Salem, Cornelius Garrett.
Both plays dir. Steven Dartnell. Des. Geoff Rose. Lgt. Gerry Jenkinson. (Mgt: Close Company.)

29 Oct. THE FALL OF THE HOUSE OF USHER. Credits as before. (Revival of production premièred at Traverse on 20 Aug.)

31 Oct. **THE IDEA AND THE IMAGE AND THE SPACE BETWEEN** – dev. Geoff Moore. Cast: Stephen Barker, John Carter, Chris Carter, Martin Lamb, Lyndon Lewis, Robin Lyons, Pamela Moore, Peter Mumford, Belinda Neave, Jill Piercy, Verena Pottell, Ruth Tansey. Dir. Geoff Moore. (Mgt: Moving Being.)

13 Nov. **THE ERIK SATIE SHOW** or 'Memoires of an Amnesiac' – dev. John Cumming and Roger Savage from the words and music of Erik Satie. Cast: Syvlia Byrne, Angus Park. Dir. John Cumming and Roger Savage. Chor. Gideon Avrahami. Des. Moshe Mussman. Lgt. John Cumming. Projections and film by Ian Dryden. (Mgt: The Pool of London in assoc. with the Pool Theatre Club, Edinburgh.)

14 Nov. **THE CAGE** by Rick Cluchey. Cast: Rick Cluchey, Lawrence Held, Richard Stewart (a.k.a. R. S. Bailey). Dir. the author. Music by Gunnar Pederson. (Mgt. San Quentin Drama Workshop.)

28 Nov. † **REQUEST PROGRAMME** by Franz Xaver Kroetz. Trans. Ruth Michaelis-Jena from 'Wunschkonzert'. Cast: Kay Gallie. Dir. David Gothard. Lgt. Neil Sandford.

29 Nov. DOCTOR GALLI. Credits as before.
MONOLOGUE by Harold Pinter. Cast for both plays: Henry Woolf. (Mgt: Henry Woolf. 'Doctor Galli' is a revival of the production premièred at the Traverse on 18 Nov. 1971.)

7 Dec. **STAKE-OUT** by Johnnie Quarrell.
HOME WORKER by Franz Xaver Kroetz. Trans. Elizabeth Bond-Pablé.
Casts for both plays: Maurice Colbourne, Penny Leatherbarrow. Both plays dir. Estella Schmid. Set des. Peter Ling. Costumes des. Gemma Jackson. Lgt. Peter Rutherford. (Mgt: Half Moon Theatre, London.)

13 Dec. † **ON THE OUTSIDE** by Thomas Murphy. Cast: Iain Agnew, Martin Black, Jane Fox, Jeni Giffen, John Glass, Patrick Lewsley, Bill Paterson, Sean Scanlan, Jeni Smith. Dir. Ian (a.k.a. Kenny) Ireland. Des. Gillian Paige. Lgt. Neil Sandford.

17 Dec. **CARITAS** – chor. Peter Darrell.

141

Cast: Susann Dinah, Philip Haigh, Fionna McPhee, Kostakis Theodossiou. Music by Cat Stevens. Des. Joyce Mellish.
CONVERSATIONS IN SPACE *– chor. Elizabeth Murdoch. Cast: Ruth Barnes, Susann Dinah, Fionna McPhee. Music by Janacek. Des. Joyce Mellish.*
POSITIVELY THE LAST FINAL FAREWELL PERFORMANCE *– chor. by Stuart Hopps (scenario in collaboration with Ian Brown). Cast: Ruth Barnes, Susann Dinah, Philip Haigh, Stuart Hopps, Fionna McPhee, Kostakis Theodossiou. Music by Glenn Miller. Des. Alan Alexander.*
Plus various improvisations by the company.
Programme dir. Stuart Hopps. Lgt. Arthur Twilight (a.k.a. Geoffrey McNab). (Mgt: Scottish Ballet Movable Workshop.)

19 Dec. **LOW TIDE** *– chor. Neil Murray. Music by Peter Brewis. Cast: Ruth Barnes, Kostakis Theodossiou. Des. Joyce Mellish. (Mgt: Scottish Ballet Movable Workshop. 'Low Tide' replaced some of the improvisations in the previous programme.)*

21 Dec. *** SEVEN FOR A SECRET THAT'S NEVER BEEN TOLD** *– dev. Rosalind (a.k.a. Ros) Clark. Music by Neil Gray. Cast: Dawn Archibald, Andrew Arkle, Susie Baxter, Neil Cameron, Neil Gray, Fiona Guild, Michelle Lassers, Malcolm Reading, Ken Wolverton. Dir. Rosalind Clark. A.D. Neil Cameron. Set. Russel Simpson. Cos. Linda Broda. Props and Masks designed by Sheila Skinner. (Mgt: Theatre Workshop, Edinburgh.)*

1975

9 Jan. **ACTION** by Sam Shepard. Cast: Susan Brown, John Dicks, Christopher Ryan, Linda Shelley. Dir. Roy Marsden. Lgt. Neil Sandford.

24 Jan. *** AN EVENING OF SCOTTISH HORRORS** by Leonard Maguire. Cast: Leonard Maguire. (Mgt: Leonard Maguire.)

11 Feb. **SAILOR** by Michael Almaz. Cast: Brendan Donnison, Martyn Jacobs, Anna Nygh, Alasdair J. Ramsay, Sally Willis. Dir. the author. Des. Terry Burton and Sue Turner. (Mgt: Monsieur Artaud Theatre Company by arrangement with the Pool of London.)

18 Feb. **† THE FANLIGHTS** by Rene Marques. Cast: Isla Cameron, Libba Davies, Margaret Heery. Dir. Doreen Cannon. Des. Guillermo Sanchez. Lgt. John Carnegie. Sound effects by Christopher Hobbs. (Mgt: Theatre 84.)

28 Feb. *** THISTLEWOOD** – A Radical Entertainment by Stewart Conn. Original Music by Adrian Secchi. Cast: David Bedard, Susan Carpenter, Meg Davies, Ron Forfar, Christopher Malcolm, Roy Marsden, Christopher Ryan, Katherine Schofield, Finlay Welsh, John Young. Dir. Mike Ockrent. Des. Poppy Mitchell. Lgt. Nick Heppel. A.D. David Gothard.

8 Apr. **TO DAMASCUS – PART ONE** by August Strindberg. Trans. Michael Meyer. Cast: David Bedard, Susan Carpenter, Meg Davies, Christopher Malcolm, Roy Marsden, Christopher Ryan, Katherine Schofield, Finlay Welsh, John Young. Dir. David Gothard. Des. Poppy Mitchell. Lgt. Jenny Cane.

8 Apr. **† TO DAMASCUS – PART TWO** by August Strindberg. Trans. Michael Meyer from 'To Damascus – Parts Two and Three.' Cast: David Bedard, Susan Carpenter, Meg Davies, Ron Forfar, Christopher Malcolm, Christopher Ryan,

Katherine Schofield, Finlay Welsh, John Young. Dir. Mike Ockrent. Des. Poppy Mitchell. Lgt. Jenny Cane. (This was a British Stage Première. The translation had already been broadcast by BBC Radio.)

9 May † **THE SUNDAY PROM-ENADE** by Lars Forssell. Trans. Harry G. Carlson. Cast: David Bedard, Susan Carpenter, Meg Davies, Ron Forfar, Lesley Mackie, Christopher Ryan, James Snell, Finlay Welsh. Dir. Roy Marsden. Des. Poppy Mitchell. Lgt. Jenny Cane.

16 May *NUMBERS by Richard Quick. Cast: Richard Quick. (Mgt: Richard Quick.)*

6 June † **GOD BLESS THE MAJOR** by Istvan Orkeny. Trans. Mari Kuttna from Orkeny's 'The Tot Family'. Cast: David Bedard, Susan Carpenter, Meg Davies, Ron Forfar, Lesley Mackie, Roy Marsden, Christopher Ryan, James Snell, Finlay Welsh. Dir. David Gothard. Des. Poppy Mitchell. Lgt. Jenny Cane.

4 July * **THE DEAD OF NIGHT** by Stanley Eveling. Cast: David Bedard, Susan Carpenter, Meg Davies, Andrew McCulloch, Christopher Ryan (rpl. David Foxxe from 14 July), James Snell, Finlay Welsh. Dir. Mike Ockrent. Des. Poppy Mitchell. Lgt. Jenny Cane. Musical Adviser: Adrian Secchi. (Toured during run to Howden Park Arts Centre, Livingston from 5 Aug.)

26 July † *ONE-MAN MASQUE by James Reeny. Cast: Lynette Hunter, Paul Kennedy. Dir. Peter Lichtenfels. (Mgt: Peter Lichtenfels.)*

6 Aug. *WILD ANIMALS FROM MEMORY by Ray Hassett. Cast: Ray Hassett. (Mgt: Sal's Meat Market.)*

15 Aug. * **GYNT!** by C. P. Taylor and the company based on 'Peer Gynt' by Henrik Ibsen. Music by Adrian Secchi. Cast: David Bedard, Susan Carpenter, Michael David, Meg Davis, Jean Faulds, David Foxxe, Andrew McCulloch, James Snell, Finlay Welsh – with Alan Ross, Charles Stoddart. Dir. Mike Ockrent. Des. Poppy Mitchell. Lgt. Jenny Cane.

26 Aug. *MOGGIE CATS AND GHOST TRAINS – play and plays for children – featuring* **THE KIL-LINGWORTH PLAY** *by C. P. Taylor. Cast: Jenny Armstrong, Lorna Barr, Jeanne Bartram, Chris Bateman, Max Roberts, David Simpson. Dir. Paul Chamberlain. Des. Jill Holmes. (Mgt: Northern Counties College Drama Group in the Traverse Courtyard.)*

26 Aug. * *EAST by Steven Berkoff. Cast: Steven Berkoff, Robert Longdon, Anna Nygh, Barry Phillips, Barry Stanton. Dir. the author. (Mgt: London Theatre Group. Revived at Traverse on 21 Oct.)*

27 Aug. * *INANNA. Scenario by Pat Douthwaite. Music by Alison Bauld. Chor. Shelley Lee. Cast: Donald Dean, Catherine Evers, Kenny (a.k.a. Kinny) Gardner, Shelley Lee, Vee Rochford, Jenny Western, Dorn Yodder. Des. Pat Douthwaite. Lgt. Gerry Jenkinson. (Mgt: Pat Douthwaite. Previewed immediately before at Third Eye Centre, Glasgow.)*

6 Sept. * *MOON – dev. and chor. Annie Stainer. Cast: Annie Stainer. Dir. and set. the author. Cos. Linda Broda. Lgt. Reg Bolton. (Mgt: Long Green Theatre Company. Revived at Traverse on 5 Jan. 1977.)*

13 Sept. **Mike Ockrent begins a year's leave of absence and Chris Parr is appointed as temporary Artistic Director with Peter Lichtenfels as Trainee Director.**

However, Ockrent never returns and Parr is later confirmed as Artistic Director. Parr's policy takes effect from the beginning of December. Lichtenfels soon becomes Associate Director – which position he holds for irregular periods up to December 1979.

21 Oct. **EAST.** Credits as before. (Revival of production premièred at Traverse on 26 Aug.)

28 Oct. *ASSASSINATIONS* by Steve Grant. Cast includes: Kevin Hughes, Robin Murphy, John North. Dir. Graham Devlin. (Mgt: Major Road.)

4 Nov. *MISTER X* by Roger Baker and Drew Griffiths. Cast: Drew Griffiths, Phillip Howells, Grant McDonald, Alan Pope. Dir. Drew Griffiths. (Mgt: Gay Sweatshop.)

11 Nov. * *THE TROUBLE WITH ANTS* by Alan Bryce. Cast: John Abbott, Richard Earth, Kenneth Garner, Cherrie Gilliam, Mollie Guilfoyle. Dir. the author. (Mgt: Overground Theatre.)

18 Nov. † *WASTE OF TIME 3* – dev. Will Spoor. Dir. Will Spoor. (Mgt: Waste of Time Inc., Amsterdam – previously known as the Will Spoor Mime Theatre.)

2 Dec. *2001 B.C. (A SALAKTIC ODYSSEY)* Cast includes: Sandra Muir. Dir. John Melville. (Mgt: Salakta Balloon Band.)

5 Dec. *EN ATTENDANT GODOT* by Samuel Beckett. Performed in French. Cast includes: Peter Allen, David McMillan, Yvan Nadeau, Michael Worton. Dir. Michael Worton. (Mgt: Les Escogriffes. New production of the play which last opened at the Old Traverse on 22 Dec. 1967.)

11 Dec. † *MASOCH* by Michael Almaz. Cast. Sally Willis. Dir. the author. Cos. Pam Martell. (Mgt: The Artaud Company.)

17 Dec. * *WOW!* – devised by the company. Cast: John Bolton, Neil Cameron, Rosalind Crowe, Sharon Erkine, Clunie MacKenzie, Ken Wolverton – with Robert Handleigh and John Sampson. Dir. Neil Cameron. Des. Ken Wolverton. Lgt. Alastair McArthur. (Mgt: Theatre Workshop, Edinburgh.)

18 Dec. *OUR MARIE* – dev. Margaret Dent from the life and work of Marie Lloyd. Cast: Margaret Dent – with a pianist. (Mgt: Margaret Dent.)

1976

6 Jan. * *LADYBIRD, LADYBIRD . . .* by David Pownall. Cast: Judith Blake, Stephen Boxer, Christopher Crooks, Mary Ellen Ray. Dir. Edward (a.k.a. John) Adams. Cos. June Thompson. (Mgt: Paines Plough.)

9 Jan. *CRATES ON BARRELS* by David Pownall. Cast: Christopher Crooks. Dir. Edward (a.k.a. John) Adams. Lgt. Chanine Yavroyan. (Mgt: Paines Plough.)

15 Jan. * *THE SEA CHANGE* by Tom Gallacher – based on Shakespeare's 'The Tempest'. Cast: Bill Bailey, David Bannerman, Roy Hanlon, Jennifer Lee, Leonard Maguire, Mark Penfold, James Walsh. Dir. Chris Parr. Des. Miki van Zwanenberg. Lgt. and Sound. Alastair McArthur.

17 Feb. * *THE GAY GORBALS* by Hector MacMillan. Cast: Martin Black, Roy Hanlon, Jennifer Lee, Ronnie Letham, Tricia Scott, Irene Sunters, Robert Trotter, James Walsh – with George Morgan, Chris Murray, Robert Pettigrew, Mike Shearer. Dir. Chris Parr. A.D. Mark Penfold. Des. Miki van Zwanenberg. Lgt. Alastair McArthur. M.D. Derek Watson. Chor. Jennifer Lee. Film by Scott Nimmo. (Rev. 20 Aug. Transfers to Third Eye Centre, Glasgow on 14 Sept.)

11 Mar.   **B MOVIE** by Robert Walker. Cast: Martin Black, Dermot Crowley, Roy Hanlon, Ronnie Letham, Tammy Ustinov – with Derek Watson. Dir. Mark Penfold. Des. Miki van Zwanenberg. Lgt. Alastair McArthur.

11 Mar.   **AND THEY USED TO STAR IN MOVIES** by Campbell Black. Cast: Martin Black, Dermot Crowley, John Finnegan, Roy Hanlon, Ronnie Letham, Trisha Scott, Tammy Ustinov. Dir. Peter Lichtenfels. Des. Miki van Zwanenberg. Lgt. Alastair McArthur.

18 Mar.   * **LAUREL AND HARDY** by Tom McGrath. Cast: Ian (a.k.a. Kenny) Ireland, John Shedden – with Derek Watson. Dir. Robert Walker. Des. Miki van Zwanenberg. Lgt. Alastair McArthur. Chor. Pat Lovett. (Returns to Traverse on 1 June during a three month tour of both weeks and one night stands to Cumbernauld, Irvine, Ardfern, Glasgow, Traverse, Hull, Erskine, Adam Smith Centre in Kirkcaldy, Craigmillar, Greenock, Kilsyth, Ayr, Biggar, Irvine, Ochtertyre and Dumfries. Rev. 20 Aug. at The Other Traverse, Old Chaplaincy Centre, Edinburgh. Transfers to Mayfair Theatre, London on 15 Nov.)

6 Apr.   *GAS by Georg Kaiser. Dir. Phil Young. (Mgt: Leeds University Theatre Workshop in assoc. with the National Student Drama Festival.)*

7 Apr.   *THE KEY by Robert Pugh. Cast includes: Robert Pugh, Kevin White. (Mgt: Rose Bruford College of Speech and Drama in assoc. with the National Student Drama Festival.)*
SWAN SONG by Anton Chekhov. Cast: Jock Stroyan, Julian Walker. (Mgt: St. Andrews

Mermaid Dramatic Society in assoc. with the National Student Drama Festival.)

9 Apr.   *GALATEA by Jacek Laskowski. (Mgt: St. Andrews Mermaid Dramatic Society in assoc. with the National Student Drama Festival.)*

10 Apr.   *COUP D'ETAT by Paul Bream. (Mgt: Keele University Drama Group in assoc. with the National Student Drama Festival.)*

13 Apr.   *THE EVEREST HOTEL (NUNS UNDRESS) by Snoo Wilson. Music and lyrics by Tim Thomas. Cast: Jan Chappell, Anna Mottram, Emma Williams. Dir. the author. Chor. Janet Amsden. (Mgt: Scarab Theatre.)*

20 Apr.   * **MESSAGES IN BOTTLES** BY John Morris. Cast: Martin Black, Ian (a.k.a. Kenny) Ireland, Muriel Romanes. Dir. Mark Penfold. Des. Miki van Zwanenberg. Lgt. Alastair McArthur.

20 Apr.   **NEXT TIME, BRING A WEE SOMETHIN' TE DRINK, SON** by Paul Vincent. Cast: Dermot Crowley, Kay Gallie, Charles Kearney, Ronnie Letham, Phil McCall. Dir. Peter Lichtenfels. Des. Miki van Zwanenberg. Lgt. Alastair McArthur. (New version of a play premièred in Glasgow in 1973 under the title 'The Discoverer'.)

27 Apr.   * **THE GRILL** by Jeremy Bruce-Watt. Cast: Roy Hanlon, Rose McBain. Dir. Callum Mill. Des. Miki van Zwanenberg. Lgt. Alastair McArthur.

27 Apr.   *THE FORK by Ian Brown. Cast: Linda Beckett, Jeffrey Chiswick, Jim Hooper, Anthony Sher. Dir. Gerald Chapman. (Mgt: Gay Sweatshop.)*

4 May   * **THE JESUIT** by Donald Campbell. Cast: Martin Black, Michael Burrell, Kenneth Drury, Roy Hanlon, David Peate, Beth Robens, Henry Stamper, James Yuill. Dir.

Sandy Neilson. Cos. Lindsey Harris. Lgt. Graeme Dott. (Mgt: The Heretics. Revived at The Other Traverse on 17 Aug.)

7 May **ME** by C. P. Taylor. Cast includes: Alan Brodie. Dir. Peter Lichtenfels, Chris Parr and Adam Strickland. (Mgt: Traverse Student Workshop.)

13 May * **OUTSIDE THE WHALE** by Robert Holman. Cast in Edinburgh: Geoffrey Jackman, Ronnie Letham, Mark Penfold, Tammy Ustinov. Additional cast in London: Matthew Vosburgh. Dir. Chris Parr. Des. Miki van Zwanenberg. Lgt. Alastair McArthur. (Mgt. of production taken over by Bush Theatre, London and revived there on 24 Feb. 1978.)

1 June **LAUREL AND HARDY**. Credits as before. (Revival of production premièred on 18 Mar.)

10 June * **THE KIBBO KIFT.** Music by J. Maxwell Hutchinson and lyrics by Chris Judge Smith. Cast: Geoffrey Jackman, Ronnie Letham, Mark Penfold, Tammy Ustinov – with George Morgan, Chris Murray, Robert Pettigrew, Mike Shearer. Dir. Chris Parr. Des. Miki van Zwanenberg. Lgt. and Sound Alastair MacArthur. (Revived on 24 August.)

29 June **SCUM** by Clare Luckham, C. G. Bond and the company. Music by Helen Glavin. Cast: Roger Allam, Ian Blower, Linda Broughton, Chris Bowler, Josephine Cupido, Helen Glavin, Gillian Hanna, Mary McCusker, Sue Todd. Dir. Sue Todd. Set. Andrea Montag. Cos. Hilary Lewis. (Mgt: Monstrous Regiment.)

8 July * **SAIGON ROSE** by David Edgar. Cast: Martin Black, Juliet Cadzow, Roy Hanlon, Godfrey Jackman, Ronnie Letham, Mark Penfold, Tricia Scott, Tammy Ustinov. Dir.

Chris Parr. Des. Tot Brill. Lgt. Alastair McArthur.

5 Aug. * **NERO AND THE GOLDEN HOUSE** by Richard Crane. Music by Robert Pettigrew. Cast: David Bannerman, Martin Black, Juliet Cadzow, Roy Hanlon, Geoffrey Jackman, Ronnie Letham, Tricia Scott, Tammy Ustinov – with George Morgan, Chris Murray, Robert Pettigrew. Dir. Chris Parr. Des. Miki van Zwanenberg. Lgt. Alastair McArthur.

17 Aug. **THE JESUIT**. Credits as before – except Stamper rpl. by Sandy Neilson. (Mgt: The Heretics at The Other Traverse, Old Chaplaincy Centre, Edinburgh. Revival of the production premièred at the Traverse on 4 May.)

18 Aug. * **WAX** by Howard Barker. Cast: Roger Davidson, Nick Edmett, Terence Frisby, Anna Mottram, Mark Penfold, Gordon Sterne. Dir. Peter Lichtenfels. Des. Miki van Zwanenberg. Lgt. Alastair McArthur. (Traverse and Bush Theatre, London. Transfers to Bush Theatre on 7 Sept.)

20 Aug. **THE GAY GORBALS**. Credits as before – except Lee rpl. Ann-Louise Ross and Walsh rpl. David Bannerman. New film is by Sidhartha Films. (Revival of production premièred on 17 Feb. Transfers to Third Eye Centre, Glasgow on 14 Sept.)

20 Aug. **LAUREL AND HARDY**. Credits as before. Traverse at The Other Traverse, Old Chaplaincy Centre, Edinburgh. Revival of production premièred on 18 Mar. Transfers to Mayfair Theatre, London on 15 Nov.)

25 Aug. **AN' ME WI' A BAD LEG TAE** by Billy Connolly. Cast: Sara Ballantyne, Margot Gillies, James Kennedy, Alex Norton, Bill Paterson, David Sands, Carey Wilson. Dir. Stuart Mungall. (Mgt: Borderline Theatre Company at The Other Traverse, Old Chaplaincy Centre, Edinburgh. Revived at Traverse on 12 Oct.)

24 Aug. **THE KIBBO KIFT**. Credits as before.

(Revival of production premièred on 10 June.)

7 Sept.   *LIGHT SHINING IN BUCK-INGHAMSHIRE* by Caryl Churchill. Cast: Jan Chappell, Linda Goddard, Robert Hamilton, Will Knightley, Colin McCormack, Nigel Terry. Dir. Max Stafford-Clark. Des. Sue Plummer. Lgt. Steven Whitson. (Mgt: Joint Stock.)

12 Oct.   AN' ME WI' A BAD LEG TAE. Credits as before. (Revival of the production which opened at The Other Traverse on 25 Aug.)

21 Oct.   † THE COLLECTED WORKS OF BILLY THE KID by Michael Ondaatje. Cast: Martin Black, Emma Chapman, Ken Drury, Ronnie Letham, Sandy Myles – with Robert Pettigrew. Dir. Peter Lichtenfels. Des. Bob Last. Lgt. Alastair McArthur. Music by Robert Pettigrew.

18 Nov.   *THE SILVER LAND* by George Byatt. Cast: Martin Black, Emma Chapman, Ken Drury, Ronnie Letham, Dolina Maclennan. Dir. Chris Parr. M.D. Dolina Maclennan. Des. Tot Brill. Lgt. Alastair McArthur. Chor. Stuart Hopps.

19 Dec.   *HELP MA BOAB* by John Bolton. (Mgt: Theatre Workshop, Edinburgh.)

★   ★   ★

Playreadings presented during the year by the Scottish Society of Playwrights.

3 Apr.   COOL DUTCH by Ian Blair.
3 Apr.   SMALL THOUGHTS FROM THE REVOLUTION by Graeme Campbell. (Premièred in production by Traverse on 5 Apr. 1979.)
4 Apr.   PASTORAL by Eric McDonald.
4 Apr.   AGNES BELFRAGE by Alisdair Gray.

1977

4 Jan.   **THE ART OF THE CLOWN** by Annie Stainer and Reg Bolton. Cast: Joseph Bolton, Reg Bolton, Annie Stainer, John Stainer. (Mgt: Long Green Theatre Company.)

5 Jan.   MOON. Credits as before – except Cos. Sue Smith. (Revival of production premièred at Traverse on 6 Sept. 1975.)

11 Jan.   LETTERS FROM K by Michael Almaz – based on Franz Kafka's letters to Felice Baver. Cast: Sally Willis.
STORY by Michael Almaz. Cast: Sally Willis.
Both plays dir. the author. Cos. Pam Martell. (Mgt: The Artaud Company.)

14 Jan.   **DOROTHY AND THE BITCH** by Marcella Evaristi. Cast: Sarah Collier. Dir. the author. (Mgt: Sarah Collier.)

18 Jan.   *THE FRIEND* by Michael Almaz. Cast: Sally Willis, Cynthia Grenville, Angela Sachs. Dir. the author. Cos. Pam Martell. (Mgt: The Artaud Company.)

25 Jan.   **MUSIC TO MURDER BY** by David Pownall. Original music by Stephen Boxer. Cast: Edward (a.k.a John) Adams, Stephen Boxer, Mary Ellen Ray, Eric Richard, Fiona Victory – with Diana Kyle. Dir. Edward (a.k.a. John) Adams. Des. Bettina Reeves. Other music by Carlo Gesualdo and Peter Warlock. (Mgt: Paines Plough.)

1 Feb.   *MOTOCAR* by David Pownall. Cast: Stephen Boxer, Diana Kyle, Joe Marcell, Eric Richard, Fiona Victory. Dir. Edward (a.k.a. John) Adams. Des. Tot Brill. (Mgt: Paines Plough.)

8 Feb.   **RECITALS OF MYSTERY, VIOLENCE AND DESIRE – THE FIRST ARABIAN NIGHT: THE LOVES OF KAMAR AND BUDUR** by the company. Based on the translation by Sir Robert Burton. Cast: Celia Booth, Christian Burgess, Pam Ferris, Bob Goody, Raad Rawi. Dir. Mike Alfreds. (Mgt: Shared Experience.)

9 Feb. **_RECITALS OF MYSTERY, VIOLENCE AND DESIRE – THE SECOND ARABIAN NIGHT: THE ROGUERIES OF DELILAH THE WILY_** – _improvised by the company. Credits: As for Part One._

10 Feb. **_RECITALS OF MYSTERY, VIOLENCE AND DESIRE – THE THIRD ARABIAN NIGHT: THE CITY OF BRASS_** _by the company. Credits: As for Part One._

15 Feb. **_HAG_** _by John Anderson. Cast: John Anderson, Tom Kingdom, Marcella Markham._
MAYDAY _by John Anderson. Cast of 4 includes: John Anderson. Both plays dir. Tom Kingdom. (Mgt: Nora Productions.)_

18 Feb. **_LIFE IN A SCOTTISH SITTING ROOM_** _by Ivor Cutler. Cast: Ivor Cutler. (Mgt: Ivor Cutler.)_

22 Feb. **_FANTASY FACTORY_** _by John Melville. Cast includes: Sandra Muir. Dir. the author. (Mgt: Salakta Balloon Band.)_

8 Mar. **_AGE OF CONSENT_** _by Drew Griffiths. Music by Tom Robinson. Cast of 6 includes: Helen Barnaby, Sarah Hardy, Gordon McDonald. Dir. Kate Crutchley. Des. Mary Moore. (Mgt: Gay Sweatshop.)_

15 Mar. _GIMME SHELTER – A trilogy of one act plays._
GEM _by Barrie Keeffe. Cast: Phillip Joseph, Roger Leach, Sharman MacDonald, Ian Sharp._
GOTCHA _by Barrie Keeffe. Cast: Philip Davis, Peter Hughes, Roger Leach, Sharman MacDonald._
GETAWAY _by Barrie Keeffe. Cast: Philip Davis, Phillip Joseph, Sharman MacDonald, Ian Sharp. Trilogy dir. Keith Washington. Des. Mary Moore. (Mgt: Soho Poly presented by The Network.)_

24 Mar. **KONG LIVES** by George Byatt. Cast: Jill Fenner, Irene Sunters, Benny Young. Dir.

Chris Parr. Des. Grant Hicks. Lgt. Alastair McArthur.

21 Apr. * **NEW REEKIE** by Ian Brown. Cast: Michael Carter, Frances Low, Ian (a.k.a. Kenny) Ireland, Muriel Romanes, Irene Sunters, Benny Young. Dir. Chris Parr. Des. Grant Hicks. Lgt. Alastair McArthur.

19 May * **THE HARDMAN** by Tom McGrath and Jimmy Boyle. Cast: Martin Black, Michael Carter, Ian (a.k.a. Kenny) Ireland, Peter Kelly, Frances Low, Ann Scott-Jones, Benny Young – with Ronnie Goodman. Cast in London: Black, Ireland, Kelly, James Kennedy, Low, Eileen Nicholas, Young – with Goodman. Radio cast: David Bannerman, Kelly, Kennedy, Low, Alex Norton, Tony Roper, Scott-Jones, Carey Wilson, Young – with Goodman. Dir. Peter Lichtenfels. Directed in London by Lichtenfels with Ian Ireland and Tom McGrath. Des. Bob Last. Re-des. in London by Grant Hicks from the original by Last. Lgt. Alastair McArthur. (Revived in assoc. with Offshore Productions at the I.C.A., London on 29 Nov. Transfers to Traverse in assoc. with The Network on 3 Jan. 1978 prior to a seven week tour of Britain. Revived at The Other Traverse, The Old Chaplaincy Centre, Edinburgh on 22 Aug. 1978. Revived at the Pavilion Theatre, Glasgow on 11 June 1979 prior to a visit to the Kammerspiele in Munich, West Germany. A radio version of the play was broadcast by the BBC on Radio 4 on 21 May 1979, on Radio 3 on 5 July 1979 and on Radio Scotland on 9 Oct. 1980. The Radio Producer was Tom Kinninmont.)

16 June * **CROWNING GLORY** – dev. Sheila Kelley and Sarah Pia

148

Anderson. Cást: Michael Carter, Frances Low, Muriel Romanes, Jimmy Yuill. Dir. Sheila Kelley and Sarah Pia Anderson. Des. Gemma Jackson. Lgt. Alastair McArthur.

24 June **THE FUNNY OLD MAN** by *Tadeusz Rosewicz. (Mgt: Eclipse Theatre.)*

19 July * **WALTER: GETTING BY** by C. P. Taylor. Cast: Joseph Greig, Peter Kelly, Peter Lincoln, Irene Sunters, Tammy Ustinov, John Young. Dir. Chris Parr. Des. Grant Hicks. Lgt. Alastair McArthur. (See also under 26 June.)

2 Aug. * **WALTER: GOING HOME** by C. P. Taylor. Cast: Joseph Greig, Peter Kelly, Peter Lincoln, Irene Sunters, Tammy Ustinov, Benny Young, John Young. Dir. Chris Parr. Des. Grant Hicks. Lgt. Alastair McArthur. (A shortened and combined version of both 'Walter: Getting By' and 'Walter: Going Home' in the Traverse production is broadcast on BBC Radio 3 on 2 July 1981 and 29 Aug. 1982 – directed for radio by Stewart Conn and featuring the original Traverse cast with the exception of Irene Sunters [rpl. Anne Kristen] and John Young [whose part was cut].)

18 Aug. * **A & R (Artists and Repertoire)** by Pete Atkin. Cast: Martin Black, Michael Carter, Paul Dalton, Terry Gilligan, Paul Haley, Mandy Moore – with Ronnie Goodman, Chris Murray, Robert Pettigrew, Mike Shearer. Dir. Chris Parr and Peter Lichtenfels. Des. Grant Hicks. Lgt. Alastair McArthur.

21 Aug. * **'AVE YOU 'EARD THE ONE ABOUT JOEY BAKER?** by Mel Smith and Bob Goody. Music by David Learner and Tony Britten. Cast: Tony Britten, Bob Goody,

Mel Smith. *(Mgt: Smith and Goody. Revived at Traverse on 8 Nov.)*

24 Aug. * **RICHARD III PART TWO** by David Pownall. Music by Stephen Boxer. Cast: Stephen Boxer, Diana Kyle, Robert McIntosh, Joe Marcell, Eric Richard, Fiona Victory, Harriet Walter. Dir. Edward (a.k.a. John) Adams. Des. Bettina Reeves. *(Mgt: Paines Plough.)*

6 Sept. * **A BED OF ROSES** – dev. Mike Bradwell. Cast: Colin Goddard, Kathy Iddon, Robin Soans, Mia Souteriou, Heather Tobias, David Threlfall, Alan Williams. Dir. Mike Bradwell. Des. Gemma Jackson. *(Mgt: Hull Truck Theatre Company.)*

11 Oct. **BLEAK HOUSE: EPISODE ONE – THE LAW-WRITER** by Charles Dickens. Adpt. the company. Cast: John Dicks, Pam Ferris, Carl Forgione, Jonathan Hackett, Eliza Hunt, Christopher Ryan, James Smith, Holly Wilson. Dir. Mike Alfreds. *(Mgt: Shared Experience.)*

12 Oct. **BLEAK HOUSE: EPISODE TWO – SHARPSHOOTERS.** *Credits: As for Episode One.*

22 Oct. * **BLEAK HOUSE: EPISODE THREE – CLOSING IN.** *Credits: As for Episode One.*

1 Nov. **WHEN HAIR WAS LONG AND TIME WAS SHORT** by Billy Connolly. Cast: Sara Ballintyne, Peter Finlay, Margot Gillies, James Kennedy, Billy Riddoch, Gaylie Runciman, Carey Wilson. Dir. Campbell Morrison. Set. Bernard Culshaw. Cos. Alan Menzies. M.D. Alasdair MacNeill. *(Mgt: Borderline Theatre Company.)*

8 Nov. **'AVE YOU 'EARD THE ONE ABOUT JOEY BAKER?** *Credits as before – except (in cast) Britten rpl. David Learner. (Revival of production premièred at Traverse on 21 Aug.)*

11 Nov. **'AN EVENING OF SAMUEL BECKETT PLAYS'.** *Quadruple bill consisting of:*

BREATH by Samuel Beckett.
THEATRE ONE by Samuel
Beckett. *Cast: Andrew Dallmeyer,*
Paul Howes.
NOT I by Samuel Beckett. *Cast:*
Andrew Dallmeyer, Vivienne
Dixon.
FROM AN ABANDONED
WORK by Samuel Beckett. *Cast:*
Paul Howes.
All four plays dir. Andrew Dall-
meyer. Lgt. Alastair McArthur.
(Mgt: Andrew Dallmeyer.)

22 Nov. *A MAD WORLD MY MAS-*
TERS by Barry Keeffe. *Cast*
includes: Gillian Barge, Simon
Callow, Paul Freeman, Robert
Hamilton, Cecily Hobbs, Will
Knightley, David Rintoul, Tony
Rohr, Jane Wood. Dir. William
Gaskill and Max Stafford-Clark.
Des. Hayden Griffin. Lgt. Rory
Dempster. Sound by Bill Cadman.
(Mgt: Joint Stock Theatre Group.)

29 Nov. *SOME ENCHANTED EVEN-*
ING by C. P. Taylor. *Cast inclu-*
des: Denis Bryson, Tim Healy,
Colin MacClacklan, George
Orwin, Anne Orwin, Max
Roberts, Dave Whitaker. Dir.
Paul Chamberlain. Des. Phil
Bailey. Lgt. Brian Hogg. (Mgt:
Live Theatre.)

2 Dec. *THE RITUAL* by Peter Hoefna-
gels. Cast: Jim House. Dir. Alis-
dair Skinner. (Mgt: City of Lon-
don Productions.)

6 Dec. * *PETER PAN AND EMILY* by
C. P. Taylor. *Cast includes:*
Denise Bryson, Colin MacClack-
lan, George Orwin, Anne Orwin,
Max Roberts, Dave Whittaker.
Dir. Paul Chamberlain. Des. Phil
Bailey. Lgt: Brian Hogg. (Mgt:
Live Theatre.)

13 Dec. DON QUIXOTE. Credits as before.
(Revival of show which last opened at
the Traverse on 26 Mar. 1974.)

14 Dec. THE SUITCASE CIRCUS – dev. Reg Bol-
ton. Cast as before. Dir. the author. (Mgt:
Long Green Theatre Company. Revival of
production premièred by Theatre Workshop,
Edinburgh at the Traverse under the title
'Son, Son, Get the Gun' on 22 Dec. 1973.)

★　　★　　★

Playreadings presented during
the year by George Byatt in
week beginning 1 March.
SOLDIER GREEN by George
Byatt.
SOME KIND OF INTELLEC-
TUAL KAMAKAZI PILOT by
George Byatt.

1978

3 Jan. THE HARDMAN by Tom McGrath and
Jimmy Boyle. Cast: Black, Ireland, Kelly,
Kennedy, Low, Nicholas, Young – with
Goodman. Dir. Peter Lichtenfels with
Ian (a.k.a. Kenny) Ireland and Tom
McGrath. Re-des, for tour by Grant
Hicks from the original by Last. Lgt.
McArthur. (Revival in assoc. with The
Network of production premièred by the
Traverse on 19 May. Presented prior to
a seven week tour to Sheffield Crucible
Studio, Liverpool Playhouse Studio,
Birmingham Repertory Brum Studio,
Brighton Gardner Centre, Manchester,
Cardiff Sherman Theatre and South-
ampton Nuffield Theatre. Revived at
The Other Traverse, The Old Cha-
plaincy Centre, Edinburgh on 22 Aug.
1978.)

10 Jan. * *DIARY OF A RAT* by Michael
Almaz. *Cast includes: Michael*
Almaz, Jenny Cryst, John Ioan-
nou. Dir. the author. Des. Pam
Martell. Lgt. Michael Almaz.
(Mgt: The Artaud Company.)

17 Jan. * *FIGHTING MAC* by Donald
Mackenzie. *Cast: Colin Brown,*
David Peate. Dir. Ian Wooldridge.
(Mgt: Seaforth Productions.)

20 Jan. *LOVE, LONELINESS AND*
LAUNDRY by Leon Rosselson
and Roy Bailey. Cast: Roy Bailey,
Leon Rosselson. (Mgt: Rosselson
and Bailey.)

2 Feb. MR JOYCE IS LEAVING
PARIS by Tom Gallacher. Cast:
Peter Adair, Margot Gillies,
Phillip Joseph, Robbie McMil-
lan (a.k.a. Coltrane), Oengus
MacNamara. Dir. Chris Parr.
Des. Grant Hicks. Lgt. Alastair
McArthur.

24 Feb. *SOON MAYBE BOOGIE. Dir.*

Paddy Fletcher. (Mgt: Incubus Theatre Company.)

26 Feb. **WORK AND OTHER DEAR GREEN FABLES** by Brian Miller. Cast: Ron Paterson. Dir. the author. (Mgt: Cottage Theatre, Cumbernauld.)

28 Feb. **WITHDRAWAL SYMPTOMS** by C. P. Taylor. Cast: Anne Godley, Chris Hallam, Mary Maddox, Anthony May, Anthony Milner, Anthony O'Donnell, Gordon Reid, Rowena Roberts. Dir. Roland Rees. Des. Adrian Vaux. Lgt. Chris Ellis. (Mgt: Foco Novo Theatre Company.)

1 Mar. * **BRITTANICA** by Tom Kinninmont. Cast: Tony Roper, John Shedden, Carey Wilson with Robert Pettigrew. Dir. Campbell Morrison. Des. Janet Scarfe. Lgt. Sheila Harborth, Alastair McArthur and Tim Trucker-Pearce. Chor. Isobel James. (Traverse at Dalkeith High School. Tour of one night stands round Lothian Region continues to Penicuik High School, Howden Park Centre, Livingston and North Berwick Primary School. Transfers to Traverse on 7 Mar.)

2 Mar. *AS TIME GOES BY by Noel Greig and Drew Griffiths. Cast: Drew Griffiths, Alex Harding, Gordon MacDonald, Philip Osment, Martin Panter, Alan Pope, Philip Timmins. Dir. Noel Greig. Des. Paul Dart. (Mgt: Gay Sweatshop.)*

7 Mar. BRITTANICA. Credits as before. (Transfer of production premièred by Traverse at Dalkeith High School on 1 Mar.)

28 Mar. **LEG WARMERS** – chor. Brian Hewitt. Music by Elton John.
* **NOCTURNE** – chor. Brian Hewitt. Music by Ramon Roper.
ASTURIAS – chor. Brian Hewitt. Music by Albeniz.
LAMENTO E VIVACE – chor. Brian Hewitt.
Casts: Fiona Alderman, Morag

Anderson, Michelle Candip, Joanna Gale, Brian Hewitt, Jonathan Kinns. (Mgt: Scottish Contemporary Dance Theatre.)

30 Mar. **VISIONS FUGITIF** – chor. Brian Hewitt. Music by Prokofiev. (Mgt: Scottish Contemporary Dance Theatre. In bill with 'Lamento E Vivace' and 'Leg Warmers'.

6 Apr. * **THE SLAB BOYS** by John Byrne. Cast: Freddie Boardley, Jim Byars, Elaine Collins, Robbie Coltrane, Pat Doyle, Billy McColl, Ida Schuster, Carey Wilson. Dir. David Hayman. Des. Grant Hicks. Lgt. Alastair McArthur. (Revived at The Other Traverse, Old Chaplaincy Centre, Edinburgh on 19 Aug. prior to transfer to Print Workshop, Glasgow in assoc. with the Glasgow Theatre Club and then to the Royal Court Theatre Upstairs, London on 18 Oct. Rev. 23 June 1982 at the Traverse. Transfers to Royal Court Theatre Main Stage, London on 17 Nov. 1982. Revived in assoc. with Glasgow Mayfest at Citizens Theatre, Glasgow on 3 May 1983.)

4 May * **STREET FIGHTING MAN** by John Bett. Cast: Peter Adair, Sharon Erskine, Roy Hanlon, Roland Oliver, Finlay Welsh, Jimmy Yuill. Dir. Ronnie Letham. Des. Grant Hicks. Lgt. Alastair McArthur. (Revived on 10 Oct. prior to transfer to Strathclyde University Drama Centre, Glasgow on 16 Oct. and then to Aberdeen Arts Centre.)

6 May * *SUGAR AND SPITE – a revue by Marcella Evaristi and Liz Lochhead. Music by Ester Allan. Cast: Ester Allan, Marcella Evaristi, Liz Lochhead. (Mgt: Allan, Evaristi and Lochhead.)*

1 June * **SOMERVILLE THE SOL-DIER** by Donald Campbell. Cast: Marian Boyes, Roy Hanlon, Roland Oliver, Beth Robens, Finlay Welsh, Benny Young, Jimmy Yuill. Dir. Sandy Neilson. Des. Tanya McCallin. Lgt. Alastair McArthur. Music by Ian Campbell.

8 June *OEDIPUS – dev. Stuart Forbes. Cast includes: Stuart Forbes, Walter Harrikoff, The Incomparable Manilla, Riza (a.k.a. Karen) McCrary, Jonathan Pope. Dir. and Des. Stuart Forbes. (Mgt: Stuart Forbes Mime Company.)*

27 June *SCENES FROM SOWETO by Steve Wilmer. Cast: Rufus Collins, Nigel Gregory. Dir. Brian Croucher. (Mgt: Group 3.)*

5 July * **THE ANDROID CIRCUIT** by Tom McGrath. Cast: Peter Kelly, Patrick Malahide, Tammy Ustinov. Dir. Robin Lefevre. Des. Grant Hicks. Lgt. Alastair McArthur. Chor. Jaye Mitchell. Synthesiser tapes by Damion O'Reilly. (Rev. on 17 Aug. at The Other Traverse, Old Chaplaincy Centre, Edinburgh prior to transfer to ICA, London.)

11 July *THE TEMPEST – adpt. Pip Simmons from Shakespeare. Cast: Rod Beddall, Sheila Burnett, Jessie Gordon, Poppy Hands, Steve Johnston, Chris Jordan, Roderic Leigh, Peter Oliver. Dir. Pip Simmons. Music by Chris Jordan with Rod Beddall and Steve Johnston. Masks by Maggie Jones. Lgt. Steve Whitson and Dick Johnson. (Mgt: Pip Simmons Theatre Group.)*

18 July *WOYZECK by Georg Büchner. Adpt. Pip Simmons. Cast: Rod Beddall, Sheila Burnett, Jessie Gordon, Poppy Hands, Steve Johnston, Chris Jordan, Roderic Leigh, Peter Oliver. Dir. Pip Simmons. Music by Chris Jordan and Rod Beddall. Cos. Roderic Leigh. Lgt. Steve Whitson and Dick Johnson.*

(Mgt: Pip Simmons Theatre Group. New production of the play which last opened at the Traverse on 27 July 1971.)

25 July *THE PEOPLE SHOW NO. 77: BILLIE HOLLIDAY SHOW PART TWO by the company. Cast: Dawn Archibald, Mike Figgis, Joy Lemoine, Mark Long, Emil Wolk. (Mgt: The People Show.)*

2 Aug. **LIVINGSTON & SECHELE** by David Pownall. Cast in Edinburgh: Joseph Marcell, Muriel Odunton, Ann Scott-James, John Shedden. Cast on Radio: Marcell, Jennifer Piercey, Shedden, Shope Shodeinde. Cast in London: Anni Domingo, Peter Kelly, Marcell, Piercey. Dir. Peter Lichtenfels. Des. Grant Hicks. Lgt. Alastair McArthur. (A radio version was broadcast on BBC Radio 4 on 10 and 16 Dec. 1979 – directed for radio by Alfred Bradley. The play was later seen at the Lyric Theatre Hammersmith Studio, London in June 1980 in a production by Peter Lichtenfels with designs by Dermot Hayes.)

4 Aug. *'ONE MAN COMEDY AND MIME SHOW' by Antonio Nodor Tome. Cast: Antonio Nodor Tome. (Mgt: Antonio Nodor Tome.)*

15 Aug. * **ROOTING** by Robert Holman. Cast: Paul Dalton, Anthony Dutton, John Normington, Roland Oliver, Pauline Siddle. Dir. Chris Parr. Des. Grant Hicks. Lgt. Alastair McArthur. (Developed by Holman from his half-hour two-hander television play 'Mucking Out'.)

17 Aug. THE ANDROID CIRCUIT. Credits as before. (Revival at The Other Traverse, Old Chaplaincy Centre, Edinburgh of production premièred at Traverse on 5 July. Transfers to ICA, London at end of run.)

19 Aug. THE SLAB BOYS. Credits as before in

152

Edinburgh. Cast in Glasgow and London: Coltrane rpl. Jake D'Arcy and Schuster rpl. by Julia McCarthy. (Revival by the Traverse at The Other Traverse, Old Chaplaincy Centre, Edinburgh of the play premièred at the Traverse on 6 Apr. Subsequently transfers to Print Workshop, Glasgow in association with the Glasgow Theatre Club and then to the Royal Court Theatre Upstairs, London on 18 Oct. Revived at the Traverse on 23 June 1982.)

22 Aug. **THE HARDMAN** by Tom McGrath and Jimmy Boyle. Cast: Black, Roy Hanlon, Kelly, Kennedy, Low, Nicholas, Sean Scanlan, Carey Wilson – with Goodman. Radio cast: David Bannerman, Kelly, Kennedy, Low, Alex Norton, Tony Roper, Scott-Jones, Wilson, Young – with Goodman. Dir. Peter Lichtenfels, Ian (a.k.a. Kenny) Ireland and Tom McGrath. Des. Bob Last and Grant Hicks. Lgt. Alastair McArthur. (Revival at The Other Traverse, The Old Chaplaincy Centre, Edinburgh of production which last opened at the Traverse on 3 Jan. Rev. 11 June 1979 at the Pavilion Theatre, Glasgow prior to a visit to the Kammerspiele in Munich, West Germany. A radio version of the play was broadcast by the BBC on Radio 4 on 21 May 1979, on Radio 3 on 5 July 1979 and on Radio Scotland on 9 Oct. 1980. The Radio Producer was Tom Kinninmont.)

29 Aug. † *DAS HELSTE JA IM KOPF NICHT AUS – a creation of Grips Theatre, Berlin. Written by Volker Ludwig and Detlef Michel. Music by Birgit Heyman and W. Siebert. Performed in German. Cast: Ute Bernskötter, Edwin Fisher, Ellen Fischer, Wolfgang von der Heide, Peter Heinsohn, Jurgen Hulnn, Johannes Joides, Astrid Ketels, Heike Körner, Hans Peters, Robert Pettigrew, Renate Rüger, Sabine Sauerer, Mick Werup, Klaus Wiegandt, Andrea Wilkens, Norbert Zipser. Dir. Andrew Neil. M.D. Robert Pettigrew. (Mgt: Theatre Wedel, West Germany in co-operation with the Scottish-German Centre/Goethe-Institute.)*

30 Aug. * *DESPAIRING, SUICIDAL . . . ? by Bob Goody, Jim Saxon and Peter Russell Brewis. Music by Peter Russell Brewis.*

Cast: Peter Russell Brewis, Bob Goody, Jim Saxon. Dir. Mel Smith. (Mgt: Smith and Goody.)

31 Aug. * *LIFE IS WHAT YOU MAKE IT by Roy Bailey and Leon Rosselson. Cast: Roy Bailey, Mike Carter, Leon Rosselson, Pam Scotcher. (Mgt: Rosselson and Bailey.)*

5 Sept. *'ODDITIES' – Triple bill consisting of:*

† *EUPHEMIA by Oddur Bjornsson. Trans. the cast. Cast: Bjorg Arnadottir, Karl Gudmundsson, Jon Juliusson, Kristin Magnus, Steinvor Mermannsdottir.*

YOLK LIFE by Oddur Bjornsson. Trans. Gudrun Tomasdottir. Cast: Karl Gudmundsson, Kristin Magnus.

† *ARIETTA by Oddur Bjornsson. Trans. the cast. Cast: Bjorg Arnadottir, Karl Gudmundsson, Kristin Magnus.*

All three plays dir. the author. Des. Jon Svanur Petursson. Lgt. Halldor Snorrason. (Mgt: The Summer Theatre, Iceland.)

10 Oct. **STREET FIGHTING MAN**. Credits as before – except Erskine rpl. Ann-Louise Ross and Welsh rpl. Sandy Neilson. (Revival of production premièred on 4 May. Subsequently transfers to Strathclyde University Drama Centre, Glasgow on 16 Oct. and then Aberdeen Arts Centre.)

15 Oct. *JESSE JIMMY – PROBABLY THE FASTEST GUN IN GOVAN by Shane Connaugton. Adpt. Morag Fullarton. Cast: Desi Angus, Betty Gillan, Stewart Preston, Billy Riddoch, Gordon Taylor, Alexander West. Dir. Morag Fullarton. Set. Janet Scarfe. Cos. Tam Harvey. Lgt. Alan J. Wands. (Mgt: Borderline Theatre Company.)*

17 Oct. *SHARED EXPERIENCE'S SCIENCE FICTIONS – improvised by the company. Cast: Sam Cox, Pam Ferris, Anthony Naylor, Raad Rawi, Ruth Seglow. Dir. Mike Alfreds. (Mgt: Shared Experience.)*

24 Oct. *** *THE SECOND COMIC AND THIRD GRAVEDIGGER SHOW*** by Russel Lane, Alex Mitchell and John Murtagh. Original songs by Sandi Easton. Cast: Sandi Easton, Isobel Gardner, Russel Lane, Alex McAvoy, John Murtagh, Tony Roper. Dir. Alex McAvoy. Des. the company. Lgt. Alex McAvoy. (Mgt: El Cheapo Productions presented by The Oil and Water Company.)

31 Oct. ***THE STREETS OF LONDON*** – dev. Edwina Dorman after the song by Ralph McTell. Dir. Edwina Dorman.
THE FISHERMAN AND HIS SOUL by Oscar Wilde. Adpt. Chris Harrowell. Dir. Pip Royall. Cos. Hilary Vernon Smith. Mime by Edwina Dorman.
Cast for both plays: Nick Dowsett, Chris Harrowell, Michael Mulkerrin, Terry Ruane, Jean St. Clair, Elaine White. (Mgt: Interim Theatre Company.)

7 Nov. **† *THE F AND H PLAY*** by Michael Almaz. Cast: Gavin Brown, Lewis Cowan, Chris Holroyd, Cheryl Law, Peter Miles, Elizabeth Phepps, Angelique Rockas, Jackie Skarvellis. Dir. the author. Des. Pam Martell. Lgt. Colin Scott. (Mgt: The Artaud Company.)

14 Nov. ***INUIT*** by David Mowat. Cast: Denise Armon, Tom Bowles, James Bryce, Su Grantley, Michael Harley, Tricia Scott, John Slade. Dir. Edward (a.k.a. John) Adams. A.D. Howard Kingston. Des. Roger Parris. Chor. Kris Plant. (Mgt: Paines Plough.)

16 Nov. *** *QUERELLE*** – A Pantomime for Jean Genet. Dev. Stuart Forbes after Genet's 'Querelle of Brest'. Cast: Peter de Burgh, Stuart Forbes, Walter Harikof, The Incomparable Manilla, Jon Pope, Mark Staford, Francis Sutor. Dir. Stuart Forbes – assisted by Tom Laurie. Des. Stuart Forbes. (Mgt: Stuart Forbes Mime Company.)

21 Nov. ***THE JUST*** by Albert Camus. Trans. Henry Jones. Cast: Rhys Evans, Christopher Frederick, Alan Gill, Poppy Hands, Sandy Neilson, Beth Robens. Dir. Francis Aiqui. Des. Chris Orvis. Lgt. Martin Palmer. (Mgt: Aico Theatre Company.)

30 Nov. ***LOVED*** by Olwen Wymark. Cast: Jill Dixon, Michael Johnson, Philip Lowrie, Priscilla Morgan, Veronica Quilligan, Sean Scanlan. Dir. Kenneth Chubb. Des. Andrea Montag. (Mgt: Wakefield Tricycle Company.)

5 Dec. ***GOGOL*** by Richard Crane. Cast: Richard Crane. Dir. and Des. Faynia Williams. Lgt. Colin Scott. (Mgt: Brighton Actors' Workshop.)

5 Dec. ***SCOTIA'S DARLINGS*** by Marcella Evaristi. Cast: David Bannerman, Monica Brady, Marcella Evaristi. Dir. the author and David Bannerman. (Mgt: Alhambra Theatre Company.)

12 Dec. ***ANCORMAN*** by Ron Hutchinson. Cast: Jack Chissick, Caroline Hunt, Will Knightley, Joseph Marcell, John Nightingale. Dir. John Dove. Des. Quentin Thomas. (Mgt: CV1 Theatre Company.)

16 Dec. ***REMEMBERING THE WORLD A LITTLE BIT*** – mime sketches by Francisco Morales. Cast: Francisco Morales and Gloria Romo. Dir. Francisco Morales. (Mgt: Theatro Chileno de Mimos, Chile.)

19 Dec. ***PETER AND PENNY AND THE MARVELLOUS MAGIC SHOW*** by Alex Norton with music by the author. Cast: David Bannerman, Elaine Collins, Gregor Fisher, Mike Halpin, Tam Harvey, Terry Neason, Simon Tait, Carey Wilson. Dir. Morag Fullarton. Des. Tony Scott. Lgt. Alan J. Wands. Chor. Conchita-del-Campo. (Mgt: Borderline Theatre Company.)

1979

3 Jan.   **ROBINSON CRUSOE** by Reg Bolton. Cast includes: Dawn Archibald, Reg Bolton. Dir. the author. (Mgt: Long Green Theatre Company.)

16 Jan.   **THE DALKEY ARCHIVE** – adpt. Allan McClellan from the novel by Flann O'Brien. Cast: John Blanchard, Arthur Kelly, Susie Kelly, Howard Lew Lewis, Allan McClelland, Oengus Mac-Namara, Steve Novak. Dir. Mike Bradwell. Des. Gemma Jackson. Lgt. Rupert Creed. (Mgt: Hull Truck Theatre Company.)

23 Jan.   **ASSASSINATIONS INDIS-CRIMINATE** – dev. the company. Cast. Patti Bee, Paddy Fletcher, Danka Gordon. Dir. Paddy Fletcher. (Mgt: Incubus Theatre Company.)

26 Jan.   **DOCTOR WELLBELOVED'S TRAVELLING ACADEMY OF HYGIENE.** Dir. Paddy Fletcher. (Mgt: Incubus Theatre Company.)

30 Jan.   **LOADED QUESTIONS** by Neil Hornick. Cast: Joel Cutrara, Peter Deman, Louise Jones. Dir. the author. (Mgt: The Phantom Captain School of Thought.)

13 Feb.   **DON JUAN** – adpt. John Retallack from the poem by Lord Byron. Cast: Valerie Braddell, Edmund Falzon, Ian Frost, Richarde Leighton, Victoria Plum, Ghislaine Rump. Dir. John Retallack. Cos. Amanda Wilson. Music by Dick McCaw. (Mgt: ATC London.)

15 Feb.   * **REQUIEM** by Stuart Forbes – based on Jean Genet's 'Funeral Rites'. Cast: Patric de Burgh, Stuart Forbes, Walter Harrikoff, Malcolm Jamieson, Riza McCary, The Incomparable Manilla. Dir. the author. (Mgt: Stuart Forbes Mime Company.)

20 Feb.   **SHARED EXPERIENCE'S GOTHIC HORRORS** – adpt. the company from J. S. Le Fanu's 'The Haunted Baronet'. Cast: Liz Brailford, Ken Drury, Michael Garner, Neale Goodrum, Sue Rogerson. Dir. John Dicks. Movement by Jane Gibson. (Mgt: Shared Experience.)

27 Feb.   **VENUS IN FURS** by Leopold von Sacher-Masoch. Adpt. Philip Oxman. Cast: Nick Birkinshaw, Katherine Gibb, Francis Rozelaar-Green. Dir. Geoff Moore. Set. Peter Mumford. Cos. Pamela Moore. (Mgt: Moving Being.)

8 Mar.   * **RENTS** by Michael Wilcox. Cast: David Bannerman, Jean Bruce, Jimmy Chisholm, Margaret Dent, Campbell Morrison, Anne Myatt, Dave Whitaker, Carey Wilson. Dir. Chris Parr. Des. Adrian Mudd. Lgt. Colin Scott. (Rev. on 28 Aug. in a rewritten version. Transfers to Lyric Theatre Hammersmith Studio, London on 17 Apr. 1982 and then to the Lyric Theatre main stage.)

5 Apr.   * **SMALL THOUGHTS FROM THE REVOLUTION** by Graeme Campbell. Cast: Peter Adair, Jimmy Chisholm, Roger Hume, Patricia Leventon, Campbell Morrison, Alison Rose, Finlay Welsh. Dir. Sandy Neilson. Des. Gemma Jackson. Lgt. Colin Scott. (This play was given a rehearsed reading by the Scottish Society of Playwrights at Newbattle Abbey on 2 Apr. 1976 and then at the Traverse on 3 Apr. 1976.)

19 Apr.   **A BIG TREATISE IN STORE** by Andrew Dallmeyer. Cast: Andrew Dallmeyer, Vivienne Dixon. Dir. the author. (Mgt: Mental Guerillas.)

24 Apr.   **CLOUD NINE** by Caryl Churchill. Music by Andy Roberts. Cast: Julie Covington, Carole Hayman, Jim Hooper, William Hoyland, Miriam Margoyles, Tony Rohr, Antony Sher. Dir. Max Stafford-Clark. Des. Peter Hartwell. Lgt. Robin Myerscough-Walker. A.D. Les Waters. (Mgt:

Joint Stock Theatre Company –
presented by the Scottish Arts
Council and the Traverse at
Moray House Theatre, Edin-
burgh.)

25 Apr. * **OVER THE TOP** by Tom
Buchan. Music by Robert Pet-
tigrew. Cast: Sue Lynne, Tony
Roper, Carey Wilson. Dir.
Campbell Morrison. Des. Grant
Hicks. Lgt. Colin Scott. (Rev. 8
May 1980.)

1 May   *THAT TIME by Samuel Beckett.*
Cast: Peter Adair.
***FOOTFALLS** by Samuel Beckett.*
Cast: Margaret Dent, Poppy
Hands.
Both plays dir. Francis Aiqui. Lgt.
Alastair McArthur. A.D. Geoff
Thorpe. (Mgt: Aico Theatre Com-
pany.)

2 May   **HESS** *by Michael Burrell. Cast:*
Michael Burrell. Dir. Philip
Grout. (Mgt: Michael Burrell.)

8 May   † *1837: THE FARMER'S*
REVOLT by Rick Salutin and
Theatre Pass Muraille. Cast:
Mary Ann McDonald, David
Papazian, Miles Potter, Booth
Savage, R. H. Thomson, Terry
Tweed. Dir. Pam Brighton from
the original production by Paul
Thompson. Des. Paul Williams.
Lgt. Paul Vallely. (Mgt: Theatre
Pass Muraille, Canada.)

18 May *VON LACHEN UBER DIE*
WELT ZUM LEBEN MIT DER
WELT – Songs, texts and poems
by Bertolt Brecht. Music by Bertolt
Brecht, Paul Dessau, Hans Eisler,
Hans Dieter Hosalla, Rudolf
Wagner-Regency and Kurt Weill.
Performed in German. Cast: Ekke-
hard Schall – with Hans Dieter
Hosalla. (Mgt: Ekkehard Schall,
German Democratic Republic.)

19 May * **THE LOVELIEST NIGHT OF**
THE YEAR by John Byrne.
Cast: Freddie Boardley, John
Breck, Elaine Collins, Robbie
Coltrane, Pat Doyle, Kay Gal-
lie, Tony Hollis, Phyllis Logan,

Ida Schuster, Carey Wilson –
with Mark Goldinger. Dir.
David Hayman. Des. Grant
Hicks. Lgt. Colin Scott. (A new
production of a rewritten version of this play entitled
'Threads' is performed at the
Hampstead Theatre Club, London on 13 Mar. 1980. It features the original Traverse cast
with the exception of Tony
Hollis [rpl. Mark Windsor] and
Kay Gallie [rpl. Claire Nelson]
and is dir. Robin Lefevre. A
radio version of the play entitled 'The Staffie' is broadcast
on BBC Radio Scotland on 1
Jan. 1981. It features the
Hampstead cast and is produced for radio by Marilyn Ireland [a.k.a. Imrie]. A further
and definitive version of the
play is produced by the Traverse on 27 June 1982 under
the title 'Cuttin' A Rug'. It
transfers to the Royal Court
Theatre, London on 19 Nov.
1982 and is rev. 4 May 1983 at
the Citizens Theatre, Glasgow
in assoc. with Glasgow
Mayfest.)

25 May *THE COCKROACH THAT*
ATE CINCINATTI by Alan
Williams. Cast: Alan Aldred
(a.k.a. Williams). Dir. Mike Brad-
well. (Mgt: Hull Truck Theatre
Company. Revived at Traverse on
21 Apr. 1981.)

31 May *MOLLY BLOOM'S SOLILO-*
QUY – adpt. Patricia Leventon
and John Quinn from James
Joyce's 'Ulysses'. Cast: Patricia
Leventon. Dir. Michael Deacon.
(Mgt: Patricia Leventon.)

11 June THE HARDMAN by Tom McGrath and
Jimmy Boyle. Cast: Ken Drury, Kelly,
Peter Lincoln, Low, Campbell Morrison,
Tony Roper, Scott-Jones, Benny Young –
with Goodman. Dir. Lichtenfels, Chris
Parr and Ireland. Des. Last and Hicks.
Lgt. McArthur. (Revival by the Traverse
in assoc. with the Glasgow Theatre Club
at the Pavilion Theatre, Glasgow of the
production last seen at The Other Tra-

verse, The Old Chaplaincy Centre, Edinburgh on 22 Aug. 1978. Subsequently transfers to the Kammerspiele in Munich, West Germany.

21 June *** THE BLACK STUFFER** by Elisabeth Bond. Cast: Peter Adair, Clare Kinsale, Irene Sunters, Rudolph Walker. Dir. Peter Lichtenfels. Des. Dermot Hayes. Lgt. Colin Scott. Chor. Pat Lovett. Music by Robert Pettigrew.

28 June *** *ACETYLENE VIRGIN* –** *Images of Sylvia Plath. Compiled from her work by Bob Macauley. Based on a concept by Barry Kyle. Cast: Jill Fenner, Jeni Giffen, Karen McCrary. Dir. Bob Macauley. A.D. George Byatt. Des. Heather Bate, Linda Broda and Lucinda MacKay. Music by David Hamilton. (Mgt: Ariel Theatre Company.)*

18 July *** TALK ABOUT IT** by John Bett. Cast: Peter Adair, Juliet Cadzow, Anthony Dutton, Roy Hanlon, Irene Sunters, Finlay Welsh, Jimmy Yuill. Dir. Ronnie Letham. Des. Dermot Hayes. Lgt. Colin Scott. (Rev. 19 Aug.)

24 July ***BANDITS*** *by C. P. Taylor. Cast: Denise Byson, Tim Healy, Brian Hogg, Ron Johnson, Pauline Moriarty, Val McLane, Anne Orwin, George Orwin, Max Roberts, Dave Whittaker. Dir. Teddy Kiedl. Des. Phil Bailey. (Mgt: Live Theatre Company.)*

31 July ***THE PEOPLE SHOW NO. 80: THE AIRPORT SHOW*** *by the company. Cast: Dawn Archibald, Mike Figgis, George Khan, Mark Long, Natasha Morgan, Emil Wolk. (Mgt: The People Show.)*

14 Aug. *** *THE WIDOWS OF CLYTH*** *by Donald Campbell. Cast: Desi Angus, Maureen Beattie, Jimmy Chisholm, Roy Hanlon, Fiona Knowles, Beth Robens, Ann-Louise Ross, Jimmy Yuill. Dir. Sandy Neilson. Set. Adrian Mudd. Cos. Mary Jane Reyner. Lgt. Ron John-*

ston. *(Mgt: Viewforth Productions.)*

19 Aug. **TALK ABOUT IT.** Credits as before except Dutton rpl. Roland Oliver and Sunters rpl. Jan Wilson. (Revival of the play premièred by the Traverse on 18 July.)

20 Aug. *** THE RED RUNNER** by Billy Connolly. Cast: Sara Ballintyne, Doreen Cameron, James Kennedy, Peter Lincoln, Alexander Morton, Tony Roper. Dir. Campbell Morrison. Des. Grant Hicks. Lgt. Gerry Jenkinson. (Traverse in assoc. with Edinburgh International Festival Society at Moray House Gymnasium, Edinburgh. Transfers to Traverse on 13 Sept.)

20 Aug. *** ANIMAL** by Tom McGrath. Cast: Richard Albrecht, Martin Black, Christian Burgess, Elaine Collins, Paul Dalton, Peter Dawson, Jill Fenner, Stuart Hopps, David Blake Kelly, Peter Kelly, Frances Low, Karen Mann, Robert Oates, Ann Scott-Jones, Josephine Welcome, Benny Young. Dir. Chris Parr. Movement by Stuart Hopps. Des. Grant Hicks. Lgt. Gerry Jenkinson. (Traverse in assoc. with Edinburgh International Festival Society at Moray House Gymnasium, Edinburgh. A production of a rewritten version of the play was premièred by the Scottish Theatre Company at the Opera House, Belfast on 14 Apr. 1981. Co-dir. Kenny Ireland and Hopps with Lgt. Jenkinson, it featured Collins, Fenner, Kelly, Low, Scott-Jones and Welcome from the original Traverse cast.)

21 Aug. **† *DER VAMPYR* –** *based on the opera by Heinrich Marschner, Byron and Polidori. Performed in German. Cast: Peter Armstrong, Heini Hartel, Ernst Haussinger, Elizabeth Kingdom, Peter Lipjewski, Robert Reim, Renate*

Reuss, Ute Ruppel, Thomas Stahl, Cielo Steltner, Nandor Tomory, Klaus Ullrich, Reinhold Wiedenmann – with Ursula Bolz, Graham Buckland, Alois Heind, Irmingard Jemiller, Wolfgang Munchs, Harald Sander, David Seaman, Jochen Sponsel, Willibert Steffens. M.D./Conductor: David Seaman. Dir. Heiney Eckardt and Pater B. Wyrsch. Des. Christa Baumgartner. Lgt. Gotz Schworer. Chor. Robert Reim. (Mgt: Opernstudio Nurnberg, West Germany.)

28 Aug. RENTS. Credits in Edinburgh as before – except without Bruce, Dent and Myatt. Cast in London: Dave Whitaker rpl. Jonathan Newth. Dir. Chris Parr. Des. Adrian Mudd. Lgt. Colin Scott. (Revival in a rewritten version of the play premièred by the Traverse on 8 Mar. Transfers to Lyric Theatre Hammersmith Studio, London on 20 Apr. 1982 and then to Lyric theatre main stage.)

4 Sept. * OOH LA LA! – dev. Mike Bradwell. Music by Stephen Warbeck with Mark Brignal. Cast: Bridget Ashburn, John Blanchard, Mark Brignal, Frances Brookes (a.k.a. Barber), Rosalind March, Hamish Reid, Stephen Warbeck. Dir. Mike Bradwell. Des. Geoff Rose. (Mgt: Hull Truck Theatre Company.)

13 Sept. THE RED RUNNER. Credits as before except Kennedy rpl. Campbell Morrison. (Transfer of play premièred by Traverse at Moray House Gymnasium, Edinburgh on 20 Aug.)

21 Sept. BENDING BODY THEATRE – an entertainment by Graham Valentine. Cast of 6 includes: Graham Valentine. Dir. the author. (Mgt: Bending Body Theatre Company, Aberdeen.)

10 Oct. * HEBUCA by Stewart Conn – derived from the 'Hecabe' of Euripides. Music by John Sampson. Cast: Isobel Gardner, Poppy Hands, Lyndy Lawson, Diana Olsson, Sue Rogerson, Carey Wilson. Dir. John Carnegie. Des. Mecheal Taylor. Lgt. John Carnegie. (Mgt: Winged Horse Touring Productions.)

17 Oct. * MEDIEVAL TALES – adapted from Chaucer and Boccaccio by Chris Harrowell. Cast: Nick Dowsett, Graeme Hattrick, Sarah Lesley, Michael Mulkerrin, Graham Peech, Terry Ruane, Jean St. Clair. Dir. Chris Harrowell. Movement by Hilary Metcalf. Set. Chris Harrowell. Cos. Hilary Vernon Smith. (Mgt: Interim Theatre Company.)

18 Oct. THE CLYDE IS RED a Poemplay by George Byatt. Cast: David Bannerman, Keith Casburn, Martin Cochrane, Cordelia Ditton, Hilary Drake, Jill Fenner, Michael McKevitt, Walter McMonagle, Jonathan Oliver, Ewan Stewart, Vari Sylvester, Benny Young. Dir. the cast, the author and Bob Macauley. (Mgt: Theatre PKF. Revived at Traverse as a playreading on 15 Apr. 1984.)

1 Nov. * MAGIC by William Grant. Cast: John Butterly, Maureen Carr, Margo Croan, Ron Paterson. Dir. Peter Lichtenfels. Des. Dermot Hayes. Lgt. Colin Scott. Chor. Stan Pettigrew. Music by John Cunningham.

2 Nov. FOREVER YOURS, MARIE LOU by Michel Tremblay. Performed in French. Cast: Sophie Clément, Rita Lafontaine, Monique Mercure, Gilles Renaud. Dir. André Brassard. Des. François Laplante. Lgt. Mario Bourdon. (Mgt: Compagnie des deux chaises, Quebec.)

9 Nov. FANNY BURNEY AND FRIENDS – adapted from the work and correspondence of Fanny Burney by Karin Fernald. Cast: Karin Fernald. Dir. David Rush. (Mgt: Karin Fernald.)

29 Nov. * THE STADIUM by Alisdair Skinner. Cast: Carole Bollard, Mark Heath, Howard Lew Lewis, Finlay Welsh. Dir. Roland Oliver. Des. Adrian Mudd. Lgt. and Sound Colin Scott.

1980

5 Mar.   * **HARD TO GET** by Marcella Evaristi. Cast: Maureen Beattie, Stephen Boxer, Peter Kelly, Maggie Shevlin. Dir. Michael Boyd. Des. Caroline Beaver. Lgt. Colin Scott. (Revived in a rewritten version on 26 Aug. A radio version is broadcast on BBC Radio 4 on 26 and 31 Jan. 1981 – directed for radio by Marilyn Imrie. A television version which includes Maureen Beattie in the cast is later broadcast by Granada TV.)

9 Mar.   *WHY DO THE WRONG PEOPLE TRAVEL?* *(Around the world in 100 minutes) – compiled by Charles Bell from tales by Nash, Coward, Betjeman, Thomas and others. Cast: Charles Bell with Peter Nelson. (Mgt: Charles Bell in the Traverse Bottom Bar.)*

1 Apr.   *MONSIEUR APOLLINAIRE ET LE CIRQUE DU ZODIAQUE – dev. Geoff Moore and including 'The Breasts of Tiresias' by Guillaume Apollinaire. Original music by Caroline Noh. Cast: Nick Birkinshaw, Jessica Cohen, Francis Rozelaar-Green, Peter Wooldridge. Dir. Geoff Moore. Chor. Geoff Moore, Jessica Cohen and Francis Rozelaar-Green. Des. Geoff Moore and Pamela Moore. Lgt. John Davis. Sound and projections by John Thorne. (Mgt: Moving Being.)*

10 Apr.   * **MOVING IN** by Alison Watson. Music by Robert Pettigrew. Cast: Sarah Collier, Lloyd McGuire, Ann-Louise Ross, Alexander West with Robert Pettigrew. Dir. John Carnegie. Des. Adrian Mudd. Lgt. John Carnegie.

25 Apr.   *THE GORGON by Mike Absalom. Cast: Mike Absalom. Dir. Rupert Creed. (Mgt: Hull Truck Theatre Company.)*

8 May   OVER THE TOP by Tom Buchan. Music by Robert Pettigrew. Cast: Russell Hunter, Tony Roper, Patience Tomlinson. Dir. Campbell Morrison. Des. Dermot Hayes. Lgt. Colin Scott. (Revival of the play premièred by the Traverse on 25 Apr. 1979.)

16 May   *JUMPING MOUSE by Brian Patten. Cast: John Bolton. Dir. John Bolton. (Mgt: John Bolton.)*

23 May   * *ASPECTS – dev. Peter Adair. Music by Susan Alexander. Cast: Peter Adair, Susan Alexander, Jules Cranfield. Dir. Peter Adair. Lgt. Alastair McArthur. (Mgt: The Adair Company.)*

30 May   *HUIS CLOS by Jean Paul Sartre. Cast: David Bannerman, Sarah Collier, Lloyd Quinan, Vari Sylvester. Dir. Sandy Neilson. (Mgt: Sandy Neilson. New production of play which last opened at the Old Traverse on 2 Jan. 1963.)*

12 June   * **TEA TENT TALK** by Kate Collingwood. Cast: Paul Anthony-Barber, Olive Ellis, Anne Orwin, Howard Lew Lewis, Patricia Stanley. Dir. Chris Parr. Des. Adrian Mudd. Lgt. Colin Scott.

19 June   *METAPHYSICS AND STRIP by Andrew Dallmeyer. Cast includes: Tam Dean Burn, Neil Cunningham, Andrew Dallmeyer, Vivienne Dixon, Susan Duffy, Kate Fraser. Dir. the author. Lgt. Colin Scott. (Mgt: Mental Guerrillas.)*

10 July   * **ROYAL FLUSH** by William Grant. Cast: Denis Agnew, Iain Glass, Lynne Miller, Melanie Wallis. Dir. Peter Lichtenfels. Des. Dermot Hayes. Lgt. Colin Scott.

1 Aug.   * **SNAPSHOTS** by John Anderson. Cast: John Anderson, Simon Attilla, Terry Dougherty, Lou Hirsch, Alastair Llewellyn, Tucker McGuire, Patricia Northcott, Robin Papas, Janene Possell, Michael Scobie, Angela Vale, Patrick Waldron, Ramsay Williams. Dir. John Normington. Chor. Charles Augins.

Des. Poppy Mitchell. Lgt. Colin Scott. M.D. Terry Dougherty. (Traverse in assoc. with Eddie Kulukundis.)

17 Aug. * *YOBS AND SNOBS by Andrew Dallmeyer. Music by Robert Handleigh.* Cast: Robbie Coltrane, Andrew Dallmeyer, Vivienne Dixon, Robert Handleigh, Sheila Latimer. Dir. and Des. the author. (Mgt: Mental Guerrillas.)

26 Aug. **HARD TO GET.** Credits as before – except Boxer rpl. Peter Wight. (Revival of a rewritten version of the play premièred by the Traverse on 5 Mar. A radio version – with the revival stage cast – is broadcast on BBC Radio 4 on 26 and 31 Jan. 1981 – directed for radio by Marilyn Imrie.)

19 Aug. * *THE ICE CHIMNEY by Barry Collins.* Cast: Chris Ettridge. Dir. John Chapman. Des. John Clark. Lgt. Steve Whitson. Sound by Mic Pool. (Mgt: Lyric Hammersmith Studio Theatre, London.)

16 Sept. **THE MISUNDERSTANDING** *by Albert Camus. Trans. Gilbert Martin from 'Le Malentendu'.* Cast: Virginia Dignam, Red Hayworth, Jackie Skarvellis, Erica Stevens, Terry Victor. Dir. Michael Almaz. (Mgt: The Artaud Company and Café Theatre.)

25 Sept. **THE SASH** by Hector MacMillan. Cast: Mary-Ann Coburn, Jon Croft, Felicity Hayes-McCoy, Anne Myatt, Jonathan Watson. Dir. Robin Peoples. Des. Peter Ling. Ass. Des. Annette Sumption. Lgt. Colin Scott.

21 Oct. **THE SEA WOLF** *by Peter Godfrey after the book by Jack London.* Cast: Dick Waring, Chris Whittingham. Dir. Brian Lipson. Lgt. Charlie Paton. Music by Camilla Saunders. (Mgt: Rational Theatre.)

28 Oct. *JACK LONDON: THE MAN FROM EDEN'S GROVE by C. R. Portz. Music by Martin Burman.* Cast: C. R. Portz. Dir. the

author. Des. Sandra Lee Marks and Kathleen L. Fredericks. (Mgt: The Labour Theatre presented by Cast Presentations Ltd.)

6 Nov. * **A NORMAL MAN** by Charles Ockrent. Cast: Richard Beale, Juliet Cadzow, Shirley Anne Field, Lou Hirsch, Ronnie Letham, Deborah Makepeace, Raymond Platt. Dir. Frank Nealon. Des. Adrian Mudd. Lgt. Colin Scott. (Traverse in assoc. with Eddie Kulukundis.)

18 Nov. **SOUND OUT** *by Terry Ruane.* Cast: Mark Colleano, Mick Dowsett, Sarah Scott, Elaine White. Dir. Jane Carr and the author. (Mgt: Interim Theatre Company.)

27 Nov. **THE CASE OF DAVID ANDERSON Q.C.** by John Hale. Cast in Edinburgh: Arthur Boland, Jon Croft, Randal Herley, Evelyn Langlands (a.k.a. Eliza Langland), Phyllis Logan, Michael Mackenzie, David Peate, Corin Redgrave. Cast in London: Arthur Boland rpl. Martin Heller and Phyllis Logan rpl. Sybil Wintrope. Dir. Chris Parr. Des. Chris Kinman. Lgt. Colin Scott (in Edinburgh). (The mgt. of the Traverse production is later taken over by the Lyric Theatre Hammersmith, London who present it in their Studio Theatre on 15 Sept. 1981.)

4 Dec. **SELF SERVICE** *by Irene Coates. Cast: Fiona Knowles, Benny Young. Dir. Bob Macauley. Lgt. Neil Sandford.* (Mgt: Ariel Theatre Company.)

16 Dec. **THE ARABIAN NIGHTS** *– dev. Justin Greene from the original stories trans. Sir Richard Burton.* Cast: Alan Finlayson, Kinny Gardner, Fay Prendergast (a.k.a. Dummer), Jon Trevor. Dir. Justin Greene. Des. Charlotte Brill. M.D. Joe McGinley. (Mgt: Scottish Mime Theatre.)

1981

17 Feb.   ***CARTOON*** *by Pip Royall. Music by Nick Dowsett. Cast: Josef Castronova, Jamie Cresswell, Nick Dowsett, Dione Inman, Gregory Koppell, Evelyn Langlands (a.k.a. Eliza Langland), Andrew McDonald, Sarah Scott. Dir. the author. (Mgt: Interim Theatre Company.)*

26 Feb.   'YOUNG PLAYWRIGHTS FESTIVAL' – sextuple bill consisting of:
   * ***HALF PRICE*** *by Alison Smith. Cast: Ann-Louise Ross, Vari Sylvester.*
   * ***GIRO*** *by Joe Mullaney. Cast: Colin Gourley, Lloyd Quinnan, Tony Roper, Ann-Louise Ross.*
   * ***ON HAWKSHAW RIG*** *by Murray S. Laverick. Cast: Colin Gourley, Laddie the dog, Murray S. Laverick, Vari Sylvester.*
   * ***THOUGHTS*** *by Julie King. Cast: Lloyd Quinnan, Tony Roper, Ann-Louise Ross, Vari Sylvester.*
   * ***THREE MEN IN A TUB*** *by Marianne Carey. Cast: Colin Gourley, Lloyd Quinnan, Tony Roper.*
   * ***WE'LL STRIVE TO PLEASE YOU*** *by Angus Reid. Cast: Colin Gourley, Lloyd Quinnan, Tony Roper, Ann-Louise Ross, Vari Sylvester. All six plays dir. Gareth Wardell. Des. Adrian Mudd. Lgt. Colin Scott. Music by Ian Robertson. (Mgt: Scottish Youth Theatre.)*

Mar.   '1-2-3' – a trilogy of related full length plays performed in rotation in repertoire:

11 Mar.   * **WHO ARE YOU ANYWAY?** by Tom McGrath.

15 Mar.   * **VERY IMPORTANT BUSINESS** by Tom McGrath.

21 Mar.   * **MOONDOG** by Tom McGrath.
   Casts for all three plays: Ron Bain, Gregor Fisher, Shelley Lee. All three plays dir. Chris Parr. Des. Jenny Tiramani. Lgt.

Colin Scott. Sound by Gregor Graham. (Trilogy transfers to ICA Theatre, London on 21, 22 and 23 Apr. respectively and then to the Young People's Theatre at the Toronto Festival, Canada on 13 May. The trilogy was jointly commissioned by the BBC and the Traverse as part of the Radio Theatre '81 Festival and broadcast on Radio 3 – with the original stage cast and Tom Kinninmont as Producer for radio – as follows: 'Who Are You Anyway' on 18 June 1982, 'Very Important Business' on 8 Mar. 1981 and 'Moondog' on 19 Dec. 1983.)

26 Mar.   ***HUMPTY DUMPTY WAS PUSHED*** *by Tom and Colum Sands. Cast: Colum Sands, Tom Sands. (Mgt: Edinburgh Folk Festival.)*

18 Apr.   **Chris Parr leaves as Artistic Director. Peter Lichtenfels is appointed as interim Director and is confirmed as Artistic Director in September.**

Apr.   'THE COCKROACH TRILOGY' – three related full length plays performed in rotation in repertoire:

21 Apr.   THE COCKROACH THAT ARE CINCINNATI by Alan Williams. (Revival of production which last opened at the Traverse on 25 May 1979.)

22 Apr.   ***THE RETURN OF THE COCKROACH*** *by Alan Williams.*

23 Apr.   ***THE COCKROACH HAS LANDED*** *by Alan Williams. Cast for all three plays: Alan Aldred (a.k.a. Williams). All three plays dir. Mike Bradwell. (Mgt: Hull Truck Theatre Company.)*

29 Apr.   * ***SHIFT WORK*** *by Donald Mackenzie. Cast: Jackie Farrell, Joseph Greig, Anne Myatt, Mary Riggans. Dir. John Carnegie. Des. Adrian Mudd. Lgt. John Carnegie. (Mgt: Winged Horse Touring Productions.)*

7 May   * **ACCOUNTS** by Michael Wil-

161

cox. Cast: Cliff Burnett, David Calder, Madelaine Newton, Tony Roper, Kevin Whately. Dir. Peter Lichtenfels. Des. Andy Greenfield. Lgt. Colin Scott. (Rev. 16 August. Transfers to Riverside Studios, London 8 Sept. A radio version is broadcast on BBC Radio 4 on 2 and 8 August 1982 – with the revival cast and directed for radio by Patrick Rayner. The play is subsequently filmed for television by Granada TV for Channel Four with some of the stage cast.)

3 June **EVERY GOOD BOY DESERVES FAVOUR** by Tom Stoppard and André Previn. Cast: Alexander Armstrong, Niall Buggy, Patrick Malahide, Robert Trotter, Tom Watson Judy Wilson – with the Scottish National Orchestra. Conducted by John Georgiadis. Dir. Peter Lichtenfels. Des. David Cockayne. (Scottish National Orchestra and the Traverse at the Usher Hall, Edinburgh. Transfers to MacRobert Centre, Stirling on 9 June and then to Kelvin Hall, Glasgow on 18 June.)

4 June *** THE ASCENT OF WILBERFORCE III** or 'The White Hell of Iffish Odorabad' – book and lyrics by Chris Judge Smith; music by J. Maxwell Hutchinson. Cast in Edinburgh: Paul Dalton, Peter Harding, Carole Harrison, Godfrey Jackman, Gordon Sandison – with Robert Pettigrew, Johnny Phillips. Cast in London: Gordon Sandison rpl. Bill Bradley. Dir. Ronnie Letham. Des. Dermot Hayes. Lgt. Colin Scott. M.D. Robert Pettigrew. Chor. Pat Lovett and Stan Pettigrew (in Edinburgh). Chor. Kenn Oldfield (in London). (The production is taken over by the Lyric Theatre Hammersmith, London and opens in their Studio on 4 Jan. 1982.)

2 July **TRAFFORD TANZI the Venus Flytrap v. the ever popular Dean Rebel** by Claire Luckham. Original music by Chris Monks. Cast: Eve Bland, Edward Clayton, Patrick Field, David Fielder, Victoria Hardcastle, Noreen Kershaw – with Chris Monks. Dir. Chris Bond. Des. Ellen Cairns. Lgt. Colin Scott. Wrestling Coaches: Mitzi Mueller and Brian McInally. (Rewritten version of 'Tuebrook Tanzi, the Venus Flytrap' which was premièred as a touring pub/club show in Spring 1978 by the Everyman Theatre in Liverpool – dir. Lou Wakefield with a cast which included Clayton, Hardcastle and Chris Martin. A new version dir. Martin entitled 'Tugby Tanzi' was toured round community centres in Leicester in Spring 1980 by the Phoenix Theatre with a cast which included Julia North. The first version of Bond's production was toured round pubs, schools and community centres in Manchester from 7 Oct. 1980 by Contact Theatre. Now entitled 'Trafford Tanzi', the cast included Hardcastle, Kershaw and Neil Pearson with designs by Cairns and music by Monks. This Manchester production was then re-written and developed into the version seen at the Traverse which became the standard version for future productions. The Traverse production was revived at the Traverse on 18 Aug. and then toured to the Birmingham Rep Studio on 26 Oct., the Belfast Festival on 9 Nov. and the Lyric Theatre Hammersmith Studio, London on 20 Nov. The Traverse pro-

duction was then taken over by the Half Moon Theatre, London and presented there in summer 1982. The production was then taken over by Freedman Panter Ltd. and Namara Ltd. in association with James and Charlene Nederlander and Richard Vos and presented at the Mermaid theatre in London opening on 30 Sept. 1982.)

9 July　*** LOTS WORSE OFF THAN YOU** by Robert Forrest. Cast includes: Tam Dean Burn.
*** GUISER MARTIN** by Robert Forrest. (Mgt: Simon John Productions.)

28 July　**WEST HAM v. HEARTS** – dev. Mike Maran and David Sheppard. Cast: Mike Maran, David Sheppard. (Mgt: Mike Maran and David Sheppard.)

29 July　*** A DRUNK MAN LOOKS AT THE THISTLE** – dev. Mike Maran and David Sheppard after the poem by Hugh MacDiarmid. Cast: Mike Maran, David Sheppard. (Mgt: Mike Maran and David Sheppard.)

30 July　**BUTTONS** by David Sheppard. Cast: David Sheppard. (Mgt: Mike Maran and David Sheppard.)

1 Aug.　**THE JOLLY BEGGARS** by Robert Burns. Music by Mike Maran. Cast: Mike Maran. (Mgt: Mike Maran and David Sheppard.)

12 Aug.　* **HEAVEN AND HELL** by Dusty Hughes. Cast: Jonathan Adams, Jimmy Chisholm, Nick Ellsworth, Hamish Glen, Celia Imrie, Jimmy Yuill. Dir. Richard Wilson. Des. John Byrne. Lgt. Colin Scott. M.D. Robert Pettigrew. Chor. Stan Pettigrew. (Transfers to Royal Court Theatre, London on 9 Sept.)

16 Aug.　ACCOUNTS. Credits as before – except Calder rpl. George Pensotti. (Revival of play premièred by Traverse on 7 May. Transfers to Riverside Studios, London on 9 Sept. A radio version is broadcast

on BBC Radio 4 on 2 and 8 Aug. 1982 – with the revival cast and directed for radio by Patrick Rayner.)

18 Aug.　TRAFFORD TANZI the Venus Flytrap v. the ever popular Dean Rebel. Credits for Edinburgh and Half Moon as before. Cast for tour and Lyric Hammersmith: Field rpl. Neil Pearson and Monks rpl. Rick Lloyd. Cast for first night at Mermaid; Field returns in place of Pearson and Rick Lloyd rpl. Richard Stone. Alternative casts at Mermaid include: Kay Adshead, Dee Anderson, Chris Darwin, Jane Lee, Brian Maxine, North, Pearson – with Mel Robinson. Casts for re-directed production at Mermaid include: Paul Abrahams, Peter Ellis, Stella Gonet, Arbel Jones, Neil McCaul, Annabel Price, James Warrior, Toyah Wilcox. Directed for Edinburgh, tour, Lyric and Half Moon by Chris Bond. Directed for Mermaid by Chris Bond and Edward Clayton. Re-directed from the original production for final cast at Mermaid by Danny Hiller. Des. Ellen Cairns. Lighting for Edinburgh, tour and Lyric by Colin Scott. Lighting for Mermaid by Brian Harris. Wrestling Coaches for Edinburgh, tour and Lyric: Mitzi Mueller and Brian McInally. Wrestling Coach for Half Moon and first Mermaid casts: Brian Maxine. Wrestling Coaches for last Mermaid cast: Howard Lester and Mitzi Mueller. (Revival of the production which last opened at the Traverse on 2 July. Toured to the Birmingham Rep Studio on 26 Oct., the Belfast Festival on 9 Nov. and the Lyric Theatre Hammersmith Studio, London on 20 Nov. The Traverse production was then taken over by the Half Moon Theatre, London and presented there in summer 1982. The production was then taken over by Freedman Panter Ltd. and Namara Ltd. by arrangement with James and Charlene Nederlander and Richard Vos and presented at the Mermaid Theatre in London opening 30 Sept. 1982. During the Mermaid run, the production was re-directed with a new cast.)

1 Sept.　*LEAVING HOME* – compiled by Barbara Ewing. Cast: Barbara Ewing, Hemi Rapata, Martyn Sanderson. Dir. Ronnie Letham. A.D. Barbara Ewing. Des. Dermot Hayes. Lgt. Rory Dempster. (Mgt: Te Wahapu Company, New Zealand.)

15 Sept.　*TAMLANE* by Edwin Stiven. Music by Richard Cherns and John Wilson. Cast includes: Mil-

ton Cadman, Sharon Erskine, Anne Lacey, Clunie MacKenzie, Una McNab, Charles Nowosielski, Garry Stewart – with Richard Cherns, Robert Handleigh, Ian Hewett, John Wilson. Dir. Charles Nowosielski. Lgt. Jeremy Webber. (Mgt: Theatre Alba.)

1 Oct. * **WEDDING BELLES AND GREEN GRASSES** by Marcella Evaristi. Cast: Sarah Collier, Valerie Fyfer, Janice Laurie. Additional cast on radio: Tony Roper. Dir. Tim Fywell. Des. Stephen West. Lgt. Colin Scott. (Transfers to Tron Theatre Club, Glasgow on 10 Nov. A radio version is broadcast on BBC Radio 3 on 1 July 1982 and 13 Feb. 1983 – directed for radio by Marilyn Imrie.)

29 Oct. * **THE HOT HELLO** by David Pownall. Cast: Vivienne Dixon, Alan Finlayson, Gerald Mannix Flynn, Illona Linthwaite, Mary Ellen Ray. Dir. Peter Lichtenfels. Des. David Cockayne and Nettie Edwards. Lgt. Brian Harris.

1982

30 Mar. *REAL TIME by Chas Bryer, Beverly Foster, Neale Goodrum, Ingrid Haskal, Derek Laskie, Frances Low, Robby Nelson, Alan Partington, Jack Shepherd, John Tams, Anthony Trent, Paul Woodrow. Cast: Chas Bryer, Beverly Foster, Neale Goodrum, Frances Low, Robby Nelson, Alan Partington, Anthony Trent. Dir. Jack Shepherd. Des. John Halle. Lgt. John Halle and Alan Day. (Mgt: Joint Stock Theatre Group presented by the Traverse at Moray House, Edinburgh.)*

13 Apr. *THE BLACK HOLE OF CALCUTTA – dev. the company and written by Bryony Lavery. Cast: Patrick Barlow, Bob Goody, Barbara Thorn. Dir. Susan Todd.*

Original music by Crannog. (Mgt: National Theatre of Brent.)

16 Apr. *CHARLIE'S A HEADCASE by Brian Miller. Music by Andy Park. Cast: Caroline Keddie, Malcolm Macilraith, Bill Murdoch. Dir. the author. Lgt. Kevin Miller. (Mgt: Stagestrux Theatre Company. Cumbernauld.)*

20 Apr. *'MEMORIES of Buck & Bubbles, Bill 'Bojangles' Robinson, Bert Williams' – devised and chor. Honi Coles and Chuck Green. Cast: Honi Coles, Chuck Green – with Tom Finlay, Kenny Macdonald, Andy Munro. (Mgt: Honi & Chuck.)*

29 Apr. * **SAILMAKER** by Alan Spence. Cast: Denis Agnew, Robert McIntosh, Ian McNicol, Nicholas Sherry. Dir. Peter Lichtenfels. Des. Sue Mayes. Lgt. Colin Scott.

7 May *TRUE CONFESSIONS – a revue by Liz Lochhead with music by Esther Allan. Cast: Esther Allan, Liz Lochhead, Siobhan Redmond. (Mgt: Allan, Lochhead and Redmond in the Traverse Bar.)*

21 May *DURTY LAUNDRY – a revue by Liz Gardiner, Morag Hepburn, Liz Lochhead, Alison Watson, Ian Crofton, Chaitanya and Warwick. Music by Graham Robb and Esther Allan. Cast: Liz Gardiner, Morag Hepburn and Graham Mendel Whitelaw. Dir. David A. Stevenson. (Mgt: Gardiner and Hepburn in the Traverse Bar.)*

27 May * **STILL LIFE** (the third part of 'Paisley Patterns' – The Slab Boys Trilogy) by John Byrne. Cast: Elaine Collins, Andrew (a.k.a. Andy) Gray, Gerald Kelly, Billy McColl, Alexander Morton. Dir. David Hayman. Des. the author. Lgt. Colin Scott. (Revived on 7 Sept. Transfers to Royal Court Theatre, London on 23 Nov. Revived on 5 May 1983 at Citizens Theatre, Glasgow in

assoc. with Glasgow Mayfest.)

23 June **THE SLAB BOYS** (the first part of 'Paisley Patterns' – The Slab Boys Trilogy) by John Byrne. Cast in Edinburgh and London: Iain Andrew, Collins, Katy Gardiner, Andrew (a.k.a. Andy) Gray, Gerald Kelly, McColl, Alexander Morton, Nicholas Sherry. Cast in London: Gardiner rpl. Jan Wilson. Cast in Glasgow: McColl rpl. David Hayman. Dir. Hayman. Des. the author. Lgt. Colin Scott. A.D. in Glasgow: Lloyd Quinnan. (Revival of play premièred at Traverse on 6 Apr. 1978. Transfers to Royal Court Theatre, London on 17 Nov. Revived on 3 May 1983 at Citizens Theatre, Glasgow in assoc. with Glasgow Mayfest.)

27 June **CUTTIN' A RUG** (the second part of 'Paisley Patterns' – The Slab Boys Trilogy) by John Byrne. Cast in Edinburgh and London: Iain Andrew, Boardley (in different role), Collins, Margo Cunningham, Katy Gardiner, Stella Gonet, Andrew (a.k.a. Andy) Gray, Gerald Kelly, Billy McColl, Alexander Morton, Nicholas Sherry. Cast in London: Cunningham rpl. Jennifer Piercey and Katy Gardiner rpl. Jan Wilson. Cast in Glasgow: McColl rpl. David Hayman. Dir. David Hayman. Des. the author. Lgt. Colin Scott. A.D. in Glasgow: Lloyd Quinnan. (Rewritten version of play premièred by the Traverse under the title 'The Loveliest Night of the Year' on 19 May 1979. Transfers to Royal Court Theatre, London on 19 Nov. Rev. 4 May at Citizens Theatre, Glasgow in assoc. with Glasgow Mayfest.)

5 Aug. *** THE BOYS IN THE BACK ROOM** by Andrew Dallmeyer. Cast: John Branwell, Jeffrey Chiswick, Neil Cunningham, Andrew Dallmeyer, Vivienne Dixon, Lou Hirsch. Dir. Peter Lichtenfels. Des. Dermot Hayes. Lgt. Colin Scott.

7 Aug. *EXCURSIONS by Fay Prendergast (a.k.a. Dummer). Cast: Fay Prendergast. (Mgt: Fay Prendergast in the Traverse Top Bar.)*

13 Aug. *SEE RED by Frank Wilson. Cast: Richard Hawley, Tyrone Huggins, Claire MacDonald, Graeme Miller, Steve Shill, Paul Wilkinson. Dir. Pete Brooks. (Mgt: Impact Theatre Co-operative.)*

19 Aug. *** BLOOD AND ICE** by Liz Lochhead. Cast: Elaine Collins, Ciaran Hinds, Jenny Michel-more, Gerda Stevenson, Andrew C. Wadsworth. Dir. Kenny Ireland. Des. Hildegard Bechtler. Lgt. Colin Scott. (Drastically rewritten by Lochhead from her play 'Mary and the Monster' which was first performed at the Belgrade Theatre Studio, Coventry in a production by Michael Boyd in Mar. 1981.)

24 Aug. † *A PRELUDE TO DEATH IN VENICE by Lee Breuer. Cast: Greg Mehrten, William Raymond. Dir. the author. Des. Linda Hartinian, Alison Yerxa and L. B. Dallas. Lgt. Linda Hartinian. (Mgt: Mabou Mines, New York.)*

24 Aug. † *WOZA ALBERT! – conceived by Percy Mtwa, Mbongeni Ngema and Barney Simon. Cast: Percy Mtwa, Mbongeni Ngema. Dir. Barney Simon. Lgt. Mannie Manin – executed by Colin Scott. (Mgt: Market Theatre, Johannesburg, South Africa.)*

7 Sept. **STILL LIFE.** Credits in Edinburgh and London as before. Cast in Glasgow: McColl rpl. David Hayman. A.D. in Glasgow: Lloyd Quinnan. (Revival of the play premièred by Traverse on 27 May. Transfers to Royal Court Theatre, London on 23 Nov. Revived on 5 May at Citizens Theatre, Glasgow in assoc. with Glasgow Mayfest.)

21 Sept. *SISTER SUZIE CINEMA – words by Lee Breuer; music by Robert Otis Telson; chor. Alison Pearl. Cast: Ben Halley Jnr. – with Fourteen Karat Soul: Reginald 'Briz' Brisbon, Russell Fox II, Le Mont Simpson, Glenny T., David Thurmond. Dir. Lee Breur. Costumes by Greg Mehrten. Lgt. Julie Archer. Sound by Craig Jones.*

THE GOSPEL AT COLONUS – adapted from Robert Fitzgerald's translation of the 'Oedipus at Colonus' of Sophocles by Robert Otis Telson (music), Lee Breuer and Ben Haley Jnr. Cast: Kevin Davis, Ben Halley Jnr., Isabell Monk, Robert Otis Telson – with Four-

teen Karat Soul: Reginald 'Briz' Brisbon, Russell Fox II, Le Mont Simpson, Glenny T., David Thurmond. Dir. Lee Breur. Cos. Rita Ryack. Lgt. Julie Archer. Sound by Craig Jones. (Mgt: Re. Cher. Chez Studio for the Avante Garde Performing Arts, New York, USA.)

28 Sept. **THE SHEPHERD BEGUILED** by Netta B. Reid. Cast: Ronnie Aitken, Alice Bennett, Heather Bennett, Natalie Bennett, Alison Boyd, Maureen Carr, Sharon Erskine, Vincent Friell, Kirsty Johnston, Anne Lannan, Clunie MacKenzie, Finlay MacLean, James O'Malley, Garry Stewart, Alexander West, John Wilson (a.k.a. Grace). Dir. Charles Nowosielski. Lgt. Jeremy Webber. Music by Richard Cherns and John Wilson. (Mgt: Theatre Alba.)

7 Oct. * **NOT WAVING** by Catherine Hayes. Cast: Carmel McSharry, Lynne Miller, Sean Scanlan. Dir. Peter Lichtenfels. Des. David Cockayne. Lgt. Colin Scott.

9 Nov. **POSTWAR** – chor. Tim Miller. Music by Big Game. Cast: Barry Davidson, Tim Miller. Projections by Kirk Winslow. Lgt. Stan Pressner. (Mgt: Tim Miller, USA in assoc. with Dance Umbrella.)

12 Nov. **DREAM SEQUENCE** – chor. Charles Moulton; music by A. Leroy. Cast: Charles Moulton. Cos. Eugenie Bafaloukas. (Mgt: Charles Moulton & A. Leroy, USA in assoc. with Dance Umbrella.)

16 Nov. 'A Programme of New Dance' – consisting of:
CONTINUOUS REPLAY –chor. Arnie Zane. Music by Brian Rulon. Cast: Arnie Zane.
SIMPLE FAITH – chor. Bill T. Jones. Cast: Bill T. Jones.
ROTARY ACTION – chor. Bill T. Jones and Arnie Zane. Music by Peter Gordon. Cast: Bill T. Jones, Arnie Zane. Lgt. Wil-

liam Yehle. (Mgt: Bill T. Jones & Archie Zane in assoc. with Dance Umbrella.)

23 Nov. Four parts from 'LIGHT' – extracts from an epic dance consisting of:
SOLO FROM 'LIGHT', PART 16 (THE DAIKON FIELD) – chor. Kei Takei. Cast: Lazuro Brezer, Kei Takei.
DUET FROM 'LIGHT', PART 8 – chor. Kei Takei. Cast: Lazuro Brezer, Luis Gonzalez.
'LIGHT', PART 10 (THE STONE FIELD) – chor. Kei Takei. Cast: Lazuro Brezer, Luis Gonzalez, Kei Takei.
DUET FROM 'LIGHT', PART 14 (THE PINE CONE FIELD) – chor. Kei Takei. Cast: Lazuro Brezer, Luis Gonzalez, Kei Takei. Lighting for all four dances by Maldwyn Pate. (Mgt: Kei Takei's Moving Earth Chamber Ensemble, USA in assoc. with Dance Umbrella.)

27 Nov. 'An Evening of Dance Solos' – consisting of:
SOLO BACH – chor. Egal Perry. Music by J. S. Bach.
HOW DEEP THE WAKING – chor. Cliff Keuter. Music by George Crumb.
BLUE GROTTO – chor. Jim Self. Design and Sound by Frank Moore.
STEEPLECHASE RAG – chor. James Waring. Music by James P. Johnson.
S'WONDERFUL – chor. Annabelle Gamson. Music by George Gershwin.
SOMEWHERE BETWEEN HOURS – chor. Manuel Alum.
KLEZMERISED – chor. Ernesto Corvino. Des. Marcella Corvino. Cast for all solos: Ellen Kogan. Lgt. Todd McConchie. (Mgt: Ellen Kogan, USA in assoc. with Dance Umbrella.)

30 Nov. 'A Programme of New Dance' – consisting of:

A WISH SANDWICH – chor. Michael Clark. Music by Eric Crermontet. Cast: Michael Clark, Owen Smith. *OF A FEATHER, FLOCK* –chor. Michael Clark. Cast: Michael Clark, Steve Goff, Owen Smith. *CRAZY DAISY AND THE NORTHERN LIGHTS* – chor. Laurie Booth. Cast: Laurie Booth. Dir. Tanya Myers. Des. Kate Owen. Tapes by Bootl. (Mgt: Michael Clark & Laurie Booth in assoc. with Dance Umbrella.)

3 Dec. **FASE, FOUR MOVEMENTS ON THE MUSIC OF STEVE REICH** – chor. Anne Teresa de Keersmaeker to existing music by Steve Reich. Cast: Anne Teresa de Keersmaeker, Michèle Anne de May. Des. Martine Andre. Lgt. Raymond Fromont and Mark Schwentner. (Mgt: Anne Teresa de Keersmaeker, Belgium in assoc. with Dance Umbrella.)

1983

16 Apr. **Jenny Killick joins the Traverse as Trainee Director.**
19 Apr. **WELCOME HOME** by Tony Marchant. Cast: Tony London, Ian Mercer, Gary Olsen, Robert Pugh, Michael Townsend, Mark Wingett. Dir. John Chapman. Des. Caroline Beaver. Lgt. Tim Speechley. (Mgt: Paines Plough.)
28 Apr. * **FUGUE** by Rona Munro. Cast: Evelyn (a.k.a. Eliza) Langland, Katherine Rogers, Gaylie Runciman. Dir. Les Waters. Des. Helen Turner. Lgt. George Tarbuck.
24 May † **TRIO** – written and compiled by Joseph Chaikin, Mira Rafalowicz, David Leveaux, Lizzie Olesker and the cast. Music by Harry Mann. Cast: Roger Babb, Ronnie Gilbert, Harry Mann. Dir. Joseph Chaikin. Des. Jun Maeda and

Mary Brecht. Lgt. Richard Lloyd. (Mgt: The Winter Project, New York. An earlier version of this production was presented in assoc. with LaMama ETC in New York under the title 'Lies and Secrets'.)

31 May † **THEATRE OF THE FILM NOIR** by George F. Walker. Original music by John Roby. Cast: Peter Blais, David Bolt, Dean Hawes, Jim Henshaw, Susan Purdy. Dir. the author. Des. Peter Blais. Lighting adapted by Peter Freund from the original by James Plaxton. (Mgt: Factory Theatre Lab, Toronto.)

9 June * **SPACE INVADERS** by Alan Spence. Cast: Tam Dean Burn, Joyce Deans, Ken Drury, Andy Gray, Jonathan Kydd, Maggie McCarthy. Dir. Peter Lichtenfels. A.D. Jenny Killick. Des. Sue Mayes. Lgt. George Tarbuck.

7 July * **BUGLER BOY** by Stanley Eveling. Cast: Hetty Baynes, Robert Morris, Joseph Peters, Tom Watson. Dir. Leon Rubin. Des. John Byrne. Lgt. George Tarbuck. (Rev. 24 August.)

4 Aug. † **MEDEA** – adpt. Barney Simon from the version of the legend of Franz Grillparzer. Cast: Clive Bell, Yvonne Bryceland, David Calder, Caroline Embling, Peggy Phango, Richard Williams, Terence Wilton and Robert Beattie, Brian Bridson, David Clark, Simon Lumsden, Graham McLeod, Sandy Nicholl, Joe Tree. Dir. Barney Simon. Des. Brian Vahey. Lgt. George Tarbuck. A.D. Jenny Killick. (Transfers to Riverside Studios Hammersmith, London on 13 Sept.)

23 Aug. **FALKLAND SOUND/VOCES DE MALVINAS** – edited by Louise Page from interviews and the letters to and from Lt. David Tinker. Cast: Marion Bailey, Paul Jesson, Lesley Manville, Stella

Maris, Julian Wadham. Dir. Max
Stafford-Clark. A.D. Simon Cur-
tis. Des. David Rodger. Lgt.
Simon Byford and Chris Toulmin.
(Mgt: Royal Court Theatre, Lon-
don.)

30 Aug. † *NASTASIA FILIPOVNA* –
adapted from Dostoyevsky's novel
'The Idiot' by Andre Wajda, Jan
Nowicki and Jerzy Radziwilowicz.
Performed in Polish. Cast: Jan
Nowicki, Jerzy Radziwilowicz. Dir.
Andre Wajda. Des. Krystyna
Zachwatowicz. (Mgt: Teatr Stary,
Cracow, Poland.)

4 Oct. *LASSIE PHONE HOME* – a
revue by Murray Ewan and
Morag Fullarton. Cast: Juliet
Cadzow, Murray Ewan, Michael
Roberts, Ann-Louise Ross, Mandy
Travis, Sandy Welch.
A NIGHT IN THE UKRAINE –
Book and lyrics by Dick Vosburgh.
Music by Frank Lazarus. Cast:
Juliet Cadzow, David Dunn, Mur-
ray Ewan, Christopher Reason,
Michael Roberts, Ann-Louise Ross,
Mandy Travis, Sandy Welch.
Revue and musical dir. Morag
Fullarton. Des. Neil Murray. Lgt.
Alan J. Wands. Chor. Celia Ham-
mond. M.D. Christopher Reason.
(Mgt: Borderline Theatre Com-
pany.)

11 Oct. *PUT IT ON YOUR HEAD* –dev.
the company. Cast: Annabel
Arden, Fiona Gordon, Marcello
Magni, Simon McBurney. Lighting adapted by George Tarbuck
from the original by Ace McCar-
ron. (Mgt: Théâtre de Complicité.)

18 Oct. *DIE HOSE (THE KNICKERS)*
by Carl Sternheim. Adpt. Jenny
Killick from the translation by
Eric Bentley. Cast: Simon Russell
Beale, Rupert Evans, Martin
Husk, Catherine Livesey, Carol
Reed – with Doreen Busbridge,
Ally Kessler, Vaughn Townhill.
Dir. and Des. Jenny Killick. Music
by Ally Kessler. A.D. Helen Ads-
head. (Mgt: Guildhall School of

Music and Drama.)

24 Oct. 'YOUNG PLAYWRIGHTS FES-
TIVAL '83' – Triple Bill consist-
ing of:
PICTURE PARADISE by Eliza-
beth Montgomery. Cast: Blythe
Duff, John Murtagh, Sheila
Macaskill (a.k.a. Greer-Smith).
(Previously produced in an ear-
lier version by TAG Theatre
Company, Glasgow.)
* **REFLECTIONS** by Fiona
Thomson. Cast: Blythe Duff,
Sandy Imlach, Teri Lally, John
Murtagh, Sheila Macaskill.
NEVER A DULL MOMENT by
Jackie Boyle and Tricia Burns.
Cast: Blythe Duff, Sandy
Imlach, Teri Lally, John Mur-
tagh, Sheila Macaskill. (Pre-
viously produced in an earlier
version by the Royal Court
Theatre, London.) All three
plays dir. Jenny Killick and
Robin Peoples. Des. Lucy Wel-
ler. Lgt. George Tarbuck. (Scot-
tish Youth Theatre and the
Traverse at Eden Court
Theatre, Iverness. After a tour
which includes Aberdeen, Kirk-
caldy, Oxenford, Ettrick Bridge,
Dundee, Glasgow, Lochgilp-
head, Clydebank, Ardrossan
and Stirling, the triple bill
transfers to the Traverse on 8
Nov.)

26 Oct. * *MEANWHILE* – an entertainment improvised nightly by the
company from suggestions by the
audience. Cast: Justin Case, Steve
Steen, Jim Sweeney, Peter Wear.
(Mgt: The Omlette Broadcasting
Company.)

28 Oct. 'A Programme of New Dance' –
including:
DECOY – chor. Robert Kovich.
PIN-UP – chor. Robert Kovich.
TARANTULA – chor. Robert
Kovich.
Casts: Segolene Colin, Robert
Kovich. (Mgt: Robert Kovich,
France in assoc. with Dance

Umbrella.)

1 Nov.   *'A Programme of New Dance' –*
consisting of:
STEPS *– chor. Dana Reitz.*
CHANGING SCORE *– chor.*
Dana Reitz.
SOLO FROM 'FIELD PAPERS'
– chor. Dana Reitz.
Cast for all three: Dana Reitz.
(Mgt: Dana Reitz, USA in assoc.
with Dance Umbrella.)

3 Nov.   **PARTS I-IV** *– chor. Michael*
Clark. Cast: Michael Clark. (Mgt:
Michael Clark in assoc. with
Dance Umbrella.)

5 Nov.   **FORMS OF RECREATION** *–*
chor. the company. (Mgt: Axis
Dance Company in assoc. with
Dance Umbrella.)

8 Nov.   YOUNG PLAYWRIGHTS FESTIVAL '83.
Credits as before. (Transfer of triple bill
premièred at Eden Court Theatre, Inverness on 24 Oct.)

★   ★   ★

Action readings presented by
David Hamilton.

25 Nov.   *THE ANSWER by David Hamilton.*
A DISGRACEFUL MISREPRE-
SENTATION by David Hamilton.

1984

31 Jan.   *A quadruple bill of monologues –*
consisting of:
THE TELL-TALE HEART *by*
Edgar Allan Poe.
THE BUCKET RIDER *–adapted*
from Franz Kafka by Steven Berkoff.
THE BIKE *(extracted from 'East')*
by Steven Berkoff.
THE ACTOR *by Steven Berkoff.*
Cast for all four: Steven Berkoff.
All four plays dir. Steven Berkoff.
(Mgt: Steven Berkoff.)

10 Feb.   **THE EEMIS STANE** *– compiled*
by Owen Dudley Edwards from
the work of Hugh MacDiarmid.
Cast: Dolina MacLennan, Sandy
Neilson. (Mgt: MacLennan and
Neilson.)

17 Feb.   **MISTERO BUFFO** *by Dario Fo.*
Trans. Ed Emery. Cast: Neil Bart-
lett, Annie Griffin, Rick Kemp,
Suzanne Odette Khuri, Banuta
Rubess, Alan Schofield. (Mgt:
1982 Theatre Company.)

21 Feb.   † **SONGS FROM THE FRONT**
a show of songs compiled by
Elaine Loudon. Cast: Elaine
Loudon – with her band. (Mgt:
Elaine Loudon.)

28 Feb.   * **GLASGOW ZEN** *– words by*
Alan Spence, slides by Mary Wal-
ters and music by Jimmy Ander-
son. Cast: Jimmy Anderson, Alan
Spence. (Mgt: Spence, Walters
and Anderson. Revived at Tra-
verse on 5 Feb. 1985.)

2 Mar.   *'AN EVENING OF TURKISH*
DELIGHTS' – a dance cabaret
consisting of:
PASHA'S HAREM *– chor. Fiona*
Dear. Cast: Fiona Busby, Christ-
ine Camillo, Wendy Dawson,
Catherine Evers, Louise Hellewell,
Paulene Laverty, Gina Long,
Sheila Manson, Jeanette Newell,
Elspeth Shaw.
ALANA'S LAMP *– chor. Louise*
Hellewell. Music by Brian Eno.
Cast: Pauline Laverty, Christ-
opher Long, Paul Tyers, Jonathan
Williams.
STUTLU KAHVE *(Arabian*
Dance from Act II of 'The Nut-
cracker') – chor. Peter Darrell.
Music by Piotr Ilych Tchaikovsky.
Cast: Christine Camillo, Lloyd
Embleton, Christopher Long, Ewan
McLeod, Paul Tyers.
THINGS HAPPEN AFTER
A . . . TURKISH DELIGHT *–*
chor. Fiona Dear. Music by Piotr
Ilych Tchaikovsky. Cast: Fiona
Dear, Robert Hampton.
HAREMESQUE *– chor. Geoffrey*
West. Music by Ketelby. Cast:
Lloyd Embleton, Christopher Long,
Paulo Lopes, Anna McCartney,
Ruth Prior.
IKI BALESI *– chor. Gordon Ait-*
ken. Music by Leo Delibes. Cast:

Noriko Ohara, Paul Tyers.
CATATURK – chor. Paulene
Laverty. Music by David Bowie.
Cast: Louise Hellewell.
BLUE RONDO A LA TURK –
chor. Peter Darrell. Music by
Dave Brubeck. Cast: Frankie Au,
Kenn Burke, Christine Camillo,
Joachim Chandler, Paulo Lopes,
Christopher Gillard, Ewan
McLeod. Lgt. Victor Lockwood for
all ballets. (Mgt: 'Iskocya Balesi'
– Scottish Ballet.)

9 Mar.   **THE INNOCENT** by Tom
McGrath. Cast at Traverse:
Willy Blair, Kevin Brock, Helen
McGregor, Lawrie McNicol,
Fiona (a.k.a. Fletcher) Mathers,
Keith Neil, Susan Oliver, Ralph
Riach, Elizabeth (a.k.a. Liz Phi-
lip) Scott, Anthony Ventre,
Alan Vicary – with George
Lyle, Tom McGrath. Cast for
revival: Blair, Brock, Tom
McGrath, McGregor, McNicol,
Mathers, Neil, Scott, Ian Sexon,
Ventre, Vicary – with Lyle,
Nick Weston. Dir. Jenny Killick.
Music by Tom McGrath and
George Lyle. Design co-
ordinated by Adrian Mudd.
Lgt. George Tarbuck (at Tra-
verse). Lgt. David Filshie (for
revival). (Traverse in assoc.
with the Royal Scottish Aca-
demy of Music and Drama. A
rewritten version of the play
first performed by the Royal
Shakespeare Company at the
Warehouse Theatre, London on
22 May 1979. The mgt. of the
production is taken over by a
cast/author/director co-
operative under the banner
'The Innocent Company' and
rev. on 10 Aug. in a rewritten
version at the Wildman Room,
Assembly Rooms, Edinburgh. It
then transfers to the Tron
Theatre Club, Glasgow in
Sept.)

20 Mar. * *ZX 'n I* – a mixture of talk, per-

formance, music and technology
by Tom McGrath. Cast: Tom
McGrath and his daughter's ZX
81 home computer. (Mgt: Tom
McGrath.)

23 Mar. * **BRASSNECK** – revue material
by Liz Lochhead with music by
Alasdair Robertson. Cast: Liz
Lochhead. (Mgt: Liz Lochhead.)

27 Mar. **PALS** by Tom McGrath. Cast:
James Gibb, Joseph Greig, Sheila
Grier, David McKay, Michael
Mackenzie, David McKay, Ann
Scott-Jones. Dir. Robert Robson.
Set. George Blackhall. Cos. Morna
Baxter. Lgt. William M. Winter.
(Mgt: Cumbernauld Theatre Com-
pany.)

3 Apr.   **BLACK MAS** by John Constable.
Cast: Trevor Butler, Carole Harri-
son, Ian Reddington, James Snell.
Dir. Roland Rees. Set. Peter Whi-
teman. Cos. Sheelagh Killeen. Lgt.
Steve Whitson. (Mgt: Foco Novo.)

12 Apr. '1984: POINTS OF DEPAR-
TURE' – triple bill consisting of:
* **THE CLEAN SWEEPS** by
Stuart Paterson. Dir. Peter
Lichtenfels.
* **PURITY** by Chris Hannan.
Dir. Jenny Killick.
* **IN DESCENT** by Simon
Donald. Dir. Jenny Killick.
Casts for all three: Simon Rus-
sell Beale, Stella Gonet, Ronnie
Letham, Ian McNicol, Caroline
Paterson, Gerda Stevenson.
Cos. Colin McNeill. Set. Kenny
Miller. Lgt. George Tarbuck.
(Transfers to Leonard Lang
Complex/Industrieterrein
Amstel, Amsterdam on 5 June
as part of 'Fairground '84' –
conceived and produced by the
Mickery Theatre, Amsterdam
and Ritsaert ten Cate for the
Holland Festival.)

12 May   **Traverse opens the Traverse
Downstairs Theatre – a 60 seat
theatre with the audience on
two sides and later (with 70
seats) on three sides of the**

acting area. The theatre is converted from the former downstairs bar which had previously been a car repair workshop.

12 May † **BARRY: PERSONAL STATEMENTS** by Frederic Mohr (a.k.a. David McKail). Cast: Gerda Stevenson. Dir. Stephen Unwin. (Downstairs Theatre. Transfers to Surgeon's Hall, Edinburgh on 29 June. Revived in Downstairs Theatre on 14 Aug.)

17 May * **78 REVOLUTIONS** by Michael Wilcox. Cast: Norman Cooley, Gordon Faith, Neil Sweattenham, Lee Trevorrow, Philip Voss. Dir. Peter Lichtenfels. Des. Dermot Hayes. Lgt. George Tarbuck. (Traverse in assoc. with Lyric Theatre Hammersmith, London. Transfers to Lyric Theatre Studio in June.)

2 June * *THE CLOWN AND THE JOCKEY* – a mime/clown show by Mark Saunders. Cast: Mark Saunders and a child. (Mgt: Mark Saunders.)

14 June * **MARK'S GOSPEL** – from W. L. Lorimer's translation of the New Testament into Scots. Cast: Sandy Neilson. Dir. Sandy Neilson and Peter Lichtenfels. Des. Adrian Mudd. (Downstairs Theatre. Rev. 21 Aug.)

21 June * **KLIMKOV: THE LIFE OF A TSARIST AGENT** by Chris Hannan. Based on Maxim Gorky's 'The Life of a Useless Man'. Cast: Christ Barnes, Michael Burlington, Kate Duchêne, Jack Ellis, Billy Fellows, Breffni McKenna, Andrew Normington. Dir. Jenny Killick. Des. Neil Murray. Lgt. George Tarbuck. (Rev. 21 Aug.)

29 June **BARRY: PERSONAL STATEMENTS.** Credits as before. (Traverse at Surgeon's Hall, Edinburgh on 29 June. Transfer of production first seen at Traverse on 12 May. Revived in Downstairs Theatre on 14 Aug.)

19 July * **THE OPIUM EATER** by Andrew Dallmeyer. Cast: Neil Cunningham, Stewart Preston. Dir. the author. Des. Adrian Mudd. (Downstairs Theatre. Transfers to Upstairs Theatre on 11 Aug. The mgt. of the production is then taken over by the author and it transfers to Mad Hatters Disco, Edinburgh on 13 Aug. Transfers to Gate Theatre, London in Dec. 1985. A radio version was broadcast on BBC Radio 3 on 11 Nov. 1984 and 24 Apr. 1985 with Preston repl. Russell Hunter. The Producer for radio was Stewart Conn.)

8 Aug. * **AN HISTORIE OF THE MACHINE** by Martyn Hobbs. Cast: Andrew (a.k.a Andy) Gray, Stephen MacDonald, Robert McIntosh, Dikran Tulaine. Dir. Peter Lichtenfels. Chor. Kedzie Penfield. Des. Andy Greenfield. Lgt. George Tarbuck.

10 Aug. † *STILL LIFE by Emily Mann. Cast: Susan Barnes, Deborah Carlisle, James Morrison. Dir. Molly Fowler. Dramaturg: James McNeil. (Mgt: Vietnam Veterans Theatre Ensemble Company.)*

11 Aug. † *SANDRA/MANON* by Michel Tremblay. Trans. John Van Burek from 'Damnée Manon Sacrée Sandra'. Cast: Simon Russell Beale, Patricia Northcott. Dir. Stephen Unwin. Des. Ashley Martin-Davis. (Transfers to Donmar Warehouse, London on 1 Oct.)

12 Aug. * **THE WORKS** by Marcella Evaristi. Cast: Marcella Evaristi. Dir. Jenny Killick. (Downstairs Theatre. Transfers to Tron Theatre, Glasgow and Third Eye Centre, Glasgow. A radio version with the original cast was broadcast by BBC

Radio 3 on 4 Sept. 1985 and 2 May 1986 – directed for radio by James Runcie.)

14 Aug. **THE HUMAN VOICE** *by Jean Cocteau. Trans. Susannah York. Cast: Susannah York. Dir. and Des. Simone Benmussa. Lgt. Genevieve Soubirou. (Mgt: Richard Jackson and Susannah York in assoc. with Espace Theatral Simone Benmussa Company.)*

14 Aug. BARRY: PERSONAL STATEMENTS. Credits as before. (Downstairs Theatre. Revival of production which opened at Traverse on 12 May.)

14 Aug. † **MELANCHOLY JACQUES** – *adpt. Jean Jourdheuil and Bernard Chartreux from 'Reveries of the Solitary Walker' and 'Letter to d'Alembert' by Jean-Jacques Rousseau. Trans. Christopher Logue. Cast: Simon Callow. Dir. Jean Jourdheuil. Set. Lucio Fanti. Cos. Patrice Cauchetier. Lgt. Bart Cossee. Music by Jean-Jacques Rousseau. A.D. Jean Badin. (Mgt: The Almeida Theatre Company.)*

14 Aug. † **BLACK DOG – INJ'EM-NYAMA** – *created by Barney Simon and the company. Cast: Kurt Egelhof, Marié Human, John Maolusi Ledwaba, Neil McCarthy, Gcina Mhlope, James Mthoba. Dir. Barney Simon. A.D. Carola Luther. Des. Neil McCarthy and Barney Simon. Lgt. Mannie Manim. (Mgt: Market Theatre, Johannesburg.)*

21 Aug. KLIMKOV: THE LIFE OF A TSARIST AGENT. Credits as before. (Revival of play premièred by Traverse on 21 June.)

28 Aug. MARK'S GOSPEL. Credits as before. (Downstairs Theatre. Revival of production premièred by Traverse on 14 June.)

28 Aug. * **HOUGH'S HALF HOUR** *by Ewan MacLachlan and Julian Hough. Cast: Julian Hough. Dir. Andrew Norton. (Mgt: David Jones Productions in the Downstairs Theatre.)*

28 Aug. **BEHIND THE OILSCAPE: PRE-19TH CENTURY** – *compiled by Anne Lorne Gillies. Cast:*

Anne Lorne Gillies. Dir. John Murtagh. (Mgt: Anne Lorne Gillies.)

29 Aug. **BEHIND THE OILSCAPE: 19TH CENTURY** – *compiled by Anne Lorne Gillies. Cast: Anne Lorne Gillies. Dir. John Murtagh. (Mgt: Anne Lorne Gillies.)*

30 Aug. **BEHIND THE OILSCAPE: 20TH CENTURY** – *compiled by Anne Lorne Gillies. Cast: Anne Lorne Gillies. Dir. John Murtagh. (Mgt: Anne Lorne Gillies.)*

18 Sept. * **ROUGHNECK** *by George Gunn. Cast: Fiona Knowles, Hugh Loughlan, Roddy Simpson. Dir. the company. Lgt. George Tarbuck. (Mgt: Theatre Pkf.)*

25 Sept. * **THE RHYMER'S PROMISE** *by Donald Gunn. Music by Richard Cherns. Cast: John Grace, Michael Hammond, Anne Lacey, Anne Lannan, Clunie MacKenzie, Garry Stewart – with Richard Cherns, Sabine Rauch, Virginia Strawson, Mushie Weston. Dir. Charles Nowosielski. Lgt. Jeremy Webber. M.D. Richard Cherns. (Mgt: Theatre Alba.)*

11 Oct. **BREAD AND BUTTER** by C. P. Taylor. Cast: Doreen Cameron, Christopher Connor, Eileen Nicholas, Alexander West. Dir. Peter Lichtenfels. Des. Andy Greenfield. Lgt. George Tarbuck. (New production of the play which last opened at the Traverse on 25 Nov. 1969.)

11 Oct. **CANDY KISSES** by John Byrne. Cast: Freddie Boardley, Nell Campbell, Jimmy Chisholm, Pat Doyle, Peggy Marshall, Brian Pettifer, Tessa Wojtczak. Dir. Robin Lefèvre. Des. the author. (Traverse in assoc. with Leicester Haymarket Theatre at Haymarket Studio, Leicester. This production was first presented by and at the Bush Theatre, London in May with designs by Byrne

and a cast which included Boardley and Marshall. Transfers to Traverse on 7 Nov. and then to Tron Theatre Club, Glasgow on 18 Dec.)

30 Oct.   **A MINUTE TOO LATE** – *dev. the company. Cast: Jos Houben, Simon McBurney, Marcello Magni. Dir. Annabel Arden. (Mgt: Théâtre de Complicité in the Downstairs Theatre.)*

7 Nov.   CANDY KISSES. Credits as before plus Lgt. George Tarbuck. (Transfer of production revived at Leicester Haymarket Theatre Studio on 11 Oct. Transfers to Tron Theatre Club, Glasgow on 18 Dec.)

22 Nov.   **NOONDAY DEMONS** by *Peter Barnes. Cast: Simon Donald, Kim Fenton. Dir. Hamish Glen. Des. Graham Johnston. Lgt. George Tarbuck. (Mgt: Writers Theatre Company in the Downstairs Theatre.)*

19 Dec.   * **SOUNDS . . . VIOLINS AND DANCERS** – *dev. Kedzie Penfield and Leonard Friedman. Chor. Kedzie Penfield. Cast: Leonard Friedman, Richard Friedman, Kedzie Penfield. (Mgt: Penfield and Friedman.)*

★   ★   ★

Playreadings presented during the year in the Upstairs Theatre by Theatre Pkf.

5 Feb.   ALL FALL DOWN by Torquil Barker.

14 Feb.   CLAXON TROMBETTE E PERNACCHIE (TRUMPETS AND DRUMS) by Dario Fo.

15 Feb.   THREE MONOLOGUES by Franca Rame.

19 Feb.   THE HEART OF SATURDAY NIGHT by Colin Macdonald.

26 Feb.   PYRATES by George Gunn.

18 Mar.   GOING HOME by Betty Stone.

25 Mar.   MAISIE BALFOUR'S APPLE TREE by Sue Matthew.

15 Apr.   THE CLYDE IS RED by George Byatt. (Revival of the poem/play which last opened at the Traverse on 18 Oct. 1979.)

29 Apr.   TWENTIETH-CENTURY FOX

by George Gunn.

Playreadings of 18 unsolicited scripts were presented in April, May and June by the Traverse in the Upstairs Theatre under the title 'Sight Unseen'.

Playreadings presented during the year in the Downstairs Theatre by Edinburgh Playwrights Workshop.

7 Nov.   AT THE DEW DROP INN by Muriel Barnett and Marjorie Harper.

10 Nov.   CONFESSIONS by Ian Rankin.

14 Nov.   THE WAL AT THE WARLD'S END by David Purves. (This was later seen in production at the Traverse under the title 'The Puddock and the Princess' on 3 Dec. 1985.)

17 Nov.   JONATHAN by Christina Johns.

Playreadings presented during the year in the Downstairs Theatre by Workshop One.

11 Nov.   THE POET – a play/poem by George Gunn. (Premièred in production by Know Alternative in the Downstairs Theatre on 20 Mar. 1985.)

18 Nov.   ORPHEUS – a play/poem by Richard Livermore.

1985

5 Feb.   GLASGOW ZEN. Credits as before. (Revival of production premièred at Traverse on 28 Feb. 1984.)

12 Feb.   **HANCOCK'S LAST HALF HOUR** by *Heathcote Williams. Cast: Jim McManus. Dir. Mark Piper. (Mgt: Jim McManus. Revived at Traverse on 26 Mar.)*

19 Feb.   'YOUNG PLAYWRIGHTS FESTIVAL '85' – *Triple bill consisting of:*
PASS THE PARCEL by *Angela Mullen. Cast: Sheila Greer-Smith, Helen McGregor, Stewart Preston, Jonathan Watson, Alexander West.*

DOON THE WATER by Kenny Grant. Cast: Sheila Greer-Smith, Helen McGregor, Stewart Preston, Jonathan Watson, Alexander West.
WITHOUT A DOUBT by George Forrest. Cast: Sheila Greer-Smith, Helen McGregor, Stewart Preston, Jonathan Watson.
All three plays dir. Alexis Leighton. Des. Robin Peoples. (Mgt: Scottish Youth Theatre.)

26 Feb. **ICKY YAH** by Andy Mackie. Cast: Louise Ballantyne, Alison Burney, Susan Clark, Wendy Cobain, Therese Dallmain, Lindsay De Vries, Craig Duncan, Ross Dunsmore, Kate Hamilton, Claire Marshall, Katie McCorkindale, Dee McRoberts, Mike Nardone, Kay Paterson, Charles Ross, Susan Ryan, Laurence Scott-Lodge, Rory Stevens, James Sturgeon, John Wright. Dir. the author and Lynn Bains. Lgt. Don Swanson. (Mgt: Kirkcaldy College of Technology in assoc. with the Scottish Student Drama Festival.)

27 Feb. **WHITEWASH?** by Haydn Davis. Cast: Stuart Borland, Karen McQueen. Dir. the author. (Mgt: Jordan Hill College, Glasgow in assoc. with the Scottish Student Drama Festival in the Downstairs Theatre.)

28 Feb. **LUNATIC AND LOVER** by Michael Meyer. Cast: John Browning, Fiona Clacher, John Hasselgren, Mary-Jane McQuillen, Nick Skipper, Irene Watson, Irene Wright. Dir. Patrick Evans. Des. Deborah Livingstone. Lgt. Jon Harvey. (Mgt: Duncan of Jordanstone College of Art, Dundee in assoc. with the Scottish Student Drama Festival.)

1 Mar. **THE SURROGATE** by Charles Barron. Cast: David Beckett, Torquil Buxton, Catherine MacBeath, Janice Stott, Andy Wilson, Ann Woods. Dir. Lorraine Hutchison.

Lgt. Gillian Forshaw. (Mgt: ACE Drama, Aberdeen in assoc. with the Scottish Student Drama Festival in the Downstairs Theatre.)

2 Mar. **MACSHEFFRAY** by Ken McPhee. Cast: Al-Hatmy, Mhari Colvin, Simon Murray, Tony Newbold, Cameron Orr, Sandra Rutherford, Terry Walls. Dir. the author. Lgt. Norman Tuddenham and Gillian Innes. (Mgt: Dundee College of Commerce Drama Group in assoc. with the Scottish Student Drama Festival.)

6 Mar. * **MORE HAPPY CHICKENS** by Michael Duke. Cast: Alan Campbell, Simon Donald. Dir. Hamish Glen. Des. Graham Johnston. Lgt. George Tarbuck. (Mgt: Abattoir Theatre Company in the Downstairs Theatre.)

7 Mar. **CAN'T PAY WON'T PAY** by Dario Fo. Adpt. Robert Walker and Alex Norton. Cast: Maureen Carr, Anne Downie, Andy Gray, Stuart Hepburn, Alexander Morton. Dir. Ian Brown. Des. Stewart Laing. (Mgt: TAG Theatre Company.)

12 Mar. **JOHN** – Book by Adele Saleem, lyrics by Sarah McNair and music by Michele Maxwell. Cast: Sarah McNair, Adele Saleem. Dir. Michele Frankel. Des. Catti Calthrop. (Mgt: Hard Corps Theatre Company.)

19 Mar. **HELEN OF TROY** by John Matthews and Mark Saunders. Cast: John Matthews and Mark Saunders. (Mgt: Tony and Derek.)

20 Mar. * **THE POET** by George Gunn. Cast: Pat Mackie, Paul Nivison. Dir. Hugh Loughlan. Lgt. George Tarbuck. (Mgt: Know Alternative in the Downstairs Theatre. Given a reading by Workshop One at the Traverse in 1984.)

26 Mar. **HANCOCK'S LAST HALF HOUR.** Credits as before. (Revival of the production which first opened at the Traverse on 12 Feb.)

27 Mar. * **THE MODERN MARINER**

by Mary Gladstone. Cast includes: Victoria Hardcastle, Anne Lacey, Bob Macauley. Dir. George Gunn. Lgt. George Tarbuck. (Mgt: Know Alternative in the Downstairs Theatre.)

2 Apr. **CABARET FAUST** *by the company. Music by John Kenny. (Mgt: TNT.)*

9 Apr. **POPPIES** *by Noel Greig. Cast: David Benedict, Stephen Ley, Gordon McDonald, David Newlyn, Richard Sandells, Peter Shorey, John Wilson. Dir. Philip Osment. Des. and Lgt. Kate Owen. (Mgt: Gay Sweatshop.)*

9 Apr. **THUNDERBOLT** *by Howard Purdie. Cast: Paul Birchard, Sedhar Chozam. Dir. the author. (Mgt: Border Reivers in the Downstairs Theatre.)*

Apr. **Jenny Killick is appointed Associate Director.**

17 Apr. † **THROUGH THE LEAVES** by Franz Xaver Kroetz. Trans. Anthony Vivis. Cast: Eileen Nicholas, Ken Stott. Dir. Jenny Killick. Des. David Neat. Lgt. and Sound by George Tarbuck. (Downstairs Theatre. Rev. 20 Aug. Transfers to Bush Theatre, London on 23 Oct.)

26 Apr. * **DEAD MEN** by Mike Stott. Cast: Kate Duchêne, Jack Ellis, David Gant, Chris Hunter, Ralph Riach, Kate Saunders, Tilda Swinton, Simon Tyrrell. Dir. Peter Lichtenfels. Des. John Byrne. Lgt. George Tarbuck. (Rev. 20 Aug. Revived at Octagon Theatre, Perth Festival, Australia in Feb. 1986.)

22 May * **WHITE ROSE** by Peter Arnott. Cast: Kate Duchêne, Ken Stott, Tilda Swinton. Dir. Stephen Unwin. Des. David Neat. Lgt. and Sound by George Tarbuck. (Downstairs Theatre. Revived on 11 Aug. Transfers to Almeida Theatre, London in Dec.)

30 May * **MACQUIN'S METAMORPH-**

OSES by Martyn Hobbs. Cast: Jack Ellis, Chris Hunter, Ralph Riach, Kate Saunders, Simon Tyrrell. Dir. Jenny Killick. Des. John Byrne. Lgt. and Sound by George Tarbuck.

27 June * **ELIZABETH GORDON QUINN** by Chris Hannan. Cast: Duncan Bell, Carol Ann Crawford, Bernard Doherty, Simon Donald, Frances Lonergan, Irene Macdougall, Eileen Nicholas, Ralph Riach. Dir. Stephen Unwin. Des. Dermot Hayes. Lgt. and Sound by George Tarbuck. (Rev. 9 Aug.)

1 July **Jenny Killick is appointed Artistic Director – to succeed Peter Lichtenfels when he leaves on 31 August.**

3 July * **THE PRICE OF EXPERIENCE** by Ken Ross. Cast: Joseph Mydell, Cyril Nri, Angela Scoular. Dir. Peter Lichtenfels. Des. David Neat. Lgt. and Sound by David Filshie. (Downstairs Theatre. Transfers to Upstairs Theatre on 27 Aug.)

1 Aug. * **LOSING VENICE** by John Clifford. Cast: Duncan Bell, Carol Ann Crawford, Bernard Doherty, Simon Donald, Simon Dormandy, Kate Duchêne, Irene Macdougall, Ralph Riach. Cast on radio: Dormandy rpl. David Rintoul. Cast in Australia: Bell rpl. Simon Tyrell and Dormandy/Rintoul rpl. Jack Ellis. Cast in Sweden, Lyceum, London and Hong Kong: Bell/Tyrell rpl. Roger Hyams, Dormandy/Rintoul/Ellis rpl. Andrew Wilde and Macdougall rpl. Penny Bunton. Dir. Jenny Killick. Des. Dermot Hayes. Lgt. and Sound by George Tarbuck. (Revived at Fortune Theatre, Perth Festival, Australia in Feb. 1986. A radio version – directed for radio by Stewart Conn – is broadcast on BBC Radio 3 on 24 June 1986. The

stage production is revived with a new set by Dermot Hayes for a Swedish tour in Nov. 1986. It transfers to the Lyceum Studio Theatre, Edinburgh on 8 Dec. 1986, the Almeida Theatre, London on 5 Jan 1987 and the Hong Kong Festival on 25 Jan. 1987.)

7 Aug. † **AUS DER FREMDE (OUT OF ESTRANGEMENT)** by Ernst Jandl. Trans. Michael Hamburger. Cast: Colette O'Neill, Raad Rawi, Philip Voss. Dir. Peter Lichtenfels. Des. David Neat. Lgt. and Sound by George Tarbuck. (Downstairs Theatre.)

9 Aug. ELIZABETH GORDON QUINN. Credits as before. (Revival of the play premièred by the Traverse on 27 June.)

10 Aug. † *TOSA GENJI* – adpt. Nagatoshi Sakamoto from the folktale by Tsuneichi Miyamoto. Performed in Japanese. Cast: Nagatoshi Sakamoto. Dir. Nagatoshi Sakamoto. (Mgt: Junko Hanamitsu, Japan.)

11 Aug. WHITE ROSE. Credits as before. (Downstairs Theatre. Revival of the play premièred by the Traverse on 22 May. Transfers to Almeida Theatre, London in Dec.)

13 Aug. † *NO SON OF MINE* A Play for Buffoons by Philippe Gaulier. Trans. Marcia Khan. Cast: Annabel Arden, Joyce Deans, Celia Gore-Booth. Dir. the author. (Mgt: Compagne Philippe Gaulier. Also plays in Downstairs Theatre [from 20 Aug.] during run.)

20 Aug. DEAD MEN. Credits in Edinburgh as before – except Hunter rpl. Raad Rawi. Cast in Australia: Rawi rpl. Valentine Pelka and Swinton rpl. Irene Macdougall. (Revival of the play premièred by the Traverse on 25 Apr. Revived at Octagon Theatre, Perth Festival, Australia in Feb. 1986.)

20 Aug. THROUGH THE LEAVES. Credits as before. (Downstairs Theatre. Revival of the production first seen at the Traverse on 17 Apr. Transfers to Bush Theatre, London on 23 Oct.)

27 Aug. *TERRESTRIAL EXTRAS* by Marcella Evaristi. Cast: Elaine Collins, Marcella Evaristi. Dir. Michael Boyd. (Mgt: Tron theatre, Glasgow in Downstairs Theatre.)

24 Sept. 'WILL YOU STILL NEED ME. . .' – Triple bill consisting of: **TOWARDS EVENING** by Ena Lamont Stewart. Cast: Martin Heller, Thelma Rogers. **WALKIES TIME** by Ena Lamont Stewart. Cast: Rose McBain, Thelma Rogers. * **KNOCKING ON THE WALL** by Ena Lamont Stewart. Cast: Martin Heller, Kenneth Lindsay, Rose McBain, Thelma Rogers. All three plays dir. Sandy Neilson. Des. Adrian Mudd. (Mgt: Prime Productions.)

10 Oct. * **THE DEATH OF ELIAS SAWNEY** by Peter Arnott. Cast: Simon Russell Beale, Carol Ann Crawford, Hilary Dawson, Bernard Doherty, Simon Dönald. Dir. Stephen Unwin. Des. Lucy Weller. Lgt. George Tarbuck. (Professional première of a play first presented by Cambridge Mummers in Cambridge in 1984 in a productiön by David Evans with a cast which included Bernard Doherty.)

11 Oct. * **HOGG: THE SHEPHERD JUSTIFIED** by Frederic Mohr (a.k.a. David McKail). Cast: Donald Douglas. Dir. Morag Fullarton. Des. Adrian Mudd. (Traverse at Kirkhope Hall, Ettrick Bridge as part of the Scottish Borders Ettrick Shepherd's Festival. Before the Festival, the production previewed in the Traverse Downstairs Theatre and subsequently tours to the following Festival venues: Bowhill Lecture Theatre, Stow Town Hall; Graham Institute, West Linton; Lauderdale Hotel, Lauder; Ashkirk Village Hall; Waverley Castle Hotel, Melrose; Tontine

Hotel, Peebles; Ednam House Hotel, Kelso; Ormiston Rooms, Melrose: Selkirk Town Hall; Tibbie Shields' Inn; Traquair House, Innerleithen; Old Gala House, Galashields; Wilton Lodge Gallery, Hawick; and Jedburgh Town Hall. It then tours to the MacRobert Arts Centre, Stirling before transferring to the Traverse on 7 Nov. Revived by Traverse in assoc. with the Edinburgh Festival Society at St. Cecilia's Hall, Edinburgh on 11 Aug. 1986. Rev. on 11 Oct. 1987 at Bowhill Little Theatre, Selkirk.)

7 Nov.   **HOGG: THE SHEPHERD JUSTIFIED.** Credits as before. (Transfer of play premièred by Traverse at Kirkhope Hall, Ettrick Bridge on 11 Oct. Revived by Traverse in assoc. with the Edinburgh Festival Society at St. Cecilia's Hall, Edinburgh on 11 Aug. 1986.)

14 Nov. *HOWARD'S REVENGE by Donald Campbell. Cast: Finlay Welsh. Dir. Sandy Neilson. (Mgt: Gyre Theatre Company.)*

3 Dec.   *THE PUDDOCK AN' THE PRINCESS by David Purves. Music by Richard Cherns. Cast: Ronald Aitken, Carol Ann Crawford, Anne Lannan, Una Macnab, Garry Stewart, Iain Wotherspoon – with Ruth Addinall, Susan Cooper. Dir. Charles Nowosielski. Lgt. Jeremy Webber. (Mgt: Theatre Alba. Given a reading – under the title 'The Wal at the Warld's End' – by the Edinburgh Playwrights Workshop at the Traverse on 14 Nov. 1984.)*

★   ★   ★

Playreadings presented during the year in the Downstairs Theatre by the Edinburgh Playrights Workshop

5 Feb.   THE EVE OF ST. PAUL by Athol Cameron.

12 Feb. EGON'S RAINBOW by Ian Tullis.

19 Feb. AGAMMEMMON'S LAW by

Richard Livermore.

26 Feb. THE TROPIC OF SOUTH KENTON by Stornoway Duns. (Premièred in production by Edinburgh Playwrights Workshop in Downstairs Theatre on 22 Mar. 1985.)

5 Mar.   SADISM AND MASOCHISM by Denise Smith.

12 Mar. ONE CHAPATY, TWO CHAPATY by Howard Purdie.

19 Mar. THE ROCK by Muriel Barnett.

26 Mar. HARD CURRENCY by Bill Costley.

PLAYREADINGS PRESENTED DURING THE YEAR IN THE UPSTAIRS THEATRE BY THE EDINBURGH PLAYWRIGHTS WORKSHOP

13 Oct. THE BALLOON ASCENT by Simon Evans.

20 Oct. A WOMB WITH A VIEW by Gabe Stewart.

27 Oct. THE RUSSIANS OF ROSS by George Gunn.

3 Nov.   SUSPICIOUS DEATH OF A MONGOL CHILD by Jessie McMurray.

10 Nov. BUSTED by John Mackenzie.

17 Nov. STALEMATE By Jim Glen.

24 Nov. A FRIEND IN NEED by Muriel Barnett and Marjorie Harper.

1 Dec.   PORTRAITS by Ian Tullis.

'ACTION' READING GIVEN IN UPSTAIRS THEATRE DURING THE YEAR BY TRAVERSE

TWO WAY MIRROR by Arthur Miller.

PLAYREADINGS PRESENTED DURING THE YEAR IN THE DOWNSTAIRS THEATRE BY KNOW ALTERNATIVE

23 Mar. TO WALK IN SUNSHINE by Betty Stone.

30 Mar. JOHNNY AND JENNY by Peter Arnott.

1986

11 Feb. *YARDSALE by Arnold Wesker. Cast: Jeannie Fisher. Dir. Eric*

Standidge. Set. Inez Nordell. Cos. Rosalind Little. Lgt. Eric Standidge. (Mgt: Jeannie Fisher.)

18 Feb. **VITA** – dev. Sigrid Neilsen. Cast: Barbara Robinson, Polly Wright. Dir. Jules Cranfield. A.D. Robyn Brown. (Mgt: Focus Theatre Company in assoc. with Lavender Menace Bookshop in Downstairs Theatre.)

25 Feb. **TO MARIE WITH LOVE** by Pauline Devaney. Cast: Pauline Devaney. Dir. Kate Harwood. Sets. Paul Gibson. Cos. Camilla Ashford. (Mgt: Century Theatre, Keswick.)

8 Mar. **PHILOTUS** – attributed to Alexander Montgomery. Edited for modern production by David Hamilton. Cast: Christopher Craig, Clunie MacKenzie, David MacKail, Una Macnab, Sebastian Mitchell, Ian Wotherspoon. Dir. David Hamilton. (Mgt: Edinburgh Playwrights Workshop in Downstairs Theatre.)

14 Mar. † **COLETTE DAME SEULE** – devised from the writings of Colette. Cast: Dominique Paquet. Dir. Patrick Simon. (Mgt: Group 3/5 Quatre-Vingt-Un Theatre and Compagnie Dramatique d'Aquitaine in assoc. with the Institute Français d'Ecosse.)

18 Mar. **ON THE EVE OF REVOLUTION** by Maxim Gorky. Dir. Lucy Conway. (Mgt: Strathclyde University Drama Group in assoc. with the Scottish Student Drama Festival.)

19 Mar. **IF IT HAD PLEASED GOD** by Patrick Evans. Cast: Sine Hood, Andrew Loudon, Mark Ritchie. Dir. the author. Des. and Lgt. Phil Cooney.
THE RAIN by Ken Davidson. Cast: Ken Davidson. Dir. and des. the author.
(Mgt: Edinburgh University Dramatic Society in assoc. with the Scottish Student Drama Festival.)

21 Mar. **ME TOO** by Lynn Bains. Music

by Ian Guthrie (with Andrew Carr). Cast: Murray Allan, Andrew Brogan, Ruth-Claire Carroll, Andrew Carr, Fiona Espie, Julie Gilchrist, Jo Grace, Teri Hernon, Tracey Henderson, Pauline Kerr, William Kerr, Arlene Knight, James Low, Angela McClune, Kevin McGregor, Caragh MacKay, Gary MacKay, Vivian McQue, Andrew Pearson, Maryanne Rarity, Lorraine Ratcliffe, Kevin Rooney, Leslie Shearer, Sameena Singh, Gavin Smith, Sharon Small, Paul Stevenson, Andrew Wilson – with Darrell Anthony, Richard Finlay, Iain Guthrie, Mike Ward. Dir. the author. Produced by Andy Mackie. Des. Paul Stevenson, Andy Mackie and the author. Lgt. Andy Mackie and Don Swanson. M.D. Iain Guthrie. Chor. the author. Sharon Small, Fiona Espie, Kevin Rooney and Gary MacKay. (Mgt: Kirkcaldy College of Technology Theatre Arts Programme in assoc. with the Scottish Student Drama Festival.)

22 Mar. * **THE TROPIC OF SOUTH KENTON** by Stornoway Duns. (Mgt: Edinburgh Playwrights Workshop in Downstairs Theatre. Given a reading at Traverse on 26 Feb. 1985.)

1 Apr. **Stephen Unwin appointed Associate Director.**

1 Apr. **ELSIE AND NORM'S MACBETH** by John Christopher Wood. Cast: John Grex, Jan Shand. Dir. Andy Jordan. Des. Candida Boyes. (Mgt: Bristol Express Theatre Company in assoc. with Birmingham Repertory Theatre.)

2 May * **KORA** by Tom McGrath. Cast: Michelle Butt, Robert Carr, Karin Cartlidge, Elizabeth Millbank, Iain Ormsby-Knox, Alison Peebles, Benny Young. Dir. Jenny Killick. Des. Neil Murray and Kevin Hannah. Lgt. and Sound by George Tar-

buck. (Rev. 10 Aug.)

6 June * **THE ORPHANS' COMEDY** by Chris Hannan. Cast: Michelle Butt, Robert Carr, Karin Cartlidge, Iain Orsmby-Knox, Alison Peebles, Nicola Redmond, Ewan Stewart. Dir. Stephen Unwin. Des. David Roger. Lgt. and Sound by George Tarbuck. Ass. Des. Rachel George. (Rev. 7 Aug.)

19 June † **BURNING LOVE** by Fitzgerald Kusz. Trans. Anthony Vivis and Tinch Minter. Cast: Leonard O'Malley, Tracey Spence. Dir. Hamish Glen. Des. Minty Donald. Lgt. and Sound by George Tarbuck and Stephen Imrie. (Downstairs Theatre. Transfers to Tron Theatre Club, Glasgow on 29 July. Transfers back to Traverse Downstairs Theatre on 8 Aug.

4 July * **LUCY'S PLAY** by John Clifford. Cast: Alan Barker, Chris Barnes, Kate Duchêne, Ida Schuster, Simon Scott, Sadie Shimmin, Ewan Stewart. Dir. Jenny Killick. Des. Bunny Christie. Lgt. and Sound by George Tarbuck. Ass. Des. Jessica Newman.

1 Aug. † **KATHIE AND THE HIPPO-POTAMUS** by Mario Vargas Llosa. Trans. Kerry McKenny and Anthony Oliver-Smith. Cast: Janet Amsden, Alan Barker, Kate Duchêne, Robert Swann. Dir. Stephen Unwin. Des. Bunny Christie. Lgt. and Sound by George Tarbuck. Ass. Des. John Reid. (Rev. on 24 Feb. 1987 at Almeida Theatre, London.)

7 Aug. THE ORPHANS' COMEDY. Credits as before. (Revival of production premièred by Traverse on 6 June.)

10 Aug. KORA. Credits as before – except Young rpl. Lawrie McNicol. (Revival of production premièred by Traverse on 2 May.)

12 Aug. † *BOPHA!* by Percy Mtwa. Cast: Sidney Khumala, Aubrey Moalosi

Molefe, Aubrey Radebe. Dir. the author. Lighting adapted by Alan Joseph. (Mgt: Earth Players, Johannesburg in assoc. with Newtown Productions in Downstairs Theatre.)

12 Aug. † *ALBERTINE, IN FIVE TIMES* by Michel Tremblay. Trans. John van Burek and Bill Glassco. Cast: Diane Belshaw, Joy Coghill, Clare Coulter, Susan Coyne, Patricia Hamilton, Doris Petrie. Dir. Bill Glassco. Des. Astrid Janson. Lgt. Harry Frehner. (Mgt: Tarragon Theatre, Toronto.)

12 Aug. † *MAINLY AFTER DARK* by Arlette Namiand. English version by Anne Devlin. Cast: Dawn Archibald, Philomena McDonagh, Cheryl Maiker, Natasha Williams. Dir. Pierre Audi. A.D. Dominic Tickell. Des. Hildegarde Bechtler. Lgt. Jean Kalman. (Mgt: Almeida Theatre Company, London.)

19 Aug. * *BODYCOUNT* by Les Smith. Cast: Tina Marian. Dir. Pip Broughton. Set. Nick Redgrove. Cos. Mandy St. Clair. (Mgt: Paines Plough – the Writers' Company in Downstairs Theatre.)

19 Aug. † *EMILY OF EMERALD HILL* by Stella Kon. Cast: Margaret Chan. Dir. Max le Blond. (Mgt: Max le Blond, Singapore in Downstairs Theatre.)

26 Aug. *BLACKBEARD THE PIRATE* – dev. Annie Griffin. Cast: Annie Griffin. Dir. Neil Barlett. (Mgt: Annie Griffin in Downstairs Theatre. Revived at Traverse on 27 Oct. 1987.)

14 Oct. *DREAMING OF BABYLON* – adpt. Kerry Shale from the novel by Richard Brautigan. Cast: Kerry Shale. Dir. Anthony Matheson. Des. Geoff Rose. (Mgt: Kerry Shale.)

28 Oct. *BURKE AND HARE* by Patrick Evans. Cast: Michael David, Andrew Greaves, Sine Hood, Alexis Leighton, Callum MacDonald, Allan Sharpe. Dir. the author. Des. and Lgt. Phil Cooney. (Mgt: Theatre Co-op.)

4 Nov.   **HOOLIGANS** by Jon Gaunt. Cast: Tom Magill, Paul Nolan, Robert Wilkinson. Dir. the author. Des. Lise Roberts. Lgt. John Laidlaw. (Mgt: Tic Toc Theatre Company.)

11 Nov. **REQUEST PROGRAMME** by Franz Xaver Kroetz. Trans. Judy Waldman from 'Wunschkonzert'. Cast: Eileen Nicholas. Dir. Nancy Diuguid. (Mgt: Eileen Nicholas. New production of play given its British Première by the Traverse on 28 Nov. 1974.)

18 Nov. **DID YOU SEE THAT?** by Krissie Illing and Mark Britton. Cast: Mark Britton, Krissie Illing. (Mgt: Nickelodeon.)

28 Nov. * **THE SILVER SPRING** by Iain Sutherland. Music composed and arranged by Joe McGinley. Cast: Stuart Bishop, Cameron Gaskell, Corinne Harris, Anne Lacey, Andrew Price, James Twaddale. Dir. Bryan Elsley. Des. Lucy Weller. Lgt. George Tarbuck.

★ ★ ★

Playreadings presented during the year in the Downstairs Theatre by the Edinburgh Playwrights Workshop

23 Feb. THE PARADISE TRUST by David Gourlay.

2 Mar.   THE DEVIL'S TRILL by Roger Musson.

9 Mar.   A FORTNIGHT IN AUGUST by Bill Dunlop.

16 Mar. THE TRIAL OF JOHN BUNYAN by Ron Biggs.

23 Mar. A radio play by Francis Hayes.

30 Mar. Two One-Act Plays by Audrey Coleman.
         IMAGINARY FRIENDS by Audrey Coleman.

6 Apr.   MCLUSKY'S LAMENT by Jim

Gracie.

13 Apr. A play by Francis Hayes.

1987

27 Jan. **THE BUSKER** by James Kelman. Cast: John Cobb, Katy Duke, Alan Tall. Dir. Ian Brown. Re-directed for this revival by the author. Des. Minty Donald. Lgt. Marian McCormick. (Mgt: Roughcast Theatre Company.)

6 Feb.   **GAMBLERS** by Nicolai Gogol. Trans. Chris Hannan and Christopher Rathbone. Cast: Jimmy Chisholm, Andrew Dallmeyer, Craig Ferguson, Kay Gallie, Jenny McCrindle, Forbes Masson, John Stahl. Dir. Hamish Glen. Set. Peter Ling. Cos. Peter Ling and Lynn Aitken. Lgt. Hamish Glen and Peter Ling. (Traverse and Tron Theatre Club, Glasgow at Tron Theatre. Transfers to Traverse on 26 Feb.)

10 Feb. * **LOOKING BACK** by John Carnegie, Monica Gibb, Isabella Jarrett, Michael Mackenzie and Garry Stewart. Cast: Monica Gibb, Isabella Jarrett, Michael Mackenzie. Dir. John Carnegie. Set. and Lgt. Alastair McArthur and John Carnegie. (Mgt: Winged Horse Touring Productions in Downstairs Theatre.)

26 Feb. GAMBLERS. Credits as before. (Transfer of production premièred at Tron Theatre on 6 Feb.)

17 Mar. **RITES** by Maureen Duffy. Cast: Jennifer Clark, Gillian Duncan, Annette Friel, Helena Gilles, Louise Ironside, Fiona James, Anne McLaughlin, Maria Miller, Lesley Morrison, Katherine Paterson, Alison Tormey. Dir. Roanna Benn. Lgt. Gary Brunton. (Mgt: Arm in Arm Theatre Company in assoc. with the Scottish Student Drama Festival.)

18 Mar. **'TIS PITY SHE'S A WHORE** by John Ford. Cast: Alison Bryce,

Douglas Clark, Craig Durham, Roger Linton, Richard McGill, Ian McGonagle, Fiona McGowan, Peter Noble, Brian O'Malley, Gillian Scott, Tanya Sensky, Alan Tait, Graeme Wilson. Dir. John Heraghty. Set. Mo Rocks. Cos. Margaret O'Hara. Lgt. Paul Moore. (Mgt: John Street Theatre, Strathclyde University in assoc. with the Scottish Student Drama Festival.)

19 Mar. *GROOMSNIGHT* by Charles A. Barron. Cast: Katie Allen, Hamish Clark, Sandra McKay, Keith McPherson, Vicky Masson. Dir. and Des. Sally Bates. Lgt. Gary Brunton. (Mgt: Edinburgh University Theatre Company in assoc. with the Scottish Student Drama Festival.)

19 Mar. *EVE SET THE BALLS OF CORRUPTION ROLLING* by Marcella Evaristi. Cast: Niall Barr, Fiona Chapman, Edward Clark, Sabine Cochraine, Claire Dowling, Angie Gray, Martha Leishman, Claire McAndrew, Sarah MacDonald, Karen Meikle, Mandy Mitchell, Kirsty Walker. Dir. Philip Howard. Set. David Hipple. Lgt. Melanie Lusher and Paddy McLaughlin. (Mgt: St. Andrews Mermaids in assoc. with the Scottish Student Drama Festival.)

21 Mar. *THE BEAUTIFUL AND THE DAMNED.* Adpt. Angus MacFadyen from the novel by F. Scott Fitzgerald. Original music by John Elliot. Cast: Tom Bradby, Aileen McFarlane, Sophie Needham, William Armstrong, Rowan Somerville, James Wallace, Sophie White – with William Armstrong, John Elliot, Kenneth Linton, Roy Percy, Brian Rennie, Richard Tipper, Graham Wood. Dir. Angus MacFayden. Set. Matthew Sleigh. Cos. Sophie White. Lgt. Dave Gray and Martin Croome. (Mgt: Edinburgh University Theatre

Company in assoc. with the Scottish Student Drama Festival.)

24 Mar. * **BLITZ!** by Jeremy Raison. Original music by Rose Milligan and James Wilson. Cast: Liane Craig, Pauline Crawford, Angela Docherty, Silvia Ferrari, Craig Fraser, Nicola Gibson, Jacqui Haddow, Karen Johnstone, Wilma Kennedy, Lynne Killin, Katrina McConnachie, Andy McLellan, Ross Milligan, Jackie Morrison, Anette Mossin, Simon Penman, Wendy Rattray, Suzanne Reid, Charlie Reston, Wendy Robertson, Catriona Sword, Derek Traynor, James Wilson. Dir. the author. Produced by Lynn Baines and Andy Mackie. Des. Heather Innes. Lgt. George Tarbuck. (Traverse and Kirkcaldy Collegé of Technology Theatre Arts Programme.)

7 Apr. * *WALLACE – GUARDIAN OF SCOTLAND* by Patrick Evans. Cast: Michael David, David Gallacher, Andrew Greaves, Alexis Leighton, Maria Macauley, Allan Sharpe, Mark Smith. Dir. the author. Des. Sine Hood. Lgt. Phil Cooney. (Mgt: Theatre Co-op.)

7 May * **ABEL BAREBONE AND THE HUMBLE COMPANY AGAINST THE GREAT MORTALITY** by Peter Jukes. Cast: Annabel Arden, Alan Barker, Celia Gore Booth, Simon Donald, David Gant, Kathryn Hunter, Roger Hyams, Richard Williams. Dir. Stephen Unwin. Set. Kristina Stephenson. Cos. Kristina Stephenson and Morna Baxter. Lgt. and Sound by George Tarbuck. (Rev. 7 Aug.)

11 June * **PLAYING WITH FIRE** by John Clifford. Cast: Annabel Arden, Celia Gore Booth, Simon Donald, David Gant, Kathryn Hunter, Richard Williams. Dir. Jenny Killick. Set.

Paul Brown. Cos. Paul Brown and Morna Baxter. Lgt. and Sound by George Tarbuck. Music by Sileas. A.D. Paul Miller. (Rev. 1 Aug.)

9 July   * **NOAH'S WIFE** by Amy Hardie. Cast: Treva Etienne, Decima Francis, Bonnie Greer, Kathryn Hunter, Wilbert J. Johnson, Leo Wringer. Dir. Jenny Killick. Des. Judy Haag. Lgt. and Sound by George Tarbuck. Ass. Des. Charlotte Seymour.

30 July   † **MAN TO MAN** by Manfred Karge. Trans. Anthony Vivis from 'Jackie Wie Hose'. Cast: Tilda Swinton. Dir. Stephen Unwin. Des. Bunny Christie. Ass. Des. Lucy Conway. Lgt. Ben Ormerod. Sound by George Tarbuck. (Rev. 4 Jan. 1987 at Royal Court Theatre, London.)

1 Aug.   **PLAYING WITH FIRE.** Credits as before. (Revival of production premièred by the Traverse on 11 June.)

7 Aug.   † **THE PROWLER** by Enzo Cormann. Trans. James Kelman. Cast: Sam Graham. Dir. Jeremy Raison. Des. Jean Kerr. Lgt. and Sound by George Tarbuck. (Downstairs Theatre.)

10 Aug.   † *LE LAVOIR* ('The Washhouse') by Dominique Durvin and Hélène Prévost. Performed in French. Cast: Gilette Barbier, Germaine Delbat, Dominique Durvin, Geneviéve Esmenard, Anne Feillet, Marie Henriau, Dominique Louyot, Elise Mongrenier, Anne-Sophie Prud'homme, Hélène Rimbaud, Christine Sandre, Christine Sureau, Claire Vidoni. Dir. and Des. Dominique Durvin. (Mgt: Theatre de la Basoche, Amiens, France at the Abbeymount Washouse, Edinburgh.)

11 Aug.   * *APART FROM GEORGE* by Nick Ward. Music by Richard Heacock. Cast: Amelda Brown, Katrin Cartlidge, Richard Heacock, Matthew Scurfield, Michael Turner. Dir. the author. Des. Fred Pilbrow. (Mgt: National Theatre Studio production presented by the National Theatre Education Department.)

11 Aug.   * *BUD* by Nick Darke. Cast: Christopher Quinn. Dir. Tony Mulholland. Des. Candida Boyes. Lgt. Jo Town. (Mgt: Liverpool Playhouse production presented by Different Drummer Theatre Company in Downstairs Theatre.)

11 Aug.   *THE SUMMIT* by Jonathon and Barnaby Stone. Cast: Barnaby Stone, Jonathon Stone. Lgt. and Sound by Gina Cascoigne. (Mgt: Ralf Ralf in Downstairs Theatre. Reworked version of show premièred at ICA, London in Apr.)

11 Aug.   † *HAVE YOU SEEN ZANDILE?* by Gcina Mhlope, Thembi Mtshali and Maralin Vanrenen. Cast: Gcina Mhlope, Thembi Mtshali. Dir. Maralin Vanrenen. (Mgt: Market Theatre, Johannesburg, South Africa in Downstairs Theatre.)

18 Aug.   * *ALMOST PERSUADED* –dev. Annie Griffin. Cast: Annie Griffin. Cos. Linda Pratt. (Mgt: Annie Griffin in Downstairs Theatre. Revived in Traversse Upstairs Theatre on 30 October.)

29 Sept.   *WHO'S LEFT* by Barry McCarthy. Cast: Maureen Beattie, Ann-Louise Ross, Judy Sweeney. Dir. Hamish Glen. Des. Graham Johnston. Lgt. Harry Lennon. (Mgt: Swaive Kinooziers.)

6 Oct.   *IN THE NIGHT* by James Kelman. Music by Alan Tall. Cast includes: Stewart Ennis. Dir. the author. (Mgt: Roughcast Theatre Company.)

13 Oct.   *THE LONG MARCH* by Khehla Phillip Ngubane, Bongani Mchunu, Isaiah Mzimande, Clement Mnguni, Jopha Mtshali, Nelson Mvelase, Thomas Shelembe, (the late) Simon Ngubane, Pete Mkhize, Mi Hlatshwayo, Debby

Bonnin, Alfred Qabula, Ari Sitas, Astrid von Kotze, Ramalao Makhene, Patti Henderson, Lawrence Zondi and Sarmcol shop stewards. Cast: Bongani Mchunu, Pete Mkhize, Clement Mnguni, Jopha Mtshali, Nelson Mvelase, Madala Ngubane, Isaiah Nzimande, Thomas Shelembe. (Mgt: Sarmcol Workers Co-operative, Howick, Natal, South Africa in assoc. with TUC and NUMSA.)

16 Oct. **THE WIZARD LADY OF BRANXHOLM** by Judy Steel. Cast: Hazel Eadie, Heather Jackson, William Steel. Dir. Lloyd Quinan. (Mgt: Borders Festival of Ballads and Legends.)

20 Oct. **POLITICS IN THE DARK** by Iain Heggie. Cast: Sheila Donald, Sheila Latimer. Dir. Bryan Elsley. Lgt. George Tarbuck. (Mgt: Words Beyond Words Company.)
JOE by Anne Marie Di Mambro. Cast: Alyxis Daley. Dir. Maggie Kinloch. Des. Robin Peoples. Lgt. George Tarbuck. (Mgt: Annexe Theatre Company.)

21 Oct. **MUM, DAD, THERE'S SOMETHING I'VE GOT TO TELL YOU** by John Binnie. Cast: John Binnie, Susan Cubie, Jilly Fraser, John Murphy, Aileen Ritchie. Dir. the author. Lgt. Caroline Hawes. (Mgt: Clyde Unity Theatre in Downstairs Theatre.)

23 Oct. **KILLING ME SOFTLY** by John Binnie. Cast: Susan Cubie, John Mooney, John Murphy, Aileen Ritchie, Stephen Simpson. Dir. the author. Lgt. Caroline Hawes. (Mgt: Clyde Unity Theatre in Downstairs Theatre.)
Performances between 27 Oct. and 6 Dec. form part of a joint Third Eye Centre, Glasgow/ Traverse collaborative season of performance art and visual theatre entitled New Work/No Definition.

27 Oct. BLACKBEARD THE PIRATE – dev. Annie Griffin. Cast: Annie Griffin. Dir. Neil

Bartlett. (Mgt: Annie Griffin. Revival of show which last opened at Traverse Downstairs Theatre on 26 Aug. 1986.)

30 Oct. **ALMOST PERSUADED** – dev. Annie Griffin. Cast: Annie Griffin. Cos. Linda Pratt. (Mgt: Annie Griffin. Revival of show which was premièred in Traverse Downstairs Theatre on 18 Aug.)

3 Nov. **HYPOCHONDRIA** by Chris and Tim Britton.
THE BRITTONIONI BROTHERS by the Company. Cast for both shows: Chris Britton, Tim Britton. Des. and Lgt. Penny Saunders. (Mgt: Forkbeard Fantasy.)

10 Nov. **THE HOUR** by Jonathon and Barnaby Stone. Cast: Barnaby Stone, Jonathon Stone. Des. and Lgt. Gina Gascoigne. (Mgt: Ralf Ralf.)

17 Nov. **S/HE** – conceived by Andy Walker. Written by Andy Walker and Jaki Rance. Music by Andy Walker. Cast: Fiona Dennison, Adrian Garvey, Soroya Kismet, Nicola McRoy, Jaki Rance, David Riley, Nicholas Timms. Dir., Des. and Lgt. by Andy Walker. (Mgt: Large Scale International.)

24 Nov. **MAN ACT 2: MIRACLES** by the Company. Cast: Phillip MacKenzie, Simon Thorne. Dir. Neil Bartlett. (Mgt: Man Act.)

26 Nov. * **HUNGER WAITS** by the Company. Cast: Anna Ingleby, Grace Morgan, Thursa Sanderson, Karen Wimhurst. Des. the Company. (Mgt: Quartet Four in Downstairs Theatre.)

1 Dec. **A VISION OF LOVE REVEALED IN SLEEP** by Neil Bartlett and Robin Whitemore. Cast: Neil Bartlett. Set. and Lgt. Robin Whitmore. (Mgt: Bartlett & Whitmore.)

6 Dec. **2AM EROTIC TIME** by the Company. Cast: Stephen Jones, Sarah Tutt, Graeme Wrench. Dir., Des. and Lgt. the company and Jed Warren. (Mgt: Dogs in Honey in assoc. with the Collective Gallery, Edinburgh.)

* ★ ★

Playreadings presented during the year in the Downstairs Theatre by the Edinburgh Playwrights Workshop

6 Oct.	THE STRATH by Bill Dunlop.
13 Oct.	McMYTH by Andrew Slimon.
20 Oct.	KENZENZABOGEY or 'The Secret History of the Japanese Economic Miracle' by Kenneth Howden.
27 Oct.	THE LONG SIX MONTHS by Margaret Macarthur.
3 Nov.	LOVE SICKNESS by Ann Kerr.
10 Nov.	THE ILL GUIDMITHER by David Purves.
17 Nov.	AZERJA by R. S. Silver.
24 Nov.	ROULETTE by Donald Gunn.
1 Dec.	THE PRIVATE LIVES OF DEACON BRODIE by Donald MacKenzie.

INDEX

NOTE: Names of people, buildings etc, are in roman, titles of plays, books, publications etc, are in italics. Where a play has been performed at, or in close association with, the Traverse, the date of its first performance there is given after the title.

Beatles, The, 12
Being an Actor (autobiography, Simon Callow), 68
Bellow, Saul (novelist and playwright), 24
Benedictus, David, (playwright), 47, 49, 53
Bett, John (playwright and actor), 80
Betti, Ugo (playwright), 18
Billington, Michael (theatre critic, The Guardian), 61
Birtwistle, Harrison (composer), 35
Bishop of Edinburgh, 59
Black and White Ball, 1964, 26
Black and White Minstrels, The (1972), 58, 61, 63
Black, Campbell (playwright), 77
Black, Isobel (actress), 22
Blackadder, Elizabeth (artist), 30
Black Dog (1984), 90
Blood and Ice (1982), 89
Bond, Chris (director), 89
Bond, Edward (playwright), 45
Bonnar, Anne (General Manager, Traverse, 1986–), 97
Bookworms Bookshop, Helensburgh, 19
Bopha! (1986), 94
Borchert, Wolfgang (playwright), 45
Borderline Theatre Company, 78
Boswell, James (Scotch biographer), 89
Boyle, Jimmy (writer), 79, 80
Boyle, Mark (artist), 30
Bradford University, 76, 77
Brandeis Interact Festival, USA, 49
Brecht, Bertholt (playwright), 23, 69
Brenton, Howard (playwright), 59
Breuer, Lee (director), 89
Broda, Paul (Traverse Committee Member, 1971), 59
Brook, Peter (director), 47
Bryden, Bill (director), 70
Büchner, Georg (playwright), 71
Buglar Boy (1983), 91
Burger Schippel, 69
Burns, Robert (poet), 24
Butterworth, Dr. (original owner, Traverse building at 112 West Bow), 50,
    76
Byatt, George (playwright), 79
Byrne, John (playwright and artist), 80, 84, 89, 90, 93

Cairney, John (actor), 24
Calder, John (publisher and Traverse Committee member), 13, 14, 18, 22,
    27, 29, 39, 45
Caledonian Hotel, Edinburgh, 56
Callow, Simon (actor), 68, 69, 74, 93
Cambridge University Theatre Company, 13
Campbell, Donald (playwright), 78, 80

Dream Play (1974), 67, 69
Drexler, Rosalyn (playwright), 47
Dryden, Ellen (playwright), 40, 46
Dubillard, Roland (playwright), 35
Dublin Fare (1965), 35, 44
Dunbar, Sandy (Director, Scottish Arts Council), 71
Dyer, Charles (playwright), 67

Eccles, Lord (Arts Minister), 59
Edgar, David (playwright), 77
Edinburgh Central Library, 60
Edinburgh Corporation (Corporation of the City of Edinburgh), 40, 61, 62
Edinburgh District Council, 71, 72, 78, 81, 87, 97
Edinburgh Evening News & Dispatch, 45
Edinburgh Experimental Theatre Group, 40
Edinburgh International Festival, 9, 12, 13, 14, 18, 23, 25, 27, 35, 39, 41, 45,
    50, 51, 57, 59, 61, 70, 73, 78, 80, 81, 83, 84, 86, 87–88, 89, 90, 91, 92, 94,
    95, 99
Edinburgh Wanderers Rugby Club, 45
Elizabeth Gordon Quinn (1985), 93
Elliott, Andrew (Traverse Chairman, 1965–66), 13, 26, 27, 29, 30, 36
Equity, British Actors' Equity, 28, 30, 63, 72
Escorial (1964), 22
Evaristi, Marcella (playwright), 80, 84, 89
Eveling, Kate (Traverse Committee member), 72
Eveling, Stanley (playwright), 18, 24, 32, 40, 44, 45, 46, 47, 49, 50, 51, 53,
    58, 59, 66, 67, 68, 69, 71, 74, 79, 91
The Exception and The Rule (1974), 69
Eyre, Richard (director), 38

Fairbairn, Nicholas, MP (Traverse Chairman, 1966–72), 29, 31, 34, 38, 39,
    40, 46, 50, 51, 52, 56, 61, 94, 96
Faithfull, Marianne (singer), 39
Fantastics, The (1965), 28
Fassbinder, Rainer Werner (writer and director), 69
Faulkner, John (Drama Director, Scottish Arts Council), 71
Ferguson, James (Traverse Committee member), 46, 59
Fielding, Fenella (actress), 58
F In Mass (1968), 40
Flett, Una (writer), 25, 29, 31, 34, 38
Foco Novo Theatre Company, 69
Follies, 73
Fordell Castle, Fife, 31, 61
Foster, Paul (playwright), 39, 45, 66
Franklyn, William (actor), 58
Fraser, John (actor), 37
Freehold Company, 47, 58, 59
Fringe, Edinburgh Festival Fringe, 13, 14, 39, 55, 56, 60, 62, 87, 88, 90, 92,
    98
Frost, David (broadcaster), 39

Fugue (1983), 91
Futz (1967), 39, 45

Gallacher, Tom (playwright), 77, 80
Game Called Arthur, A (1970), 58
Gateway Theatre, Edinburgh, 15
Gay Gorbals (1976), 77
Geliot, Michael (director), 22, 23, 27
Gerber, Joe (Traverse Chairman 1972–73), 46, 61, 67, 72, 79, 90
Ghelderode, Michael de (playwright), 22, 59
Glasgow Herald, The, 91
Glasgow Theatre Club (Tron Theatre), 81
Gorky, Maxim (novelist and playwright), 92
Gothard, David (director), 91, 96
Grabbe, Christian Dietrich (playwright), 18
Graham, Ranald (playwright), 40, 41, 46
Graham, Roderick (Chair, Scottish Arts Council Drama Committee), 88
Granada Television, 35, 36, 40, 43
Great Northern Welly Boot Show (1972), 61, 70
Green Julia (1965), 24–25
Greenwood, Diana (designer), 67
Griffiths, Trevor (playwright), 59
Grotowski, Jerzy (director), 48
Guard, Philip (actor), 58
Guardian, The, 39
Gwilym, Mike (actor), 58
Gynt! (1975), 68

Hale, John (playwright), 81
Hall, John (playwright), 35
Halliwell, David (playwright) 58, 67
Hampstead Theatre Club, 25, 62, 63, 86
Handke, Peter (playwright), 69
Hannan, Chris (playwright) 92, 93, 94
Happy Days are Here Again (1965), 24
Happy End (1964) 23, 25, 35
Harborth, Sheila (Traverse Stage Manager, Production Manager and
    Administrator (1971–84), 67, 71, 72, 75, 78, 82, 83, 91
Hardman, The (1977), 79, 80, 84, 86, 89
Hard to Get (1980), 80, 84
Hare, David (playwright), 59
Harewood, Earl of (Edinburgh Festival Director), 18
Harrison, Carey (playwright), 46, 47
Harvieston House, by Edinburgh, 44
Havergal, Giles (Artistic Director, Glasgow Citizens' Theatre), 36
Hawthorne, Nigel (actor), 58
Haygarth, Tony (actor), 51
Hayman, David (actor and director), 80, 88
Haynes, Jim (Traverse Chairman, 1963–65, Artistic Director 1964–66) 9–40,
    42, 44, 46, 51, 53, 56,57, 61, 66, 70, 80, 84, 95, 96, 98, 99

Haynes, Viveka (later Viveka Wallmark), 16
Heaven and Hell (1981), 89
Henry IV 56, 58
Heretics Theatre Company 78
Heron, Patrick (artist) 30
Hessian Corporal, The (1967) 42, 66
Hitler Dances (1972), 59
Hobson, Harold (theatre critic, Sunday Times), 9, 14, 34
Holm, Ian (actor), 58
Holman, Robert (playwright), 77, 80
Howard, Alan (actor), 58
Hughes, Dusty (playwright), 89
Human Voice, The (1984), 93
Huis Clos (1963), 9, 17
Hutchinson, J. Maxwell (composer), 77

Ice Chimney (1980), 84
In a Cottage Hospital (1969),47
Inadmissible Evidence (1966), 37
In the Heart of the British Museum (1971), 59
Inert, The (1967), 46
Innocent, The (1984), 90, 92
International Writers' Conference, Edinburgh Festival, 1962, 14, 21
Investigation, The (1966), 35, 66
Ionesco, Eugene (playwright), 18, 35, 45
Ireland, Dr Kenneth (Director, Pitlochry Festival Theatre, Traverse
    Committee member), 34
Ireland, Kenny (a.k.a. Ian) (actor and director), 70, 88

James, Polly (actress), 58
Jarry, Alfred (playwright), 18, 39, 45
Jeanetta Cochrane Theatre, London, 27
Jefford, Barbara (actress), 58
Jenks, Eric (Traverse General Manager, 1965–66), 27, 35
Jesuit, The (1976), 78
Johns, Jasper (artist), 30
Johnson, Dr. Samuel (lexicographer, harmless drudge), 89
Johnstone, William (artist), 30
Joint Stock Theatre Company, 44, 54, 69
Jones, Michael (playwright), 46
Jonic, Bettina (singer), 23, 35
Joseph, Stephen (theatre director), 15, 16
Judge Smith, Chris (writer), 77

Karge, Manfred (playwright),94
Kathie and the Hippopotamus (1986), 94
Kelsall, Moultrie (actor), 12
Kemp, Lindsay (mime artist and director) 24, 28, 58, 62
Kemp, Roger (actor), 69
Kent, Nicholas (Associate Director, Traverse, 1971–73), 43, 61, 64,67

Mitchell, Poppy (designer), 67, 73
Mitchell, Tom (Traverse President, owner of Traverse building, James Court), 12–13, 14, 15, 17, 22, 25, 28, 44, 49, 50, 51, 62
Moffat, Alistair (Fringe Administrator, writer, broadcaster), 56, 62
Monsieur Artaud 1969, 51
Moore, Geoff (director), 24,72
Moore, Jack Henry (Traverse stage manager/director, 1965–66), 26, 28, 30, 32, 66
Moray House Gymnasium, Edinburgh, 81
Mourning Becomes Electra (1967–68), 41
Moving Being Company, 24, 68, 72
Moving In (1980), 80
Mowat, David (playwright), 47
Mrozek, Slawomir (playwright), 22
Mtwa, Percy (playwright), 89
Muggeridge, Malcolm, 41
Muir, Andrew (Traverse Committee member), 13, 15
Muir, Bill (Traverse Stage Director, 1963–70), 72
Mully, George (director), 24
Munro, Rona (playwright), 91

Nastasia Filipovna (1983), 89, 91
National Theatre, 63
Nero and The Golden House (1976), 77
Next Time Bring a Wee Somethin' Tae Drink, Son (1976), 79, 80
Neville, John (director), 55
New Society, 10
Noble, Ian (Traverse Committee member), 46
Norton, Alex (actor and playwright), 88
Nottingham Playhouse, 55
Novelist, The (1971), 58
Nuns, The (1973), 67
Nye, Robert (playwright, novelist), 47

Obaldia, Rene de (playwright), 35
Ockrent, Michael (Artistic Director, Traverse, 1973–75), 35, 42, 51, 66–74, 77, 78, 79, 83, 86, 91, 97, 99
Of Hope and Glory (1965), 27
Oh Gloria! (1965), 35
Oh Starlings (1971), 59
Old Chaplaincy Centre, Edinburgh, 77
Ondaatje, Michael (playwright), 79
O'Neil, Colette (actress), 9, 17
O'Neill, Eugene (playwright), 41
Open Space Company, 47, 58
Open Space Theatre, 70
Open Theatre, 48
Orange Souffle (1965), 24
Orisons (1963), 9
Orwell, George,77

Osborne, John (playwright), 37
Other Traverse, Old Chaplaincy Centre, 78, 80, 81
Oxford Playhouse, 43
Our Sunday Times (1971), 59, 60
Outside the Whale (1976), 77

Palace Cinema, Royal Mile, Edinburgh, 15
Palmer, Bob (Drama Director, Scottish Arts Council), 87, 91
Pantagleise (1971), 59, 63
Paperback Bookshop, Charles Street, Edinburgh, 11, 12, 13, 15, 21
Paradise Foundry, 68, 69
Parr, Chris (Artistic Director, Traverse, 1975–81), 51, 60, 64, 67, 70, 71, 73,
    75–85, 86, 88, 89
Paterson, Bill (actor), 88
Paterson, Stuart (playwright), 92
Paterson's Shortbread Show (1966), 35
Pemberton, Antonia (actress), 58
Penciulescu, Radu (director), 69
People Show, 47, 48
Perry, Clive (theatre director), 38
Perth Theatre, 66, 67
Pinget, Robert (playwright), 22
Pinter, Harold (playwright), 22, 25, 50
Pirandello, Luigi (playwright), 45
Pitlochry Festival Theatre, 14, 15, 34
Play (1969), 47
Playing With Fire (1964), 21
Poliakoff, Stephen (playwright), 59
Pollitt, Clyde (actor), 17
Pollock Hall, Edinburgh, 23, 29
Pool Theatre, Edinburgh, 70, 77
Portable Theatre, 59
Primrose, Deirdre, Lady (Traverse Committee member), 46, 57
Primrose, Neil, Lord (later the Earl of Rosebery) (Traverse Chairman,
    1973–75), 57, 61, 71
Priestley, J. B. (playwright and novelist), 18
Prince of Wales Theatre, London 71
Pryde, Bill (director), 70

Radziwilowicz, Jerzy (actor), 89
Raeburn, Susie (Traverse Committee member), 83
Relapse, The (1972), 58
Rents (1979), 80, 84
Restoration of Arnold Middleton (1966), 37
Reynolds, Gillian (journalist, critic), 39
Richardson, Penny (Traverse General Manager, 1970–73), 60, 63
Rifkind, Malcolm, M.P., 61
Riverside Studios, London, 91
Rooting (1978), 80, 84
Rosebery, Neil, Earl of (previously Lord Primrose) (Traverse Chairman